From Guerrillas to Government

Eastern African Studies

From Guerrillas to Government

The Eritrean People's Liberation Front

DAVID POOL

James Currey
OXFORD

Ohio University Press
ATHENS

James Currey Ltd
73 Botley Road
Oxford
OX2 0BS

Ohio University Press
Scott Quadrangle
Athens, Ohio 45701

1 2 3 4 5 05 04 03 02 01

British Library Cataloguing in Publication Data
Pool, David, 1944–
    From guerrillas to government : the Eritrean People's
Liberation Front. - (Eastern African studies)
        1. Eritrean Liberation Front 2. Eritrea - Politics and
    government - 1962-1993
I. Title
963.5'06

                    ISBN 0-85255-852-X (James Currey cloth)
                    ISBN 0-85255-853-8 (James Currey paper)

Library of Congress Cataloging-in-Publication Data
Pool, David.
    From guerrillas to government : the Eritrean People's Liberation Front/David Pool.
            p. cm -- (Eastern African studies)
    Includes bibliographical references (p.) and index
    ISBN 0-8214-1386-4 (Ohio University Press: alk. paper) -- ISBN 0-8214-1387-2 (Ohio
    University Press : pbk. : alk. paper)
    1. Eritrean People's Liberation Front. 2. Eritrea--History--Revolution, 1962-1993. 3.
    Eritrea--History--1993- 4. National liberation movements--Eritrea. I. Title. II. Eastern
    African studies (London, England)

DT397.P66 2000
963.507

                                                                        00-053028

Typeset in 10/12 pt Baskerville
by Long House Publishing Services, Cumbria, UK
Printed and bound in Great Britain
by Woolnough, Irthlingborough

To Hannah Azieb

Contents

Contents

Maps

Note on province boundaries
In 1997 the Eritrean government redrew the maps of Eritrea's provinces. Throughout the text reference is made to the earlier provinces as reproduced on the map.

Notes on Transliteration & Currency

The spelling of Eritrean personal names and place names varies considerably in the sources and on maps, a function of diverse transliteration methods from Tigrinya and Arabic into English. Diacritical marks have been dispensed with as much as possible save where they might be helpful in the bibliography. The author is indebted to his copy-editor, Matthew Seal, for his rigour in bringing consistency to the diversity.

birr and $E (Ethiopian dollar) are used interchangeably. In 1997 the Eritrean government introduced its own currency: the *nafka*.

ix

Abbreviations

BANA	Eritrean Women War Veterans Association
BMA	British Military Administration
CCE	Constitutional Commission for Eritrea
CPEPMB	Creating a Popular, Economic, Political and Military Base
DM	Destruction Movement
EIJ	Eritrean Islamic Jihad
ELA	Eritrean Liberation Army
ELF (1)	Eritrean Liberation Forces
ELF (2)	Eritrean Liberation Front
ELM	Eritrean Liberation Movement
ELNA	Eritreans for Liberation in North America
EPFP	Eritrean People's Forces Party
EPLA	Eritrean People's Liberation Army
EPLF (1)	Eritrean People's Liberation Forces
EPLF (2)	Eritrean People's Liberation Front
EPRP	Eritrean People's Revolutionary Party
EPSP	Eritrean People's Socialist Party
ERA	Eritrean Relief Association
EUP	Eritrean Unionist Party
FM	Foreign Mission
FO	Foreign Office
GC	General Command
GS	General Secretariat
LPP	Liberal Progressive Party
MA	Mass Administration
ML	Muslim League
NDP	National Democratic Programme
NGO	Non-Governmental Organization
NUEW	National Union of Eritrean Women
PA	People's Assembly
PB	Political Bureau
PFDJ	People's Front for Democracy and Justice
PLF	Popular Liberation Forces
RC	Revolutionary Command
RICE	Research and Information Centre for Eiritrea
TPLF	Tigray People's Liberation Front
UN	United Nations
UP	Unionist Party

Glossary

al-tanzim	the organization
baito	village committee
baraka	blessing/charisma
chikka	village head
Derg	military committee
demeniale	state land
diesa	collective village landownership
diglal	chief of Beni Amir
dura	grain
enda	lineage
Etiopia tikdem	Ethiopia First
fallul	anarchists (lit.), group which split from ELF
fasila	platoon
Fateh Mogareh	customary law
fidayin	urban guerrillas
Ge'ez	orthodox church script
hadith	sayings of Prophet Mohammed
haile	military force
hedareb	Beja
helewah sawra	defence of the revolution
kashi gebez	chief priest
kebele	urban residents' association
kebessa	highlands/plateau
khalwa	Islamic school
Khatmiyya	Eritrean and Sudanese religious order
kikkiya	Ottoman administrative title
ma'askar hibu'an	camp of ghosts
makalai ailat	newcomers to village
manqa	bat: EPLF dissident group
megeba'aya	village meeting
metahit	lowlands
nabtab	aristocrat in tigre areas
na'ib	Ottoman administrative title
omda	tribal section chief
qadi	judge in Islamic court
restenyat	those who inherited land

risti	inheritable land
Selfi Natzinet	Liberation Party
sha'biyya	popular
sharia	Islamic law
shaykh	title of both religious and tribal leader
shumagulle	clan elder
sufi	Islamic mystic
tabot	ark of covenant
takhlit	rotation of military units
tariqa	Islamic mystical order
Tigray	northern Ethiopian province
Tigre	language
tigre	serf
tsilmi	family ownership
Wahhabi	orthodox Islam of Saudi Arabia
waqf/ awqaf (p)	Muslim endowment
yamin	rightist
zemacha	Ethiopian educational conscription

Acknowledgements

The list is long and is a consequence of my prolonged period of support for Eritrean self-determination and statehood and lots of discussions along the way. Institutions include the Nuffield Foundation, the University of Manchester, the Minority Rights Research Group and the Eritrean People's Liberation Front (EPLF) in its many guises. My original interest in Eritrean politics was sparked by Semere Russom and the very hard-working cadres who called by my apartment in Khartoum in the mid-1970s. They had no idea that this book would result. I have conducted numerous interviews over the years outside and inside Eritrea, and would like to thank many unnamed Eritreans, from peasants to pastoralists and from Eritrean Liberation Front (ELF) *fallul* to EPLF fighters, who helped my understanding. Many of those I mention will totally or partially reject the analysis. I would thank Asghedet and Meriem particularly, two Semeres, Ermias, Petros Tesfagiorgis and the indefatiguable group of Eritrean Relief Association (ERA) people in London in the 1970s, Ali, Wadi Bashai and AndeMichael and AndeBurhan.

In independent Eritrea Zemheret Yohannes presented the views of the Popular Front for Democracy and Justice and an informative retrospective on the ELF. In independent Eritrea, hospitality and friendship came from families in Addi Hawasha and the Ghirmazion family, particularly Abraha, who subjected me to more football matches in a day than I had seen in several years; Andom, whom I met through Ralph Horne, was a gracious host in Asmara and Decamhare, and helped me in liberated Addi Hawasha village. Sporadic discussions have taken place over the years with Trish Silkin and Lionel Cliffe, and Christopher Clapham's comments at seminars and workshops have always been provocative.

Thomas and Lydia are the only children in their school who know where Eritrea is. My sisters, Linda and Debra, do too. Eileen Fry and Jessica Wannamaker have encouraged me at different times over the years. Michael 'Micky' Unger, more than a friend, knew when not to ask whether it was finished.

Introduction

In 1991 the army of the Eritrean People's Liberation Front (EPLF) entered Asmara, completing the total liberation of Eritrea from Ethiopian rule. The armed struggle had been initiated by a small band of guerrillas in western Eritrea with a few antiquated rifles and little ammunition. This small group evolved into the Eritrean Liberation Front (ELF) from which the fighters who formed the EPLF split in 1970. Thirty years after the first shots were fired, the Eritrean People's Liberation Army (EPLA), with its infantry divisions and artillery and armoured brigades, completed the liberation struggle. In 1993 Eritrea became an independent state. Gaining independence was an immense achievement. Both international and African diplomatic norms opposed the emergence of new states in Africa. Ethiopia had a much larger population and a longer historical existence as a political entity than many European states. Until the emergence of the EPLF, Eritrean nationalist movements and the first liberation front, the ELF, continuously fragmented and undermined the national project of independence. This work does not do justice to the ELF, and a full-length study of the ELF would fill many gaps in the account of Eritrean nationalism.

Through a focus on the EPLF, this book seeks to explain the path to independence and assess the political character of the post-independent Eritrean state. It is divided into three interrelated parts. In Part One the first chapter presents an interpretation of Eritrean society and historical sociology and a second deals with communal politics and early nationalism. The chapter on Eritrean society serves two functions. Firstly, it provides an interpretation of the social and historical context of Eritrean nationalism and, secondly, it presents an outline of the obstacles to the emergence of a unified liberation movement. The second chapter follows from the first and examines the articulation of social conflicts into the politics of the British Military Administration (BMA) period and of the early years of the ELF. It has two purposes: firstly, to indicate the way in which social cleavages were politicized and, secondly, to illuminate how an understanding of these periods influenced the character of the EPLF. It is argued that it was an analysis of this past and reaction to it that shaped the ideological framework and political education programme into which EPLF recruits were inducted and which subsequently formed the political orientations of the younger generation of fighters. Although the period from the 1940s to the late 1960s is interesting in its own right, one of the factors that was central to the organizational discipline of the EPLF was its incorporation of members through its induction programme of political education, in which great stress was given to Eritrean society, history and politics. This programme shaped the consciousness of front members, and acceptance of it was as much a symbol of organizational commitment as the carrying of a Kalashnikov.

These two chapters provide a basis for part of the explanation of the character of the EPLF. While the early nationalist movement of the BMA period and the first authentic liberation movement, the ELF, were rent asunder by tensions arising from socio-economic cleavages both deeply and shallowly rooted in Eritrean society and history, the EPLF was of a different stripe. It was a political organization with a marked degree of autonomy from both past and contemporaneous society, and its development into one of the most formidable liberation movements in contemporary history was a function of its capacity to penetrate society rather than be riven by its social conflicts.

Part Two provides an account of the way in which the EPLF became an autonomous organization largely immune from the divisive and conflictual impact of communal cleavages. One element of that process was through political education combined with separate structures of internal control that combined strong internal discipline with a degree of latitude for individual initiative. It is divided into three chapters that examine the early years of the EPLF, stressing the construction of internal organizational and ideological discipline, the expansion of the front into Eritrean society and its capacity to turn political and military adversity to its advantage. These three interlinked topics illuminate the processes whereby the front took on characteristics of 'stateness' and was able to maintain that capacity and reproduce the man and woman power to sustain the struggle for a prolonged period and 'against all odds', as one close observer of the EPLF entitled his book.

Oddly for a non-state organization, the EPLF came close to Charles Tilly's notion of a state: differentiated from organizations operating in the same territory; autonomous; centralized; with internal structures coordinated with one another.[1] Although Tilly focuses on state-making

---

[1] C. Tilly (ed.), *The Formation of States in Western Europe*, Princeton University Press, Princeton, 1975, p. 70.

in Western Europe and asserts the irrelevance of the European pattern for states that came after, these characteristics have a striking resemblance to the major characteristics of the EPLF. The ideological framework and the organizational characteristics of the EPLF cannot be isolated from the pragmatic imperatives of military victory, the fundamental rationale for any movement pursuing a strategy of guerrilla war.

In Part Three, I examine the strains and problems deriving from the intersection of the liberation front with a liberated national society, sections of which had been connected loosely or not at all with the front and its organizational structures. This final part provides a preliminary assessment of the transposition of the EPLF into the government of the new Eritrean state, and the character of the new political system operating in a world of states and an international economy.

I have followed relatively conventional academic sourcing for the analysis of past and contemporary events. Given the necessity of secrecy in a bloody liberation struggle, a strong tradition of silence about the front and its activities has developed, and this has been perpetuated into post-independent Eritrea. Conventional kinds of sourcing have had to be abandoned at times. The reader will have to allow a degree of trust to the author, particularly on areas which remain sensitive some years after liberation. Some of the information is based on stories and incidents related in confidence. Even after liberation it is preferable not to identify individuals who are not in the leadership.

This work, then, is a first step in exposing the EPLF to the light of day. There are many Eritreans and EPLF members who know far more and, eventually, different analyses that progress beyond this one will appear in critical reaction to it. It is written with a modesty reinforced by a comment sincerely rather than critically made: 'Only a handful of people know the whole story and organization of the EPLF; not many members do.' One element is missing in this account: the scale of the personal tragedies involved in the long and bloody liberation struggle. The cold statistics of martyrs, disabled and refugees mask the brutality of death from war and famine, murder and rape, the disorientation resulting from constant uprootedness and the need to survive in alien surroundings and the impact on those who got to 1991 of the parents, children and comrades who did not. If the final part of this study appears in part critical of the political order emerging in Eritrea, it is sympathetic to those who brought independence and are bound by the ingredients of its success and the darker memory of those who never saw it.

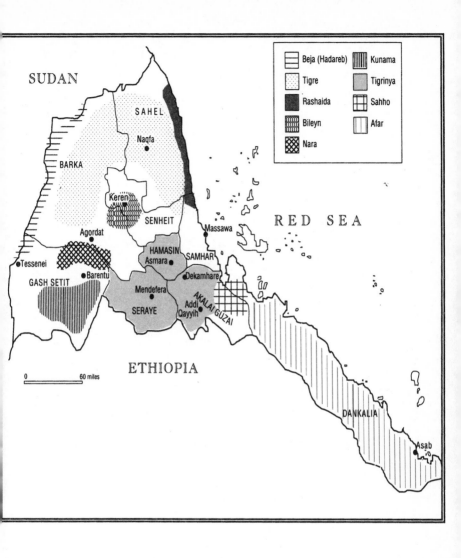

MAP 1 Provinces, main towns and ethno-linguistic groups of Eritrea

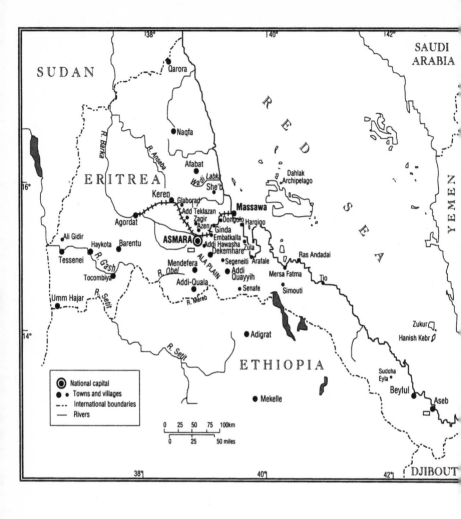

MAP 2 Eritrea: showing places mentioned in the text

I

Reaction to the Past

These two introductory chapters covering Eritrean history and society provide background for the armed struggle and an essential part of the explanation of the formation and shaping of the Eritrean People's Liberation Front (EPLF). The characterization of the past and the weight given to communicating it in the political education programmes of the EPLF are an index of the political and ideological import of history for the leadership of the front. The stress on the past derives from the dialectic relationship between multi-faceted socio-historic sources of disunity and conflict and the political imperative to forge both national unity and a unified nationalist movement.

What might appear as a strange obsession with history had deep roots in the formation and erratic course of Eritrean nationalist movements and nationalist ideology. Success in liberating Eritrea from Ethiopian control in 1991 was not the inevitable outcome of a 'natural course' of nationalist struggle following a historical tide similar to African liberation from European colonial rule. The obstacles to unity and independence were, at different historical periods, overwhelming. Whereas many liberation fronts are nurtured in a favourable environment, neither the social nor the political context from which the EPLF emerged were conducive to the creation of the most successful liberation front to fight on African soil.

It would appear paradoxical that such a disciplined and unified movement originated from a society that had been sharply fragmented and with a history of nationalism marked by division and violent conflict. Divisions between Eritreans were, in part, a factor in Eritrea's incorporation into the Ethiopian empire rather than the more 'natural course' of independence; they were at the root of two civil wars between the EPLF and the ELF, and have played an important role in shaping the agenda of the post-independence government.

Communal cleavages are not necessary incendiaries for political conflicts. Eritrea, however, has them in good measure: clans, 'tribes', ethno-linguistic groups and nationalities[1] and distinct religious communities. With the proviso that these cannot be treated in isolation from other social cleavages like status and class, from the ecological regions which they inhabit, nor from their relationship with political structures (empires, colonial states, liberation fronts and the independent government of Eritrea), such has been their importance that an analysis of the regions and communities of Eritrea is a necessary starting point. It must be emphasized that listing the communities in Chapter 1 does not imply that they have been constant politically coherent groupings, and we shall demonstrate their historic fluidity and political malleability. Neverthless, these varying communal sources of political solidarities have episodically wreaked destruction on Eritrean political organizations.

In Chapter 2 we shall also present an interpretation of the impact of these cleavages on the politics of Eritrea during the British Military Administration (BMA) and the first decade of the ELF, in addition to a presentation of the EPLF's reading of the history of these periods. The relevance of distant swathes of history for understanding a twentieth-century liberation struggle might be questioned. However, the process of Eritrea's creation by Italian colonization, the politics of the colony's disposition after Italy's defeat in World War II, the cultural orientation and practices of Eritrean liberation fronts and the form of government established after liberation in 1991 are inextricably linked to social cleavages and perceptions of them. Contemporary political regimes (colonial, liberation and the independent government) have both drawn on and reacted against conceptions of the historic impact of the process and formation of Eritrean society and politics, and the trajectory of nationalism and unity.

Many writers have stressed the salience of religious division as the determinant of Eritrean political conflicts. Some writers and commentators on Eritrea have stressed the broader multi-dimensional division into lowland pastoralist Muslim and highland peasant Christian as the major social, cultural and political cleavage: a triumvirate of ecological context, mode of livelihood and the religio-cultural. Others have stressed regionalism. As we shall demonstrate, mountains, deserts and coastal plains have no distinctive political voice and, in many parts of

---

[1] The EPLF has consistently analysed Eritrean society on the basis of nationalities defined in terms of a common language. We shall return to this topic.

Eritrea, the populations inhabiting particular regions have been markedly fluid. Regions have been significant in three respects. Firstly, they possess different material resources and have undergone uneven social and economic development, deepened through the impact of colonial and post-colonial policies. Political regionalism or the politicization of regionalism in Eritrean politics has masked competition between socially differentiated ethnic, tribal or sectarian communities and provided a material basis for their political mobilization. Secondly, different areas of Eritrea have been shaped by varying administrative connections to external empires. Thirdly, the liberation struggle resulted in differential ties between the peoples of particular areas and the ELF and EPLF, on the one hand, and the liberation fronts and the Ethiopian authorities, on the other.

Most of the writings since the 1950s, however, assume sealed and congealed categories of ethnic, tribal and religious community. The EPLF's conception of nationalities is a contemporary variation of this assumption, and is intended to mould Eritreans into a particular form of social cooperation. This premise permeates the assumptions of many independent Eritrean government policies. Leaving aside 'being Eritrean', an impossibility before its creation as an Italian colony in 1891, religious communities provide the largest potential reference point for community identity and political action, and they have been the most harped upon. In most parts of the Third World – and Eritrea is no exception – distinct tribes, ethnic or cultural–linguistic groups reside in particular regions. The political and administrative histories of different areas of Eritrea have not so much shaped culture as fused with it. The starting point, then, is to weave together local community history (language, culture and religion) with broader historical processes.

One

*The Social
& Historical Context*

Introduction

Climate and ecology, and modes of production deriving from them, have combined with the impact of competing empires to produce a complex regionalism. The most important distinction perceived by Eritreans is between highlands (*kebessa*) and lowlands (*metahit*), but there are important contrasts within these categories and the lives of the peoples who inhabit them. There have been considerable changes in both ecology and livelihoods and significant population movements as a result of war and famine and periodic variations in rainfall. One marked change from the beginning of this century has been the continuing sedentarization of pastoralists. In listing the different regions, the communities which have inhabited them will be mentioned briefly, followed by more detailed analysis of ethnography and religion. It makes sense to provide information on the two separately because there is not a neat fit between regions and particular communities. This chapter provides an essential background for the analysis of Eritrean nationalism and problems of national unity in general, and the EPLF's conception of the nature of social cleavages in particular.

Geography and Regions

The Kebessa, Central Highlands or Plateau. These different names have been used for this region of Eritrea, which is 2,000 metres above sea level. It suffers from severe environmental degradation, brought about by soil erosion and population pressure. Rainfall is irregular and unevenly distributed. The three former highland provinces of Akalai Guzai, Hamasin and Serai were historically linked to Ethiopian empires, and the inhabitants are Christian, village-based, peasant cultivators.[1] Agriculture is based on cultivation using simple ploughing methods utilizing teams of oxen to break up the hard soil. As a result of the limited grazing in many parts of the highlands, many of the villagers move their animals seasonally to pasture on the escarpments between the western and eastern lowlands. This region is the most urbanized part of Eritrea.

Senheit, the Semi-Lowland Bridge. Most accounts of Eritrea place the former Senheit province as part of the *metahit*. It is in fact a geographical and social 'bridge' between the plateau and western and northern Eritrea. Centred on the market town of Keren, it is a highly mixed area: peasant farmers and agro-pastoralists, the minority Bileyn community, Tigre-speaking Muslim tribes and Christian Copts who have, over time, migrated from the plateau.

The Northern Highlands, Sahel. These are a geological extension of the central highlands, which begin in Senheit province, extend to the Sudan border through Sahel province and overlook the latter's Red Sea coastal plain. The land is largely barren mountains cut by deep valleys through which run seasonal streams. On the eastern escarpment there are fertile areas irrigated by spate flow. The population is mostly dependent on agro-pastoralism, although there has been increasing settlement around the small towns of Naqfa and Afabat. It was in these rugged mountains of Sahel where the EPLF established its main base area and where decisive battles were fought in the 1980s.

The Southwestern Lowlands. They have relatively good, albeit unpredictable, rainfall compared to other parts of Eritrea and, in areas close to the Gash and Setit rivers, are relatively fertile with opportunities for arable agriculture. The population both rears livestock and practises shifting cultivation. It is an area where, in the past, there have been conflicts between pastoralists and village cultivators, particularly between the minority Kunama and Nara, Beja and Tigre tribes. Today many of the villages are mixed, a consequence of the sedentarization of the latter. A large number of the inhabitants of this area

---

[1] It should be noted that in 1995 the provinces mentioned here were abolished. Since the former are referred to in all the literature on Eritrea, I have retained their names here. The administrative changes will be dealt with in Part III.

fled to Sudan during the war, and it is anticipated that refugees would return there.

The Northwestern Lowlands. These have limited rainfall, are very sparsely populated and are an area of agro-pastoralism: livestock rearing with patches of settled cultivation. Agro-pastoralists frequently move between Eritrea and the Sudan.

The Red Sea Coastal Plains. This arid area, along the 1,000 kilometre Red Sea coast, has extremely limited rainfall and high humidity levels. The southern inhabitants of the former Dankalia province are Afar pastoralists, although some villagers on the coast between Massawa and Asab, the two main Eritrean ports, are involved in fishing.

The Eritrean People:
Ethnicity and Nationalities

The Italians created a colonial state composed of distinct tribal, ethnic and linguistic groups, a distinctiveness often reinforced by their residence in the different ecological settings mentioned above. The main ethno-linguistic groups are generally referred to as nationalities in Eritrea and as such have been the basis of EPLF cultural and language policies.[2] They can be divided into two dominant ones, the Tigrinya and Tigre speakers, and seven small minorities. None are absolutely homogeneous, and all have some internal cultural, religious or socio-economic cleavages.

The Tigrinya

The Tigrinya speakers reside in the three former provinces of Hamasin, Akalai Guzai and Serai. They are mostly Coptic Orthodox Christians, a religion they share with Ethiopian Christians. There are, however, converts to Protestantism and Catholicism, a function of nineteenth-century missionary activities on the part of, respectively, the Swedish Mission and the Italian Catholic church, and the some-what culturally separate communities of Jiberti Muslims in the highland towns and villages. Tigrinya is a semitic language, a derivative of

---

[2] The most useful, if outdated, overview of Eritrean ethnography is S.F. Nadel, *Races and Tribes of Eritrea*, British Military Administration, Eritrea, 1944.

classical Ethiopian *Ge'ez*, and although now confined to liturgical use written Tigrinya is in the *Ge'ez* script and is occasionally the source of modern Tigrinya words. It is also spoken in the northern Ethiopian province of Tigray, from where many of the highlanders trace their origins. The great bulk of Tigrinya speakers are subsistence peasants, and because of population pressure on the land many have moved to other areas of Eritrea.

The Tigre

Tigre speakers reside in a large arc around the highlands: in the western lowlands, the northern highlands and the northeastern low-lands. Like Tigrinya, their language is semitic and derives from *Ge'ez*. Prior to the war, the great bulk of this community were pastoralists and agro-pastoralists. Some settled in agricultural communities and in towns like Ginda, Keren and Massawa. Tigre speakers are over-whelmingly Muslim and are divided into several tribes. These include sections of the Bani Amir of the western lowlands, the Marya, the Bayt Juk and the majority of the Mensa of the area around Keren, the Habab, Add Takles and Add Tamariam of the northern highlands and the inhabitants of the Massawa and Harqiqo areas. Some of these tribes were originally Christian and converted to Islam, while others trace their origins to Arab Muslim pious men who, according to their traditions, came from the Arabian peninsula and married locally. Commerce across the Red Sea over the centuries has also resulted in the development of Arabic in Tigre-speaking areas like Massawa and Harqiqo. Tigre tribes like the Bani Amir, Mensa and Marya have developed multi-faceted connections to the Arabic-speaking northern Sudan and provided many early ELF fighters.

Afar

Afar is a Cushitic language and its speakers inhabit Dankalia, the southern desert coastal lowlands of the Red Sea that stretch from south of Massawa to Asab. They are Muslim, organized in clans and share a culture and language with the Afar of Ethiopia and Djibouti. Although there have been pan-Afar nationalist factions emerging from time to time, such nationalism has been counterpoised by the Islamization policies of the Ethiopian Afar sultan of Aussa. The northern Eritrean Afar of Dankalia have been oriented towards Massawa and have pro-duced several key EPLF military leaders and fighters for the early ELF.

Bileyn[3]

The Bileyn live in Keren and its surrounding villages, historically known as the land of the Bogos. They are equally divided into Christian (both Catholic and Orthodox) and Muslim, and some are bilingual or trilingual, speaking Bileyn as well as Tigre and Tigrinya. Oral traditions suggest a connection to the Agaw of Lasta in Ethiopia. They are divided into two sections, the Bayt Tarqe and Bayt Tawqe, which are based on clans under the authority of elders rather than a centralized political authority. Many early ELF fighters were Bileyn.

Beja or Hadarab/Tu-Bedawi

This Hamitic-speaking language group is found among some tribal sections of the Bani Amir of western Eritrea. According to S. F. Nadel, writing in the 1940s, many of the Beja-speaking sections of the Bani Amir are bilingual in Beja and Tigre. Some of the sections have traditionally pastured across the Sudan border, as Beja-speaking Sudanese tribes have pastured into western Eritrea. Like southeastern Tigre-speaking Bani Amir, some sections of this group have taken up sedentary cultivation.

Kunama

The Kunama speakers are a Nilotic people and reside in settled peasant communities in villages between the Gash and Setit rivers and in Barentu town. They follow traditional religion, and there has been significant conversion to Christianity and Islam. Some of their kin live over the border in Ethiopia. There has been longstanding animosity between the settled Kunama and both the Nara and neighbouring pastoralist Bani Amir.[4] As a result of Bani Amir and Nara involvement with the independence movement the Kunama developed close ties with Ethiopian governments and were little involved in the independence struggle, and were a source of recruits to fight against it.

---

[3] See M. Ghaber, *The Blin of Bogos*, Baghdad, 1993.

[4] This tension has been deep-rooted. In the nineteenth century, when the Bani Amir paid taxes to the Egyptian governor of Kassala, it was reported that they asked for military assistance against the Kunama, and there were many incidents of slave raiding and trading from the Kunama through Massawa. F. L. James, *The Wild Tribes of the Sudan*, Dodd Mead, New York, 1883, pp. 67–8, 138.

Nara

The Nara speakers, like the Kunama a Nilotic people, reside in villages in the western lowlands east of the Gash river. A sometimes-used but unacceptable derogatory term for them in Tigrinya is Barya, implying 'negroid slaves'. They were Islamized in the nineteenth century and had a traditionally hostile relationship with the Kunama, often allying with the Bani Amir in raids against the former.

Rashaida

The Rashaida are a small pastoralist Arabic-speaking Muslim tribe that came from the Arabian peninsula in the nineteenth century They have preserved both their language and pastoralist traditions.

The Sahho

The Sahho, a Cushitic language people, live on the eastern edge of the plateau and in the foothills of Akalai Guzai province. Sahho speakers also reside in the northwestern parts of Tigray province of Ethiopia. They are both agro-pastoralists and settled agriculturalists. They are loosely tribally organized, with the main tribes being Assaorta, Miniferi, Hazu and Debremela. Although there are only differences in dialect between these tribes, the Assaorta view themselves as distinct from the others on the grounds of their Arabian descent and separate lineage. With the exception of a small clan of the Miniferi, they are Muslim. There has been a past history of animosity, based on conflict over land and grazing, in southeastern Akalai Guzai, between Sahho and the local Tigrinya Christian population.

There are no reliable statistics on the proportions of these communities nor for the total population of the country. Population figures, from the Italian period to the present, have been based on estimates and vary considerably. Current population estimates range from 2.5 million to more than 3 million. In 1995, the department of education based its statistics on a figure of 3,081,000.

The UN Commission Report of 1950 provided estimates based on combined criteria of community (ethnic, religious and language) and region, ignoring the internal diversity of regions, and gave separate figures for the urban population. Extrapolating from these, crude percentages for 1950 would be:

Tigrinya Highlanders: 47.5%
Tigre Lowlanders: 34.5%
Afar and Sahho: 10.5%
Nara and Kunama: 4%

A CIA estimate of 1994 gave the following percentages (oddly including the Kunama with Tigre speakers):

Tigrinya: 50%
Tigre and Kunama: 40%
Afar: 4%
Sahho: 3%

Eritrea, then, has two dominant linguistic communities, Tigrinya and Tigre. Both of these estimates make Tigrinya speakers the largest single community and give a relatively equal balance between Muslim and Christian. Religion has been a significant historic source of community and political identification, and there is a high correlation between Christianity and Islam and the Tigrinya and Tigre speakers, respectively. Most analysts of Eritrea view the major divide between Eritreans as based on differences of religion and language and forms of production, that is agro-pastoralist lowland Muslims and peasant highland Tigrinya Christians. It is to these two socio-economic categeories that we now turn.

The Plateau, the Peasantry and Christianity

We have mentioned that the majority of the inhabitants of the plateau are Christians, the bulk of whom are Orthodox Ethiopian Coptic, one index of their religious and cultural links to Ethiopian empires.

The existence of Muslim communities in the plateau area and within the Tigrinya-speaking community cuts against religio-cultural homogeneity. Contrasting and, at times, conflictual modes of livelihood (merchants and peasants and pastoralists and peasants) have provided sources of friction. The Muslim Jiberti community, like the Christian, traces its origin to Ethiopia, but is distinct from the latter in religious belief and the cultural values and practices associated with Islam. In terms of ethnicity and language they are the same people but have a strong sense of community and rarely marry outside of it.

The Jiberti were the most economically advanced of the Muslim communities. Like the Jews of the Pale of Settlement, a historically embattled minority in an area under the sporadic control and arbitrary edicts of a Christian empire, Imperial Ethiopian prohibitions against landownership sent them into crafts and petty trade in the villages and entrepreneurial and mercantile business in the towns. These were economic activities frowned on by the land-obsessed highland peasantry, even though the latter were forced into debt relations with Jiberti merchants during times of hardship. Despite the relative prosperity of this mercantile group in relation to the peasantry, the former were subordinated to the latter under the terms of provincial customary laws when resident in Christian villages.

Today, there remains a clearly delineated Muslim quarter surrounding the main mosque in Asmara. A survey of language use in the grain and vegetable market of Asmara in the late 1960s showed that 15 per cent of transactions were in Arabic, providing a further index of the different cultural orientation between the Asmaran merchant group and the majority Christian Tigrinyans.[5] At the fringes of the highlands there are also minorities of Tigre-speaking Muslims in western Serai province and Muslim Sahho-speakers at the eastern edge of the plateau. Both of these communities were agro-pastoralists, and on occasions came into conflict with peasants over grazing land.

It is as much peasant social structure and the connections between the peasantry, the church and the priest as shared religious practice and belief that have shaped the highland Christian community. Much of the following description is based on a report written in 1942 about the province of Hamasin by Kennedy Trevaskis, a British administrator,[6] supplemented by the better-known survey by S.F. Nadel, a British anthropologist employed by the BMA.[7] The picture presented here changed little in qualitative terms until the 1970s, although there has been a long process of urban migration and increased connection to the towns.

[5] R.L. Cooper and S. Carpenter, 'Language in the Market' in M.L. Bender (ed.), *Language in Ethiopia*, OUP, London, 1976, p. 249.

[6] Trevaskis Papers, *Hamasein*.

[7] Both Nadel and Trevaskis were astute observers of Eritrea, and although the latter came to favour partition between Sudan and Ethiopia, his writings on the ethnography of the area from Keren northward to the Sudan border and the Hamasin province are based largely on what he was told. Their reports were based on a combination of both first-hand observations and interviews, and provide a reliable source from which it is possible to draw conclusions about how the past was believed to have been shaped and contemporary social and political structures. Given the importance of community memory, they provide a benchmark, even though they were written by British colonial officials whose government had its own agenda for the future of Eritrea. Where relevant both indicate sketchiness of evidence.

Land tenure systems in the highlands were complex and mixed.[8] Three basic types have been distinguished: *diesa, tsilmi* and *demeniale*.[9] The first two are different forms of risti, a term signifying hereditary ownership. *Diesa* is collective village ownership, but in this system land is periodically distributed to *endas* (village clans). *Tsilmi* is individual family ownership, but authority over land inheres in the *enda*, with the effect that individual families were usually constrained from selling land. *Demeniale* was introduced during the Italian period and converted large tracts of village land into government land. Much of the latter comprised fertile irrigated areas.

The three provinces of Akalai Guzai, Hamasin and Serai have somewhat different historical traditions based on ancestral descent and distinct customary laws, but they shared one significant social division. The peasantry were divided into two classes: *restenyat* (derived from *risti*) and *makalai ailat*, respectively, those who owned and inherited land and those who did not. The latter were generally defined as immigrants into already established villages, with the ownership and inheritance of land the privilege of the former who were descended from the village founders. These later immigrants were granted land if all village land could not be cultivated and if they could prove residence of 40 years. There was originally a degree of flexibility, then, but with increasing population pressure on the land more rigid distinctions developed. Where they were granted land as cultivators, it could not be inherited through their clan. They were second-order villagers. From these families came those involved in crafts, a rather despised occupation compared to agriculture. They could not be represented on the village council and thus had no formal voice in village affairs. If they left the village they had no automatic right of re-entry.

The core of village social structure was the *enda* and it was from *restenyat endas* that the village council was formed. By the early 1940s the *chikka* (village head) had lost much of his power and was essentially the middleman between government and elders from the endas of the village, collecting tribute and passing on orders. His particular powers lay in his role as judge/mediator in village disputes. The role of judge and tribute and tax collector symbolized the duality of the village: an autonomous self-regulating social and economic unit linked to the state through the collective payment of tribute and tax. The latter had

---

[8] A clear account of the complexity can be found in Nadel, *Races and Tribes of Eritrea*, pp. 35–6.
[9] There are considerable variations in and mixes of individual, family and collective tenures in the highlands and in Serai province *diesa* is called *shehana*.

historically been the main index of Ethiopian imperial and state power. In the late nineteenth century and in the 1940s, the historic extraction of tax underpinned the Ethiopian claim to its territorial-state boundaries.

A key village institution was the *shumagulle* (clan elder), a committee of whom was elected from the *restenyat endas* and was responsible for the allocation of building sites, the distribution of land for cultivation and pasture, and the supervision of church finances. The committees' responsibility for building sites was particularly important in that they assessed the status of those who wanted to build a house and thereby determined membership of the village political community.

The church remains the most prominent building in any highland Christian village, with its importance symbolized by its position on high ground above the village or slightly apart from it. The building of the church was a mark of the power of the *restenyat* insofar as land on which to construct it had to be set aside, and only landowning clans were able to do that. Similarly, the living of the priest was provided for by cultivable land set aside for him. Such provision marked the right of a particular descent group to acceptance as *restenyat*. A further index of the centrality of the church to power was that when a new church was constructed the *makalai ailat* would attempt to participate in its foundation to gain recognition as *restenyat*.[10] The *tabot*, the symbol of the ark of the covenant paraded under a canopy on special holidays, was held in an inner sanctum and had inscribed on it the names of the *endas* originally endowing the church land and setting aside land for the living of the priest. Only the priests could view the *tabot* and give a judgement on whose names were inscribed, a decisive role for the church in allocating power in the village.[11]

The priests of villages officiated at christenings, marriages and burials, and generally came from the *restenyat* of the village. Although Nadel pointed out that the peasants were often cynical about the spirituality of the priesthood and that disputes between villagers and priests were common, the church had the 'formidable weapons of excommunication and refusal to celebrate mass'.[12] The power of the priest to deny communion for transgressions has remained an important means of social control. Priests can punish transgressors by demanding that the miscreant fast and pray. It would be difficult for villagers to disobey as the priest could publicly shame them by naming

[10] Trevaskis Papers, *Hamasein*, p. 35.

[11] *Ibid.*

[12] Nadel, *Races and Tribes of Eritrea*, p. 33.

14

them in general village meetings.[13] The priest also taught village children verses of the Bible and *Ge'ez*,[14] and played a healing role by administering draughts of holy water to the sick or pinning parts of scripture on their doors. Priests were numerous: in 1942, the large village of Add Teklazan, to the north of Asmara, had 31 priests. Even smaller villages like Addi Musse, with a population of 804, had nine.

The permanent property of the church was untouched in the *diesa* system of tenure and, in villages where there was no shortage of land, priests were given land for religious services additional to that which they received as ordinary community members.[15] A further connection between the privileged strata and the church derived from the administration of church finances. These were overseen by the senior priest, the *kashi gebez*, or, in many villages, a committee of church wardens drawn from the *restenyat*.[16]

Much of the customary law of the highlanders was linked to religion. For example, the periodical sharing out of communal village land in Akalai Guzai was fixed for every seven years in Lent, and the nomination of village officials involved in the parcelling out of land and overseeing other agricultural activities was fixed on a particular feast day. Even the date for the provision of seed by a peasant who had others work the land for him was fixed on a feast day.[17] The customary law of Akalai Guzai, first written in the 1820s, was shaped into a new collection in the 1940s by 29 district chiefs and 83 'experts in law' selected by villagers. All of those who assembled to formulate the new compilation were *restenyat*.

The most important conclusion to be drawn from these analyses of the church and the villages is that the church and the priesthood were linked to the *restenyat* and were bonded together through their mutual benefits of landownership, social privilege and political power and the exclusion of the *makalai ailat*. Although there was a democratic and cooperative ethos to much of village politics through village meetings, the representation of families, the rotation of office through consensus

---

[13] I have been informed that a particular insult would be that so-and-so had been behaving like a Muslim.

[14] See H.G. Dagne, 'Non-Government Schools in Ethiopia' pp. 339–49 in M.L. Bender (ed.), *Language in Ethiopia*, for an account of the formal structure of religious education in the Christian areas of Ethiopia.

[15] EPLF, Research and Information Center on Eritrea, *Creating a Political Base*, p. 35.

[16] Trevaskis Papers, *Hamasein*, pp. 35–8.

[17] The Law of Adghentegheleba, Chapter XXXIX Rules Concerning Land Held in Risti, Supreme Court, Government of Eritrea 1944.

and the role of committees in village affairs, it was exclusionary, clan-based and male. As we have also shown, it was infused with religious values, traditions and practices.

Urbanization in the highlands was largely initiated during the Italian colonial period, when settlements like Asmara, Mendefera (Addi Ugri) and Decamhare took proper urban form and attracted the surrounding peasantry and, subsequently, communities from many parts of Eritrea, as well as from Tigray province. 'Native quarters' developed around Italian residential and manufacturing areas. The biggest increase occurred in the 1930s. The Eritrean population of Asmara, for example, grew from 15,000 to 120,000 between 1935 and 1941.[18] The process of urbanization tended not to result in the rupture of ties to villages of origin. Many urban migrants retained claims on rural production in addition to their wage and, for the few, salary and entrepreneurial profit. Those of *restenyat* origin were entitled to a share of the produce deriving from their hereditary village landownership. In consequence, part of the emergent urban social structure combined an income from employment supplemented by an income in cash or kind as petty absentee landowners. Class and strata-based cleavages included those of workers and peasants and rural and urban and, within the latter, between established urbanites and newcomers.

Although it has been argued that Italian colonial rule for the most part perpetuated pre-capitalist social structure and only had a decisive but short-lived impact during the Fascist period in preparation for the invasion of Ethiopia in 1936, there was large-scale mobilization of the peasantry out of subsistence. Many villagers joined or were conscripted into the Italian colonial army and provided the labour for building the transport infrastructure of the colony, some leaving forever their rural way of life. Others were employed in the Italian-owned factories and workshops. Just prior to the post-war slump, there were 27,000 Eritreans employed in industrial enterprises in 1944–5.[19]

We have depicted the structural links between founding village *endas*, village political power and the church and priesthood because of their subsequent decisive political role in determining Eritrea's unification with Ethiopia. As we have demonstrated, Orthodox Christianity was not, as Jordan Gebre-Medhin simplistically put it: 'the pillar and custodian of feudal high culture'.[20] Rather, it was at the very

---

[18] T. Killion, 'The Eritrean Economy in Historical Perspective', *Eritrean Studies Review*, Vol. 1, No. 1, Spring 1996, p. 102.

[19] *Report of the UN Commission for Eritrea 1950* p. 63.

[20] J. Gebre-Medhin, *Peasants and Nationalism in Eritrea*, Red Sea Press, Trenton, NJ, 1989, p. 46.

heart of peasant village life. Ties of solidarity between Tigrinyans were based on a sense of shared ancestry on the part of residents of the three provinces, language, Christianity and similar village-level administrative and legal practices. These were reinforced by many highland villagers being linked to collateral *endas* living in neighbouring villages. Despite the religio-cultural homogeneity of highland Christians, the internal stratification of villages and lack of socio-economic solidarity deriving from differential access to land that we have noted was an important factor, among others, in enabling the EPLF to mobilize the rural poor, as we shall demonstrate.

Lowlands, Islam and Pastoralists

The Muslim community has been traditionally cast as inhabiting the lowlands of Eritrea, where they live as pastoralists and agro-pastoralists moving between grazing areas with their cattle and camels. The picture is more complicated. There are distinctions between the different lowland areas and ethnic and linguistic differences between lowlanders, as we have indicated at the beginning of this chapter. The latter distinction has had implications for different politico-historical orientations.

The interrelationship between rural lowland Eritrea, particularly the western part, and forms of Islam is important to examine for several reasons: the independence movement found most support among Eritrean Muslims and the armed struggle was launched in the west by individuals who were embedded in western society or originated from there. The social context of the latter region was to influence its early dynamic.

The most salient historic cleavage within Muslim communities derived from a historically determined division based on property relations, save that the property was human and animal rather than land. The Tigre-speaking tribes, until the twentieth century, were divided into two castes deriving from a distinction between a ruling group of migrant conquerors and indigenous conquered: *shumagulle* and *tigre*, conventionally translated as master and serf. This kind of caste division cuts against the usual conception of tribe as a community organised on the basis of a sense of common descent and, as we shall see in the first part of the following chapter on the BMA, the tribe in Eritrea was a highly malleable construct.

The *tigre* rendered services and paid dues to members of the ruling caste. Depending on whether the subjects were pastoralists or agriculturalists, dues were paid in milk, animals and portions of slaughtered animals or a share of the crop.[21] An example of the kinds of demands placed on the *tigre* is best illustrated from a listing of the principal obligations of the Marya documented in the early 1940s: annual payment of eight gourds of butter, the gift of a tongue and breast of any animal slaughtered and of a calf on the occasion of a *shumagulle* marriage. More bizarre was the payment of one Maria Theresa dollar when the *shumagulle* contracted syphilis. The obligations of the *tigre* of the Bayt Asghede, a trans-tribal descent group which separately ruled the Habab, Add Takles and Add Tamariam, were even more onerous. Those of the Add Takles were obliged to undertake the daily milking of the *shumagulle*'s cattle.[22] The proportions of *tigre* to *shumagulle* varied from tribe to tribe. It was estimated that for those ruled by the Bayt Asghede it was one to 20, for the Marya one to 10 and the Mensa one to two. The higher the proportion of *tigre* to *shumagulle* the weaker the latter became. In western Eritrea, among the Bani Amir the caste division was differently named: *nabtab* for the ruling group and *tigre* or *hedareb* for the ruled.[23]

It is worth examining the Bani Amir in some detail, as they provide an illustration of an additional obstacle to political unity deriving from the political economy of agro-pastoralism. They were one of the largest tribes with an estimated membership of 30,000 to 40,000 in the 1940s. Most of the early fighters of the ELF came from it or its close associate, Bayt Ma'ala. The Bani Amir were fragmented into *nabtab* and *tigre/hedareb* and into sections and clans. In the mid-1940s, they were divided into somewhere between 17 and 21 tribal sections. Some spoke Beja, the majority Tigre, and some a combination of the two mixed with Arabic. The strongest bonds arose from a sense of common descent, customary law and the Islamic religion. Although there has periodically existed an overarching political authority in the chiefly institution of the *diglal*, the power of the latter was essentially based on his role as tax-collector for whichever empire or colonial rule was in control of Bani Amir lands. From Italian times onward tribute collection, organized downwards from the paramount chief through *omdas* (section heads), was a major attribute of Bani Amir political unity. However, even in this important sphere unity was minimal with

[21] Trevaskis Papers, *The Social Organisation of the Tigre Speaking Peoples*, p. 29. Acccording to this source, there were variations in the treatment of the subject peoples as between those who were conquered and those who asked for the 'protection' of the conquerors.
[22] *Ibid.*, pp. 42 & 56.
[23] S.F. Nadel, 'Notes on Beni Amer Society', *Sudan Notes and Records*, No. 26, 1945, pp. 56–7.

section chiefs unable to collect without armed force. Their explanation was that

> they and their clans-fellows are like brothers and the chief's words count for little ... The clan chiefs have to contend also with the ambitions of their sub-heads, who arrogate to themselves positions of semi-autonomy. They collect tribute or issue orders within their smaller groups and regard the clan chief only as an intermediary between them and the paramount chief. Often too, from jealousy or personal hostility, they ignore and by-pass the clan chief.[24]

This account by Nadel is worth quoting in full because of the congruence, in form if not in content, between the structure of authority of agro-pastoralist social organization and that of the ELF in the mid-1960s. The character of the latter resulted in an internal crisis which was formative of the contrasting structure of authority of the EPLF, a topic that we examine subsequently. Despite the sense of descent from a common ancestor, the nature of agro-pastoralism provided a basis of tribal fragmentation. Nadel claimed that the tribesman was ignorant of 'the migrations of his brother clans; even clan chiefs often show a strikingly inaccurate knowledge of the seasonal dispersal of the tribe.'[25] The economy of the pastoralists and agro-pastoralists, based on the imperative of grazing clan-owned animals, was in tension with the broader ethno-political unity of the tribe. The society and economy of a tribe like the Bani Amir were an unlikely basis for the establishment of a disciplined liberation movement. Although Nadel's comment cited above could be ascribed to the reluctance of informants to give information to evade tribute, there is a remarkable lack of stateness and orientation towards a state deriving from such a social organization.

The Bani Amir domain was also populated by client tribes. Many of these had earlier migrated from the east and the northern highlands. Although they amalgamated with the Bani Amir some retained a sense of their origins and earlier solidarity into the contemporary period.

We have demonstrated the multiplicity of cleavages dividing the arc of peoples residing around the highlands. The overwhelming majority of them were Muslim in belief and practice: they generally followed *sharia* principles of inheritance, for example. Islam, however, provided only a loose cultural solidarity rather than an organizational one deriving from a religious institution or religious hierarchy. There was nothing comparable to the Orthodox church. Muslim institutions, like

[24] *Ibid.*, pp. 62–3.
[25] *Ibid.*, p. 60.

19

awqaf administration,[26] until very recently were localized.[27] In 1943, a degree of administrative coherence was established when the BMA gave the mufti of Eritrea the power of appointment to the *awqaf* committees of Keren, Massawa and Asmara. The mufti devolved upon the *sharia* qadis (religious judges) of the main Muslim towns the power of establishing and of appointment to *awqaf* committees.[28]

The sprawling geography of the lowlands, the varying and contradictory combinations of the artificiality and malleability of some tribal groupings and the occasional strong solidarity of others together with the relative independence of sub-tribal clans all worked against the unity of Eritrean Muslim society. The main overarching structures which linked Muslims in a broader Islamic community originated in the role of pious individuals and families at the head of religious orders. In Eritrea, several families, but two in particular, have played such a role: the Mirghani family of the Khatmiyya *tariqa*[29] and the Add Shaykh. Unfortunately, there has been no detailed study of Islam in Eritrea, other than that of J. S. Trimingham, whose treatment is rather cursory but nevertheless deals with an aspect of Islam that has been ignored by analysts of Eritrean politics,[30] the majority of whom have been Europeans or Christian Eritreans without much knowledge of or contact with Muslim Eritreans.[31]

In the absence of detailed studies, the following analysis of the role of pious families and sufi orders is supplemented by conclusions drawn from comparable societies dominated by pastoralism. Although social patterns drawn from other historical contexts cannot compensate for the lack of Eritrean material and cannot be a substitute for Eritrean explanations of Eritrean circumstances, the structural similarities are sufficiently strong to be suggestive.

The argument of anthropologists like Gellner and Evans-Pritchard is that pious men and their descendants play a mediating role between

---

[26] *Waqf (plural: awqaf)* are endowments, usually made by the wealthy and pious, for the upkeep of mosques, shrines and schools.

[27] See Yasin M. Aberra, 'Muslim Institutions in Ethiopia: the Asmara Awqaf', *Journal of the Institute of Muslim Minority Affairs*, 1983–4.

[28] Only after the Ethiopian revolution of 1974 was *awqaf* administration given authority over a range of activities broader than endowments. *Ibid.*, p. 209.

[29] *Tariqa* is Arabic for 'path' but is used for a sufi or mystic order.

[30] J.S. Trimingham, *Islam in Ethiopia*, OUP, Oxford, 1953.

[31] My impression is that there has been a general lack of contact between Christian Eritreans and Muslims. Most do no not have friends who are from other communities, although this situation was changed under the liberation fronts, which provided an umbrella for such mixing. It is also perhaps different in mixed urban communities like Keren.

clans over grazing rights. They provide the scriptural basis for Islamic beliefs and practices in illiterate societies through their learning and their knowledge of Islam. In return, pastoralists support, through gifts and reverence, the spiritual and mediatory role of the pious families.[32] In the Eritrean context, they have provided a reform of and, to a certain degree, Islamic legitimation for tribal customary laws. In addition to ritual and spiritual functions, these families have played a significant role in religious education and thus in the provision of a basic degree of literacy.

The Add Shaykh are a 'tribe' (a problematic term, as will become clear) that traces its descent from a holy man, Shaykh al-Amin ibn Hamad.[33] The history of the Add Shaykh illuminates both the difficulties involved in the concept of tribe and the strange dynamics of tribal formation. Shaykh al-Amin arrived in Sahel at the beginning of the nineteenth century. His preaching and reputation for miracles brought a following from the Muslim *tigre* of the, then Christian, ruling caste of the Bayt Asghede, as well as other disaffected clans in the area. According to Trimingham, the tribe developed a social structure similar to other groups based on a division between masters and serfs. Although Shaykh al-Amin remained the focus of a cult, the tribe followed the pattern of others and, as it grew, became increasingly segmented with groups splitting off, and members of the family, with some exceptions, failing to retain their *baraka* (charisma/blessing). The split of the Faidab Add Shaykh, who attached themselves to the Bani Amir, produced Sayyid Mustafa wad Hasan (also known as Sayyidna signifying 'our' religious master) who wielded considerable religious influence among the latter.[34]

The history of the Add Shaykh contrasts with that of the Mirghani family, which remained insulated from the 'tribalization' process which subverted the broader religious appeal of the Add Shaykh. In part, this appears to be a function of the former retaining the *baraka* and piety of the sufi but combining it with an Islamic orthodoxy. The Khatmiyya spread to Eritrea at the beginning of the nineteenth century when Muhammad Osman al-Mirghani brought the message of his sufi master, Ahmad ibn Idris al-Fasi of Mecca. The latter was sympathetic to Wahhabi puritanism and thus, while remaining within the mystic tradition of sufism, was also a reformer of sufi excesses. For Muhammad

---

[32] E.E. Evans-Pritchard, *The Sanusi of Cyrenaica*, OUP, Oxford, 1949; E. Gellner, *Saints of the Atlas*, University of Chicago Press, Chicago, 1969.

[33] Much of the following is based on Trimingham, *Islam in Ethiopia*.

[34] In 1997 a descendant of the family was governor of Keren/Senheit.

Osman, the path to mysticism was grounded on a knowledge of the orthodoxies of the Quran, the *hadith* (sayings of the Prophet Muhammad) and *sharia* law. On the death of Ahmad, the Khatmiyya became an independent *tariqa*. Muhammad Osman's sons were sent out to spread the message of their father and expand the influence of the order. From Sudan, al-Hasan became an influential figure among the Bani Amir and the Habab, and his shrine at Kassala an important place of pilgrimage. Apart from the border town of Kassala, both Keren and Massawa became Khatmiyya centres.

The Khatmiyya sufi order and its lodges existed in many parts of Eritrea as well as in Sudan. One of its main lodges in the latter was located in the border town of Kassala, subsequently the organizational locus of the ELF. The Khatmiyya enjoyed a large following among Eritrean Muslims, both pastoralists, rural settled and urban. In the early 1950s, the Keren Khatmiyya *shaykh* was Sayyid Ja'far, a great grandson of Muhammad Osman. Another descendant, Sayyid al-Hashim, has a burial shrine north of Massawa, where the anniversary of his death was widely celebrated. In addition to the Bani Amir and Habab, the Khatmiyya was influential among the Add Takles, Add Tamariam and Sahho.[35]

The interweaving of Islamic law with the social norms and practices of tribes and clans was common throughout Muslim Eritrea. The existence of clans combining expertise in religious law with piety and mysticism has been noted among the Sahho of the eastern escarpment: the me Embera, Bayt Khalifa and Bayt Shaykh Muhammad, who trace their origin to Arab migrants, became 'holy sub-groups'.[36] In addition, certain holy clans, like the Intile Shaykh Are, provided Quranic teachers and mediators among all the Sahho tribes, and the Bayt Qadi supplied religious judges for the five Assaorta sections. The revision of the Bani Amir customary law of 1958 was prepared by a religious notable, begins with a Quranic invocation and ends with a prayer to Almighty God to 'guide us to anything that brings success to ourselves and our people'.[37]

The lowland regions of Eritrea, except for the Massawa area, had several socio-economic characteristics in common: they had low levels of urbanization and fewer modern economic activities relative to the plateau. If the Eritrean plateau was a periphery of an Ethiopian

---

[35] In my visit to Keren in spring 1996 I was informed that I had just missed a Khatmiyya celebration held at a mosque attended by followers from these tribes, an indication of the continuing loyalty to the order although the scale of attachment is difficult to estimate.

[36] Trimingham, *Islam in Ethiopia*, p. 177.

[37] New Customary Law of the Beni Amir Tribes, 12 February 1958.

empire increasingly centralized in the Amharan province of Shoa, low-land Eritrea was a periphery of a periphery. Its peoples were pastoralists, recently settled former pastoralists and some long-established peasants, mostly in the Nara area. With the development of commmercial agriculture in the west and in neighbouring Sudan there was a move away from these traditional economic pursuits. People from the west and north took labouring jobs on agricultural schemes in Sudan and Italian-owned plantations in Eritrea. The area had a few small towns, Agordat, Barentu and Tessenei, which were little more than large villages. By the mid-1940s, Barentu had a population of 1,000 and Tessenei and Agordat 4,000 each. Of the latter two the inhabitants were of mixed geographical origin, with only tribal chiefs, prosperous merchants and religious notables from the indigenous local population drawn there when the Italian rulers established them as administrative centres and military posts. They developed into small market towns along trade and transport routes from Sudan into the plateau, semi-lowlands of Senhit and the northern highlands.

The handing-over notes of the BMA administrative officer of Agordat, written in 1952, only nine years before the launching of the armed struggle in the surrounding rural areas of the town, illustrate the low level of urbanization, social organization and services, and the salience of petty trade. Municipal tax was collected by three chiefs of quarters: Bani Amir, Sudanese and 'Abyssinian' (that is, highland Tigrinyan). The Bani Amir, in recognition of their greater numbers, had to pay the most and, according to the handing-over notes, still had the most to pay! Tobacco and fuel were the monopolies of two merchants. Five merchants dominated the dura grain trade. The one clinic was funded largely by taxes from the animal market, and was staffed by a nurse and a servant. There were five schools in all of Agordat district: one for boys with 200 pupils and seven teachers and one for girls with 50 pupils. The three other schools at Keru, Algaden and Bisha had one teacher each and 115 pupils altogether. Employment, other than in animal herding, agriculture and administration, was in industries processing rural products. For the most part these were Italian-owned: a button factory employing about 530 Eritreans, a rope factory employing 200, a timber factory employing 100 and a bottle-making factory employing 30, all of whom were female. Women were involved in the weaving of mats from dum palm, the bulk of which was domestic labour with the products exported to Asmara. Only three enterprises mentioned were Eritrean-owned: all were lime factories outside Agordat and employed casual temporary labour.

There was a sizable merchant community of 600, the great majority of them involved in petty trade.

This area of the west, so central to the beginnings of the armed struggle had no significant rural–urban cleavage. The inhabitants of Agordat with links to the local population were from the Bani Amir and paid taxes through their Agordat chief. The president of the Agordat council was the Bani Amir *diglal*. When the liberation struggle broke out it was within a wholly rural context, with the presence of the state limited to administrative structures organized on tribal lines through *shaykhs* and their deputies in tribal sections. The system had been formalized in the Italian period and persisted through the BMA. As in other colonial systems of control, a native administration was an inexpensive method of providing law and order, extracting tax and tribute and providing mechanisms of punishment.

By the 1940s, this administrative system in both the west and north was in some disarray because of a rural class conflict between the ruling castes and serfs or client tribes. In the course of this conflict, as we shall demonstrate in the analysis of the politics of the BMA, Islam came to play a mobilizing role for the serfs and set it in tension with the chiefly administrative structure. Ultimately, Islam became identified with serf liberation and with the course of Eritrean nationalism. Even though early nationalism as an idea flourished in Muslim areas, the society of those areas had organizational characteristics that were in tension with those of a national state. The social organization of agro-pastoralists and the traditions of sufi religious orders are antipathetical to state organizations and the territorial character of the state. Borders are irrelevant for grazers and for transnational religious organizations. This lack of orientation to the state can be linked to regionally differentiated patterns of incorporation into the empires that competed for tribute and, from the late nineteenth century onwards, for a territorially defined statehood. Of particular importance is the march area of Senheit, caught between an expanding and resurgent Ethiopia and the Muslim north and west.

Mosaic Regions and Peripheral Minorities

The Senheit: Land of the Bogus

In the post-World War II period, this area was a crucible of nationalism. At its centre was Keren, a town which had been the seat of the short-lived but well-organized Egyptian government in the nineteenth century and an important administrative and military centre during the Italian period. Like other towns, its population was drawn from various areas of Eritrea, but by the mid-1940s about a third of its 9,000 population were from the local Bileyn people. It has a position as market centre for both the immediate surrounding region and a trading centre linking the west, the northern highlands and the central highland plateau.

It was from here that Ibrahim Sultan connected rural social struggles of the serfs against the aristocrats and the independence struggle against the unionists. It was a city which was in the forefront of the struggle against Ethiopia and a flashpoint of strikes and demonstrations as the Ethiopian government dismantled the federation arrangement. A significant part of the population were supporters of the ELF, although it came under EPLF control for a short period in 1977. It was and is a city of some political magnitude in nationalist history, and its strategic setting, resembling an amphitheatre surrounded by stark mountains, and cultural make-up have ensured its strategic and political significance. It was also, and remains today, a centre for the Khatmiyya family.

Keren and the area around it was a microcosm of Eritrea, with its social mix of groups related to highland Christians and Eritrean minorities, like the Bayt Juk, sharing the Tigre language and Islam with other Tigre speakers to the west and north. The Bileyn, with their distinctive language, culture and particularly vibrant traditional music, are divided into two tribes/descent groups: Bayt Tawqe and Bayt Tarqe. Indicative of the cultural flux of Eritrea, they were originally Coptic Christian but in the nineteenth century some adopted Islam. Some remained Coptic, some reconverted from Islam to Christianity and, in the twentieth century, some converted to Catholicism. Though few in number the Bileyn produced many who were engaged in early nationalist politics. Keren and its surrounding villages were an ethnographic, cultural and economic bridge between the highlands and the pastoralist west. Not only was this area of strategic importance, it was also of political importance for the liberation movements. Recruiting support from its mixed population could only enhance the representativeness and inclusionary nationalist character of the movements competing for control over the armed struggle.

Competing Empires, Imperial Remnant and State-Connectedness

In pursuing an independent state the EPLF sought to create an organization which was autonomous not only of Eritrean society but impenetrable by external forces. The magnitude of the problem with regard to the latter has deep historical roots originating from the area out of which Eritrea was carved. Trevaskis crudely described the creation of Eritrea through Italian colonialism thus: 'The Italians had lopped off the extremities of their neighbours, cobbled them together and called them Eritrea.'[38] Parts of these extremities, however, had historically been component parts, if peripheral ones, of imperial bureaucratic states and, thus, different regions of Eritrea had varying links to neighbouring empires.[39]

We shall briefly describe these because they have a triple importance for several lines of argument that occur throughout the analysis of the EPLF. Firstly, one aspect of the success of the EPLF was the creation of organizational autonomy free from divisive external state influences. Secondly, the core groups of fighters who formed the EPLF came from regions where there had been relatively stable connections between settled populations and coherently organized imperial tributary rule. We shall draw some conclusions from this to reinforce an explanation of the state-like character of the EPLF. In our later discussion of the EPLF, we shall stress its organizational capacities and the process through which it took on attributes of 'stateness' during the liberation struggle. While it is difficult to link the imperial experiences of the Eritrean peoples to subsequent politics and ascribe a political culture or orientation, there is a certain congruence between those peoples and regions which were territorially organized and tribute-payers to relatively stable empires and those pastoralist clans organized on the basis of kinship who were periodic tax-payers to unstable imperial systems. Thirdly, these varying links to empires are part of the historic roots of the difficulties involved in framing education and language policies in the post-independence period.

The Muslim communities of Eritrea, with some exceptions, were not under the rule of Ethiopian empires until the inauguration of the Ethiopian–Eritrean Federation in 1952. The Asab area of southern

---

[38] Trevaskis Papers, *The End of the Italian Empire*, Part II, p. 5.

[39] For more detail see D. Pool, 'Ethiopia and Eritrea: The Pre-Colonial Period' in *The Eritrean Case*, Research and Information Centre on Eritrea, Rome, 1982.

Dankalia was under the control of the local sultan of Aussa until purchased by the Italians in 1869. Massawa and the surrounding areas were ruled by the Ottomans from 1557, an area to which the Egyptians succeeded. By 1872, the latter had expanded its control from the coast to Keren and the Senheit. Until then Senheit had been a march area between the Christian highlands and the Muslim west and north. In the areas around the Gash–Setit and Barka rivers, some of the peoples of western Eritrea had occasional tributary relations with the Sudanic Funj kingdom of Sinnar from the sixteenth century to the nineteenth when the Egyptians took control, while others at times paid tribute to the rulers of Tigray province. The highland plateau provinces paid tribute to Ethiopian emperors and governors of Tigray province, which was at times autonomous of the imperial centre.[40]

The settled peasants of the central highlands and the peoples of the Massawa and Harqiqo area were connected directly and for long periods to relatively well-organized imperial systems and, as long-settled peoples, were more easily taxed and conscripted. The Massawa and Harqiqo areas of the former Samhar province were at the core of the Ottoman administration on the Red Sea coast and the local ruler, the *na'ib* (deputy of the Turkish commander), responsible for the collection of imperial tribute. The family of the *na'ib* came from the Tigre-speaking Bellu people and, following the Egyptian succession to the Ottomans, remained powerful. The Bellu were at the core of a sub-imperial quasi-military administration under the *kikkiya*, another Ottoman administrative term. Indicative of the level of institutionalization and the fusion with a form of clan organization, the descendants of these officials used these administrative titles as family names.[41]

Until the Italian occupation, the highland areas had paid tribute to Ethiopian empires ruled by Amhara or Tigrayan emperors or princes through a set of local ruling families.[42] Furthermore, and as we have

---

[40] See the article by Alemseged Abbay, 'The Trans-Mareb Past in the Present', *Journal of Modern African Studies*, Vol. 35, No. 2, 1997, which is based on the assumption that there is some kind of fixed and objective identity resulting from 'history' between the Christian highlander and the people of the Ethiopian Tigray province. The author's analysis could equally well draw the conclusion that, though the concept of identity is extremely problematic, it is highly malleable if evidence is drawn from collective action.

[41] Members of these families were represented in the EPLF central committee and hold high positions in the post-independence political and administrative institutions.

[42] For an interesting analysis of the systematization of tax and its links to the militarization and centralization of Ethiopia in the nineteenth century see T. Tegenu, *The Evolution of Ethiopian Absolutism*, Studia Historica Upsaliensa 180, Uppsala, 1996, and for references to the Eritrean region, pp. 119, 137–8.

shown, the Eritrean highland village had a stable administrative order, with its committees and councils and village officers to supervise and police land and animals. The Eritrean peasant lived in and, when he or she joined the liberation struggle, came from a background and culture that had been highly regulated and organized. As a consequence, there was a lengthier history of administration and state-connectedness for both these parts, unlike northern and western Eritrea. In the north and west, the history was one of attenuated chieftainship, as in the Bani Amir, or relatively autonomous tribal or community councils. We have also mentioned the role of sufism in the west. Generally, the pious sufi leader would seek autonomy from the state to preserve the autonomy and traditions of the order. There was, thus, a kind of ideological symmetry between these two forms of social and religious organization in terms of state–society relations.

It is obviously very difficult to establish with any conclusiveness that a sense of stateness, in terms of being connected to a continuous system of power, authority and duties like those of tax and tribute, shaped the consciousness of people inhabiting particular areas, but there is a remarkable coincidence between the respective areas from which the early EPLF recruited and those of the early ELF.

If there is an explanatory gap between the imperial past and the beginnings of the armed struggle, it should be noted that these different imperial experiences of Eritrean regions were subsequently underpinned by socio-economic ones, as we have pointed out. The Massawa/Harqiqo area and the central highlands, on the one hand, and the western lowlands, northern highlands and the southeastern Red Sea coastal regions, on the other, were differentially affected by the impact of Italian colonialism.

Descent, Language and Religion

Although we have stressed the problematic nature of the concept of tribe, the rationale for this form of communal solidarity was a belief in common descent. The latter impinged on senses of cultural identity, religion, language and linguistic orientation. All had implications for nationalist politics, the politics of the armed struggle, and education and language policies after independence. The western pastoralists spoke mainly Tigre, a language akin to Tigrinya in structure and grammar but with significant accretions from Arabic. In this largely illiterate pastoralist context, literacy was in the 'higher' referent

28

language culture of Islam: Arabic. It was the language of the Quran and the written language of the *sharia* courts. Speaking some Arabic was not unusual for any pastoralist trading animals and animal products across the Sudanese border, the petty merchants of the north trading in Port Sudan or the peasant-pastoralists of the northern highlands migrating for work to the Gash cotton planatations over the border. Any child who had received a basic Quranic education would at least be familiar with the sounds and phrasings from the memorization of verses from the Quran.

Insofar as descent from a common ancestor was a source of solidarity, the character of that ancestral line had implications for broader trans-national solidarities. Many tribes that were Muslim traced their descent to Islamic holy men originating from the Arabian peninsula who then married into local communities. Whatever the veracity of these memories, they were recounted in their oral traditions in the 1940s. Such literacy as did exist came through the teaching of the Quran, the sayings of the Prophet and the words and wisdom of holy men, and was in Arabic. Under the British Arabic had equal status with Tigrinya, and increasing numbers of Eritrean Muslims sought education outside Eritrea: in the Sudan, Egypt and Saudi Arabia. The low level of educational provision in the Muslim areas of Eritrea did not fit the aspirations of even the very small numbers seeking secondary and higher education in the Ethiopia of the 1950s. Muslim intellectuals and educated from the majority Tigre speakers, as well as those from Muslim minority communities, frequently use Arabic, the language of the Quran, as a *lingua franca* and the Arabic script. Although Arabic provides a basis of affinity between the different Muslim communities of the lowlands it was the language of a small strata of educated and traders. Although religion provides an additional affinity between Muslim lowlanders, Eritrean Muslims are fragmented geographically and, for the mass, linguistically. Moreover, they are constituted of different tribes with different histories, cultures and customs.

Migrations, Descent and
the Problems of Culture and Ethnicity

Compounding the fluidity of historical imperiums and varying tributary relations, the historic migrations of the peoples of Eritrea are illustrative of the malleability of religious and cultural allegiances and identifications. This malleability has provided nationalists with opportunities to shape and reshape the past in changing contemporaneous circumstance and thereby bolster both distinct communal histories and a shared Eritrean one. Eritrea was not simply a land of imperial extremities, it was also a land of migrants, a melting pot which many twentieth-century political leaders stirred.

At times, the language, culture and religion of migrants changed and, at times, the culture and religion of indigenous peoples into which migrant conquerors came changed. We have mentioned the particular social formation in the Tigre- and Beja-speaking parts of northern and western Eritrea. As tribes moved into the areas outside the highlands, conquered peoples and the retainers of the conquering clans became subject peoples with a status akin to slavery which, over time, ameliorated to that of serfdom. The conquered peoples became incorporated into the conquering tribes and, as serfs, had feudal dues to pay and services to provide. All of these obligations were incorporated into the various customary laws. Many northern Muslim tribes trace their genealogical origins to both highland Christian Ethiopia and Arab ancestors.

For example, both the Mensa and Marya trace their origin to Zed, a member of the Quraysh, the tribe of the family of the Prophet Muhammad, who migrated from the Arabian peninsula to Dankalia.[43] At some point in their travels from Dankalia and their residence in Senheit they became Ethiopian Orthodox Christians. By the latter part of the nineteenth century the majority adhered to Islam.[44] Like the Mensa, the Marya converted to Orthodox Christianity through the influence of the host society in which they settled. In the nineteenth century, they converted to Islam.[45] After settling to the north of Keren, both Mensa and Marya began speaking Tigre. Illustrative of the problems of defining either ethnicity or nationality on the basis of descent traditions or on language, both the Marya and Mensa claim a shared ancestry with the Assaorta and Hazu, Sahho-speaking tribes.

According to their legends, the Add Takles trace their descent from Bumnet, whose ancestors came from Akalai Guzai to Carneshim in Hamasin province and subsequently moved down the Anseba river northwards. Both their place of origin and the names of ancestors confirm their initial adhesion to Orthodox Christianity and membership of Tingrinya-speaking communities. They share a common

---

[43] Trevaskis Papers, *The Tribes and Peoples of the Cheren District* p. 22. The Sahho of eastern Akalai Guzai trace a similar origin despite the linguistic difference between them and the Tigre-speaking Mensa and Marya.

[44] Some were converted to Protestantism and Catholicism.

[45] Trevaskis, *op. cit.,* pp. 43.

descent from Bumnet's son, Asghede, and, through him, kinship with the Bayt Asghede of the Habab and the Add Tamariam tribes of the northern highlands. Like the other Bayt Asghede, the Add Takles converted to Islam in the nineteenth century. In contrast, the Add Shaykh, traditionally resident between the Add Takles and the Habab, trace their descent to a late eighteenth-/early nineteenth-century immigrant of Quraysh stock from Arabia. Over time all of these were Islamicized and changed their original languages to Tigre, that of the people they conquered. Some took on the dress and facial markings of local communities.[46]

Although I have stressed differences between the peoples of Eritrea and mentioned the cultural, religious and historic links between the Christian highlanders and Christian highland Ethiopians, there were also historic links between the peoples of the plateau and those inhabiting areas north of it who had been subject to Muslim empires or Muslim local rulers. The recollected history of the geographical origin of the Hamasin people – and one has no grounds for thinking that the other provinces of the highlands were that different – is essentially Tigrayan or from further south into Abyssinia/Ethiopia. However, there were subsequent migrations northwards, linking the people of the plateau to those of the Keren district and the northern highlands in Sahel province and these south-to-north migrations were clearly recollected in the memories of the 1942 generation. The political consequences will be examined below.

Spheres of Interaction

Although we described the social structure of the highlands and lowlands separately, we have pointed out the existence of connections between the Tigre and Tigrinya in the discussion of migrations. In addition to historic links, there were a variety of social, economic and cultural interactions between the plateau orthodox Christians and Christianity and the rest of Eritrea that have been the basis of both cohesion and conflict. We have mentioned that several of the communities residing north of the plateau trace their origin to the same ancestors as plateau Tigrinyans and claim kinship with Sahho people. Secondly, there are Tigrinya Orthodox Christian peasants inhabiting both the southern rural areas of Senheit province adjacent

---

[46] It seems that Bani Amir styles were particularly modish and were imitated by other tribal groups in north and northwest Eritrea.

to Hamasin, for whom Keren is the main economic centre, and the towns of most areas outside the plateau. There is limited statistical evidence for the latter but by the early 1940s about 15 per cent of the population of Keren were from Hamasin, Serai and Akalai Guzai provinces.[47] By 1950, two-thirds of the Eritrean urban population were Christian,[48] and of the one-third Muslim the great majority were Tigrinya-speaking Jiberti. The spread of Tigrinya-speakers has continued: by 1995, of the 213 primary schools in non-highland provinces the language of instruction in 80 was Tigrinya.[49]

This spread of Tigrinyans to the lowlands and semi-lowlands was partly a function of land shortages and partly the lack of self-sufficiency in grain.[50] Only four districts in Hamasin (North and South Carneshim, Tekhle Ageba, and Kebessa Tchewa) were self-sufficient with the others, like Miname Zeraye, at 80 per cent and North Anseba as low as 20 per cent. The differences were made up by varying combinations of animal sales and wage-labour. Trevaskis linked the insufficiency of production to land tenure and the absentee *restenyat* living and working in Asmara. With regard to the former, he has argued that in places with similar soil conditions communal land was not as productive as the two areas with individual *tselmi*, but that the *restenyat* would oppose root and branch the introduction of individual *tselmi* if the *makalai ailat* were included. Whatever the case, highlanders migrated to towns in both the plateau and all areas of the lowlands from Tessenei in the west to Asab in southern Dankalia.

A third sphere of interaction between highlanders and lowlanders derives from grazing patterns. Many plateau villagers pasture their cattle and oxen seasonally in areas where the bulk of the inhabitants are Muslim. A peasant agriculture based on the plough was one that for ecological and demographic factors took some highland peasants to the western and eastern lowlands for grazing and into competition with the lowlanders who were Muslim. It was not the classic confrontation of the desert and the sown, the pastoralist and the peasant. The settled peasant was also something of a seasonal pastoralist, adding a further potential for conflict over grazing between highlander and lowlander. The Christian peasant as partially agro-pastoralist reverses the conventional stereotype of Muslim lowlanders as an exclusively pastoralist group. Although this kind of movement led to conflicts at

[47] Trevaskis Papers, *Tribes and Peoples of the Cheren District*, Appendix e.
[48] *Report of the UN Commission*, 1950, p. 24.
[49] *Basic Education Statistics, 1994–5*, Ministry of Education, Asmara, 1996, p. 50.
[50] Trevaskis Papers, *Hamasein*.

times there were institutionalized mechanisms of mediation which worked successfully in areas where highlanders grazed. Where conflict over land and grazing was particularly intense and reinforced by religious and ethnic differences, there was a tendency for outside political actors to exploit these cleavages.

The fourth arena has limited contemporary relevance but a degree of resonance in the histories of the two leading religious communities. The Coptic church played a role in sustaining Christianity in areas where, in the nineteenth century, an Islamic revival appeared to be making inroads into orthodox Christianity. Trevaskis accorded the Coptic church, through the role of the monasteries, the function of protectors and sustainers of Christianity against this Islamic revival. He cited those of Debrebizen and Zaabadan in the Anseba, the most westerly and northerly areas of Coptic Christianity.

Conclusion

There is a dichotomy between ethnicity (in the sense of a consciousness and memory of common descent) and being subject to an empire, one of the defining characteristics of which was religion. Part of the explanation lies in the historical sociology of Eritrea and the ethnic, linguistic and religious intermixing brought about through past migrations of peoples in combination with shifting lines between competing imperial orders. In the absence of territorial states with clearly demarcated boundaries, the shifting lines were based on imperial capacities to extract tribute from the different peoples living in the area and, at times, voluntary payment of tribute to secure protection against other predatory imperial orders.

Insofar as competing empires required an administrative structure, no matter how loose, to extract tax and tribute and that it was based on local chiefs, the powers and autonomy of the latter were periodically enhanced. Given that the most important empires were Islamic (the Ottoman, the Egyptian and the Sudanic Funj) and Christian (the Ethiopian), religious practice and belief were frequently fused with collective tribute payment. At times, tribute was collected where a particular empire could mobilize sufficient force; at times religious conversion and migrations of communities brought dramatic shifts in tribute payment from one empire or another; and, on some occasions, the religious orientation of a particular empire resulted in the conversions of communities.

Although there was a degree of convergence between religious profession and being subject to a particular empire, ethnicity, in the sense of a consciousness of common descent from an ancestor, blurred the picture, as did shifts in languages used by communities. Although some of these changes took place hundreds of years ago, memories of them remained extant in the twentieth century. In certain periods, these memories became instruments for imperial and colonial rulers and sources of mobilization for competing Eritrean nationalist forces. There are many examples where memories of particular collectivities were created.

What, then, forms a community in Eritrea? From the above account, it is apparent that there are multiple historic sources, based on popular and subjective versions of their histories, for cohesion and conflict between the peoples of Eritrea. The introduction of criteria for delineating communities on an objective basis has generally been a purposive political action. Given the changes mentioned here, our original classification of peoples as separate cultural entities or nationalities suggests an unreal fixity. It is clear from my interpretive analysis of Eritrean society and history that social groups, be they ethnic, linguistic, religious or tribal, have been fluid. This is not to deny that such affinities have not had a significant impact on Eritrean politics and nationalism.

Although differences in modes of livelihood (settled cultivators, pastoralists and agro-pastoralists) have diminished during this century, the lowlands have been the heartland of Muslim pastoralist and agro-pastoralist communities and the highlands the heartland of Christian Tigrinya-speaking peasant cultivators. Differences between the two were compounded by the deeper impact of Italian colonization on the highland area, the results of which produced significant socio-economic differences between the lowlands and the highlands and between Eritrean communities inhabiting these regions. For pastoralists and sufi organizations alike, state borders were of limited significance and at most a hindrance. While Christianity in the highlands played a role in social subjugation and preservation of privileges of the *restenyat* and property-owning monasteries, Islam played a more radical role in its connection to social strata and tribe. The western lowlands, the long eastern coastal plain and the northern highlands were all populated by agro-pastoralists and, except for the Massawa and Harqiqo areas, lacked a territorially based administrative system and a rootedness in the land in contrast to the settled highlanders. While the latter were combined in conflict over village land and locked into a legal system of a territorial nature, grazing and animal wealth were at the heart of the lowland pastoralist economy. Its social organization, cultural orientation and ecology provided the context for the early phase of the armed struggle led by the early ELF. The settled highlands and the Massawa–Harqiqo areas provided the social context for the second phase of the armed struggle led by the EPLF. While we shall argue that the latter was important in terms of the social base of a highly organized and disciplined liberation front like the EPLF, of equal importance was the creation of an ideological and cultural framework which gave some sense to the complex and cross-cutting cleavages of Eritrean society. The task was a particularly urgent one by the late 1960s as the historic fluidity and malleability of the component parts of Eritrean society had congealed into a more rigid reflection of tribe and religion in politics.

In the following chapter, we shall examine this process. The politics of the BMA period was marked by political conflict and fragmentation which was one determining factor in Eritrea's federation with Ethiopia and its subsequent incorporation into and subordination to the Ethiopian imperial central government. Although Eritrean nationalist historiography has frequently linked the fragmentation to both British and American strategic designs and Ethiopian subversion, much of the evidence suggests that there was a social, cultural and political division within Eritrean society of longer historical standing that these external interventions both fuelled and fed. The character of nationalist politics in this period shaped the nature of the armed struggle of the 1960s and 1970s, the policies of the fronts and the political education programme of the EPLF, particularly its history component. It is not inaccurate to state that there was a dialectical reaction against the past and a purposive reconstructive analysis of it to reshape the political consciousness of nationalists.

Two

The Political Context
The Historical Roots
of Discipline & Autonomy

Introduction

Following from our analysis of the social, ethnic and regional structure of Eritrea, we shall examine the ways in which religion, ethnicity and politics became entwined during the period of the BMA and the 1961–70 period of ELF-led liberation struggle. The BMA was a temporary administration (1941–52) intended to last until the Four Powers (Britain, France, the Soviet Union and the US) determined the disposition of the former Italian colony. The Four Powers were unable to agree, and the issue was passed to the United Nations. The UN Commission of Investigation (1950) recommended a federation with Ethiopia, which began in 1952. From 1952 onwards the Ethiopian government together with the pro-Ethiopian Eritrean Unionist Party undermined most of the federal provisions and abrogated the federal arrangement in 1962, when Eritrea became an Ethiopian province. There was increasing nationalist agitation from the mid-1950s onwards, culminating in strikes and demonstrations in 1958 when the Ethiopian flag replaced the Eritrean.

In 1958, the Eritrean Liberation Movement (ELM) was established by nationalist activists resident in Sudan.[1] The founding leaders were of Muslim background but secular and influenced by the Sudan Communist party. The ELM, the members of which were organized in secret cells of seven, spread to the Christian highlands, becoming a secular Muslim–Christian organization reflecting the multi-sectarian

---

[1] See T.H. Faddab, *Harakat al-Tahrir Iritiriya wa Masiratihya al-Tarihkiyya* (Arabic: The Eritrean Liberation Movement and its Historic Fate) Sharuf Press, Cairo, 1994 and R. Iyob, *The Eritrean Struggle for Independence: Domination, Resistance Nationalism 1941-1993*, CUP, Cambridge, 1995, Chapter 3.

cooperation in nationalist protest at the subversion of the federation. Its initial strategy of peaceful struggle brought no dividends and was subsequently replaced by a *putschist* strategy to be carried out by the Eritrean police. In competition with the ELM, the ELF was formed in Cairo in 1960. The first shots of the armed struggle were fired in 1961 marking the beginnings of the 30-year war of liberation. This bare account of the development of Eritrean nationalism does little justice to the deep divisions which occurred within the Eritrean political movements. Here we are interested in the reflection of Eritrean social divisions in two crucial episodes: the nationalist politics of the BMA period and the early years of the ELF.

The politics of the BMA period were marked by such intense conflict and sharp fragmentation that they became a determining factor in Eritrea's federation with Ethiopia and its subsequent incorporation into and subordination to the Ethiopian imperial central government. Although Eritrean nationalist historiography has frequently linked the fragmentation to both British and American strategic designs and Ethiopian subversion, there was a social, cultural and political division within Eritrean society of longer historical standing which these external interventions both fuelled and fed. The character of nationalist politics in this period shaped the nature of the armed struggle of the 1960s and 1970s, the policies of the fronts and the political education programme of the EPLF, particularly its history component. There was a dialectical reaction against the past and a purposive reconstructive analysis of it that was intended to shape a new nationalist political consciousness. Similarly, and in a parallel reactive fashion, the character of the early ELF was a formative influence in shaping the organizational structure and ideology of the EPLF.

British rule initiated a politics based on regionalism and sectarianism when it permitted the formation of political organizations prior to the consultation exercise on the future of Eritrea with the Four Power Commission and subsequently the UN Commission. In varying forms, the impress of these cleavages was carried into the politics of the federal period, bedevilled the ELF and resulted in a series of splits within the Eritrean field. It has generally been argued by Eritrean nationalists that the introduction of sectarian divisions into Eritrean politics was the responsibility of the British who, in their desire to partition Eritrea between Sudan and Ethiopia, mobilized Islamic sentiment for the former, while the Ethiopian government in its desire to return Eritrea to the 'motherland' mobilized Christian sentiment. Subsequently, the internal opposition which emerged in the ELF in the mid-1960s argued that the organizational basis of the ELF reinforced sectarianism, tribalism and regionalism.

Although the politics of the BMA and the ELF are interesting in their own right and have been the focus of much writing on Eritrean nationalism, our main stress is on how the experiences of the party period and the formative years of the ELF shaped the organizational form of the EPLF and its policies and ideology, and particularly the latter's emphasis on unity, secularism and reform. These guiding principles, however, brought the EPLF into tension with significant segments of Eritrean society and produced an imperative to insulate organizational members from their own society. By focusing on these two experiences, the intention is to illuminate how the founders of the EPLF initiated the process of creating an organizational and institutional autonomy in two dimensions: an internal one free from the impact of Eritrean social divisions and an external one free from the influence of regional states.

Both historical experiences had a significant impact on the trajectory of Eritrean nationalism and account in part for the weight given by the EPLF to political education, and within that to a particular vision of Eritrean history and society. Drawing attention to these connections involves more than an analytic linkage between ideology and social and historical analysis. Firstly, the social and political divisions of the BMA resulted in the failure of early nationalists to secure independence and, secondly, the fragmentation of the ELF weakened the Eritrean nationalist cause after armed struggle was substituted for political means.

The BMA and the Politicization of Religion

In 1941, the British took responsibility for the temporary administration of Eritrea as Occupied Enemy Territory until a decision was made on the disposal of the former Italian colony. British rule lasted until 1952, when the UN proposed a federation with Ethiopia under the authority of the Ethiopian Emperor. A combination of factors shaped this outcome and there has been a considerable literature on this topic dealing with the interplay between Eritrean divisions, Ethiopian interventions and international interests, as they developed between 1941 and 1952.[2] There is no doubt that the British policy of

---

[2] See G.K.N. Trevaskis, *Eritrea: A Colony in Transition, 1941–52*, OUP, Oxford, 1960; O.

the partition of Eritrea between Ethiopia and Sudan, the Ethiopian campaign to return Eritrea to its motherland, the interest of the US in securing the Kagnew military base at Asmara and US influence at the UN were important factors in denying Eritrea independence and drawing a veil of diplomatic silence over the subversion of the federal provisions.

Our concern in this section is the relationship between Eritrean society and politics and, in particular, the role of religious communities and political parties. British officials and Eritrean authors have portrayed this polarization of unionists and independentists in different ways. A major source for these interpretations is Kennedy Trevaskis. In his account, a combination of economic crisis, Ethiopian nationalist activity and the pro-Ethiopian position of Orthodox church leaders brought forth an alliance between Christian sectarianism and the Ethiopian government in pursuit of unity with Ethiopia.[3] This process was deepened by bloody clashes between Eritrean Christians and the Sudan Defence Force made up of Sudanese Muslims and used by the BMA as an instrument of law and order. The result of these different processes was the formation of the Unionist movement. In response, a nationalist movement emerged from the Muslim community when the Muslim League was formed in 1946 to oppose union with Ethiopia. Although there was a Christian political organization, the Liberal Progressive Party, opposed to union and some Muslim members of the Unionist Party, Trevaskis argued that, by 1947, 'the Eritreans had rallied under their rival religious banners and now stood divided against one another in opposing Moslem and Christian factions'.[4] Ultimately, this division provided the domestic basis of the UN's federation compromise, eschewing both partition between Ethiopia and Sudan and complete incorporation within Ethiopia.

Jordan Gebre-Medhin closely followed Trevaskis's account but provided a different interpretation. He placed great stress on Ethiopian and Orthodox Church intervention, arguing that the former fragmented Eritrean national unity and delivered the urban strata to the Unionists, and that the latter delivered the highland peasantry through religious coercion. He further argued that the basis of Muslim opposition to union was their exclusion from national political discussions and

[2] (cont.) Yohannes, *Eritrea, A Pawn in World Politics*, University of Florida Press, Gainesville, 1991; Gebre-Medhin, *Peasants and Nationalism*; T. Negash, *Eritrea and Ethiopia: The Federal Experience*, Nordiska Afrikainstitut, Uppsala, 1997.

[3] Trevaskis, *Eritrea*, Chapter III.

[4] *Ibid.*, p. 76.

violence used against them by unionists. Underlying Gebre-Medhin's interpretation is a class analysis. He argued that the Eritrean ruling class favoured union and that this class, including Muslim feudal chiefs and Christians, was multi-sectarian. The Muslim nationalists favouring independence were based on and closely linked to the bulk of their followers organized in the serf emancipation movement. The Christian peasantry, on the other hand, were manipulated. Thus, the pro-independence movement was a mass one and the unionist movement was elitist, violent and an instrument of the Ethiopian Crown and Church which through coercion and spiritual pressure neutralised the Christian peasantry.

This line of analysis effectively negates an assumption of sectarian identity and consciousness as the motor of Eritrean politics and, in this respect, differs from that of Trevaskis. Gebre-Medhin's analysis is similar in nature to that of the EPLF. It was expressed succinctly and polemically by the Eritreans for Liberation in North America, supporters of the EPLF:

> Even though the Unionist party represented the interests of the British colonialists, the Ethiopian expansionists and domestic exploiting classes, through demagogy, threats of excommunication from the Coptic church and terrorism, it coerced certain sections of the toiling masses into joining them.[5]

The EPLF version of this period of Eritrean history was the following:

> As the colonial and expansionist forces arrayed against national independence were stronger than the subjective forces of the Eritrean people, each of these external forces hatched its own plot ... to prevent independence ... British colonialism ... inflamed non-basic religious, tribal and regional contradictions ... [and the Ethiopian regime] used the church [and the] Unionist Party ... exploiting religious differences and imposing religious pressure on the masses.[6]

In using the term 'non-basic contradictions' to characterize the divisive role of religion in politics, the EPLF recognized that there were tensions based on religion but identified the basic contradictions as those of class.

Tekeste Negash, an Eritrean exile historian, basing his analysis largely on the British archives of the period, has produced a revisionist account of Eritrean nationalism. He argued that sentiment for unity was not a function of church and imperial ideological manipulation

---

[5] *In Defence of the Eritrean Revolution*, Eritreans for Liberation in North America, p. 48.
[6] *Memorandum*, EPLF, April 1978, p. 6.

and coercion but derived from a deeply rooted consciousness among Eritrean Christians.[7] He presented the UP not as an Ethiopian creation but as an 'Eritrean organization' and argued that the churches and their adherents, Orthodox, Catholic and Protestant Evangelical, began working for union immediately after the end of Italian rule,[8] and that the 'leadership of the UP was permeated with deeply religious people belonging to different denominations'.[9] In contrast to Gebre-Medhin, Negash argues that the movements and parties which favoured independence were the creatures of the British and the Italians: the former supported the LPP, based on Christians of Akalai Guzai and Asmara, and the ML, and the latter both supported and funded the Independence Bloc. Below we shall present an interpretation that explains the political orientations of the two communities with reference to the entwined combination of culture, religion and rural class structure.

The major problem with Negash's version is not that his argument (that Christians supported union and operated through the UP) is wrong but that to analyse the UP solely as a mass movement based on deeply religious sentiment, that is, a pure sectarian consciousness, is misconceived. Firstly, he misses the bigger picture by neglecting the links between the character of the rural political economy of highland Eritrea and its relationship to the Orthodox church and unionism. The mediating mechanism was the fusion of village church and the *restenyat*. As we have shown, the latter formed the village committees, represented the villagers to the outside and were part and parcel of the administration of village religious affairs. While the UP leaders are convincingly portrayed as deeply religious by Negash, this dominant stratum in the highland villages had every reason to support the UP given the interconnection between social, economic and religious structures.

In the same way, it is an artifice of Gebre-Medhin to analyse the social structure of the highland Tigrinyans without incorporating the long-established fusion of the social and the religious. In the second place, Negash neglects the symbiotic relationship between the rural political economy of the highlands and that of the lowlands, particularly the demonstrative effect of the serf rebellion on the Christian Tigrinyan 'Abyssinian districts' between Hamasin and Keren. The latter was the political centre of serf agitation against the

---

[7] Negash, *Eritrea and Ethiopia*, Chapter 2.

[8] *Ibid.*, p. 38.

[9] *Ibid*, p. 47.

dominant ruling group within the Muslim community, a division we have treated in the preceding chapter.

Neither Gebre-Medhin nor Negash examine the resonance of this class struggle in the march area between Islam and Christianity. Developments there, however, give some indication of how the serf demands began to have an impact on the *restenyat-makalai ailat* relationships in areas peripheral to the highlands. In some parts of the Abyssinian districts, the arrival of newcomers from Hamasin province promoted a move to individual ownership whereby the original village founders would receive *risti* land and the latecomers would not. The latter favoured the communal system through which they would receive access to communal land, albeit without the political rights in village institutions. Part of the move to protect the privilege of the *restenyat* was a demand to adopt the Bileyn Bayt Tarkae customary law, on the grounds that the Tigrinya-speaking Adirbe and Bileyn Bayt Tarkae were descended from a common ancestor.

What is particularly interesting in these developments is a blurring of any religious consciousness or Tigrinya Christian separateness. Sections of the Bayt Tarqe were Muslim and their customary law, the *Fateh Mogareh*, was one of the identifying marks of being Bileyn.[10] A further mark of the domino effect of the serf dissidence was the emergence of a similar kind of rebelliousness among the Nara, where there were no such class distinctions, against the chiefly family appointed by the Italians. One tactic of the Nara dissidents was a call for union with tribes of the Agordat district on the spurious grounds of common kinship.[11]

These kinds of incidents provide further evidence for the imprecision and blurring of concepts of tribe and ethnic group, and are indicative of the malleable nature of religion, law and ancestry as marks of community solidarity when economic and political interests were at stake.[12] In a general way, these developments undermine the interpretation of Eritrean nationalism as wholly a function of a collective consciousness and action based on religious and ethnic blocs.

While asserting the authentic Eritrean character of the unionists, Negash is overly dismissive of the nationalists of the same period as

---

[10] Trevaskis Papers, *The Tribes and Peoples of the Cheren District*, pp. 109, 127. The British were against the change on the grounds of the administrative chaos it might cause.

[11] Trevaskis Papers, *A Report on the Tribal Reorganisation of the Western Province*, pp. 20–1.

[12] Negash is critical of Trevaskis's interpretation and argues that he was rewriting history from the perspective of the subversion of the federation. The Trevaskis papers, on which the book is substantially based, however, make it clear that this was not the case.

externally created. Crucial to understanding the development of the trend of Eritrean nationalism which pursued separation from Ethiopia is the serf rebellion. We have treated in the preceding chapter the structure of this division into masters and serfs in those areas outside the plateau.

Negash's notion that the creation of the Muslim League was of British inspiration is stated explicitly: they 'twisted the arms of the Moslem leaders in Eritrea to form the ML towards the end of 1946'.[13] The only evidence produced, and Negash takes some pride in his evidential basis for criticizing other interpretations, is a quote from the monthly political report concerning a tour by the military administrator stating that he convinced Eritrean Muslims that unless they 'think for themselves, the Plateau Christians will do their thinking for them'.[14]

The analysis of the foundation of the Muslim League has wider implications insofar as most historians argue that the ELF grew organically from the ML and, as a consequence, was rooted in a Muslim consciousness from which it was never able to free itself.[15] Gebre-Medhin has portrayed this more accurately, arguing that the ML made the plight of the serfs a cornerstone of its political activities.[16] He ignores the linkage between this social protest movement and Islam. In fact, the serf movement leaders used the ML as a political instrument of its leadership, but in doing so linked together Islam, social reform and national independence in an ideological cluster that was to have a profound impact on the forging of a unified nationalist movement in the early 1960s.

We now turn to the linkages between nationalism and Islam.

My interpretation of the popular and orthodox character of Islam and the serf movement illuminates a more significant socio-historical continuity between the social basis of the ML and the early ELF than simply that of a political orientation deriving from Muslim–Christian division and a degree of continuity of leadership. As Gebre-Medhin has correctly argued, the economic basis of the master–serf relationship had long been eroding under Italian colonial rule even if political structures were retained. What Gebre-Medhin does not touch on, however, is a continuity of religio-cultural factors deriving from this social conflict. Rather, he stresses the EPLF's succession to the

---

[13] Negash, *Eritrea and Ethiopia*, p. 31.

[14] *Ibid.*, p. 44.

[15] *Ibid.*, p. 149.

[16] Gebre-Medhin, *Peasants and Nationalism*, pp. 151–2.

radicalism of the serf emancipation movement devoid of any religio-cultural content, and thus misses the linkage between radicalism, Islam and nationalism. As a consequence, he produces a simplistic critique of the ELF, at the core of which is a contrast between the ELF's lack of revolutionary ideology and the EPLF's possession of it. To stress the continuity on a single dimension, however, is to distort the complex legacy for the armed struggle of the socio-cultural basis of the serf movement and the ML. In the first place, the serf movement created the minimal conditions for the spread of the armed struggle through the Muslim community. In the second place, however, it was a legacy which made it difficult for the ELF to establish an autonomy from the society which it was attempting to liberate, and points out one of the major contrasts between it and the EPLF: the latter's capacity for autonomous action.

One of the main impacts of the expansion of mixed populist and orthodox Islam in the nineteenth century was in the realm of law. Sufi leaders and religious clans during the nineteenth-century Islamic revival attracted followers on the basis not only of their reputation for piety and *baraka* but for their introduction of *sharia* legal principles. These principles were in marked contrast to the bulk of customary law of the tribes which had developed through conquest. By the 1940s, the impact of *sharia* on customary tribal law exhibited some variations in the legal practices of the different Muslim communities. Although there was inequality before the law in terms of gender, in other respects the incorporation of *sharia* principles modified and ameliorated the relationship between conqueror and conquered. With some exceptions,[17] the settlement of blood disputes and principles of inheritance among the Tigre-speaking tribes were based on *sharia*.[18] For the Muslim components of the Bileyn, the *sharia* had made some headway but customary law predominated and frequently set the judgement of the *qadi*'s court against that of the tribal.[19] With regard to the Bileyn, Trevaskis cites the example of the friction between *qadi* and custom over the breaking of the marriage contract.

One index of the appeal of Islam to serfs was the desertion of Bayt Asghede *tigre* to the Add Shaykh. Trevaskis has described this process as follows:

> dissident serfs were attracted to Shaykh El Emin and his family both because they respected him as a form of saint, and because they

[17] The Marya, Mensa and Bayt Juk.
[18] Trevaskis Papers, *The Tribes and Peoples of Northern Eritrea*, pp. 33–4.
[19] *Ibid.*, p. 57.

followed him as subjects and not as serfs. This relationship has endured and such dues as the ruling family have received are voluntary offerings and not obligatory payments.[20]

As we have pointed out, there was a contrast here with the Mirghani family which attracted followers from the Tigre and the tigre but did not become a ruling tribal family, as the Add Shaykh became a 'tribe'.[21]

The leavening effect of Islam, linked to the impact of Italian colonialism and the development of a cash economy in Eritrea and Sudan, subsequently had important consequences for the development of nationalism. Alternative economic opportunities emerged for serfs with the advent of colonialism and new forms of production. Nadel cites the Bani Amir serfs joining the Italian army.[22] Italian control also increased security, reduced the need for protection offered by tribal agglomerations grouped around conquering clans, encouraged the drift of pastoralists away from the traditional areas of pasture and, as a consequence of these processes, undermined semi-feudalism. In addition, from both northern and western Eritrea, migration to cotton schemes in Sudan provided a livelihood independent of the semi-feudal social relationships existing in their localities.[23]

The subversion of this kind of society continued under the British when the serf leaders linked serf emancipation to national independence or, at least, anti-unionism. Given the historic tensions between *sharia* and customary law, between Islamic teachers and preachers and the conquering clans who were beneficiaries of customary law, it was not surprising that close ties emerged between both formal and popular Islam and serf emancipation leaders. When the leaders of the serfs linked their fortunes to the independence movement organized in the Muslim League, however, they carried with it an Islamic orientation.

Trevaskis's unpublished memoir provides a more detailed and personal account of the dynamics of the formation of the ML than that found in his book.[24] It differs from the version of Negash, which portrays the ML as a British creation. According to Trevaskis, then

---

[20] *Ibid.*

[21] This process illustrates the problems of the concept of tribe which at minimum should denote some sense of common descent.

[22] S. F. Nadel, 'Notes on Beni Amer Society', *Sudan Notes and Records*, 1945, p. 72. As we shall later point out, serving in colonial armies was to provide a boost to the inauguration of the armed struggle.

[23] Such opportunities were also taken by those from the ruling groups.

[24] Trevaskis Papers, *Eritrea: The End of Italian Empire, Part II.*

political officer in Keren, Ibrahim Sultan, the serf movement leader, approached him and asked for assistance in freeing the *tigre* in order that they could become the basis of a party opposed to union. The overriding concern of the BMA was that emancipating the serfs would bring insurmountable administrative problems and require large-scale involvement in land disputes. Ibrahim Sultan proposed resurrecting the old pre-conquest tribes. Thus, Ibrahim Sultan provided Trevaskis with a 'feasible alternative to anarchy'[25] by fulfilling the British appetite for cheap colonial administration through the rule of tribal chiefs over tribal agglomerations and resolving worries about social and political disruption in what was meant to be a temporary military administration.

As we have pointed out, the Muslim religious establishment and sufi orders were in constant tension with the customary order, and the major beneficiaries of that were the masters. Many of the latter had joined the unionist camp on the grounds that their privileges would be confirmed under an Ethiopian feudal order. When Ibrahim Sultan and the serf movement linked their fate to nationalism, so Islam, in both its Sunni legal orthodox and popular forms, and nationalism became fused. It is these longer-term developments which underpinned the emergence of the ELF in that they created the social basis of a nationalist movement in Eritrean Muslim society largely but not wholly free from chiefly domination. The scale of the changes was immense. Twenty-eight new tribes were formed affecting a total population of 180,000. Like the ML and the serf movement, the ELF was multi-tribal. This multi-tribal character was a consequence of the intertwining of the egalitarian face of Islam, which provided a degree of unity for the Muslim community, long fragmented on a 'tribal' basis under the *shumagulle*. In reconstructing the *tigre* tribes, many educated urbanites of serf origin became the chiefs of the newly formed serf tribes. As Trevaskis put it, the best way to solve the problem of selecting new chiefs was 'to make those grand Pasha-like emissaries of Ibrahim chiefs'.[26] Thus, the British retained the 'tribe' as a principle of social and administrative organization. According to Trevaskis, Ibrahim Sultan was pleased with his politicking and arrived in his office saying call me 'Sultan Ibrahim Sultan'.

Although the British had rejected Ibrahim Sultan's request for financial support, sectarian tensions in the highlands resolved the

[25] *Ibid.*
[26] *Ibid.*, Chapter 12, p. 7.

46

problem of finance for the ML. The Jiberti community, particularly that of Asmara, bore the brunt of unionist attacks and discrimination. Tedla Bairu, a UP leader, even suggested that the Jiberti not be consulted by the UN Commission because they were Ethiopians. This relatively wealthy urban merchant community sought the protection of the ML and provided money.[27] Eventually the ML fragmented, and a major factor in its division was the *tigre* issue: Ibrahim Sultan made a tactical alliance with the Christian nationalists of the LPP and the remaining Italian community, and formed the Independence Bloc, which was largely financed by the Italian government. Since the Italian government was associated with the maintenance of the feudal order, the *tigre* tribes formed the Muslim League of the Western Province, one of the moving spirits of which was the *qadi* of Keren.

The Legacy for the ELF

The social changes which occurred in the Muslim community were a prerequisite for the launching of the armed struggle in 1961. They provided an egalitarian social basis for mobilizing individuals into joining and supporting an armed movement distinct from the hierarchical, caste-like social system that had existed for hundreds of years. It was believed that union with Ethiopia would resurrect and reinforce that system. According to Trevaskis, the serf leaders preferred the 'modernity of Egypt to the primitive disorder of Abyssinia'.[28] There can be no doubt, however, that nationalism and its links to social radicalism had become coloured with an ethos linked to Islam and that the ELF, in its early stages, was influenced by it, even if it was not an explicit part of its stated aims. The continuity can be noted, firstly, in the links between Islamic personalities and organizations and the Cairo-based founders of the ELF and, secondly, in the competition between the ELF and the secular nationalist Eritrean Liberation Movement (ELM).

More research is required into the continuity between Eritrean Islam and nationalism, and although our major purpose is to illuminate the historical background of Eritrean nationalism and the influence of it in shaping the EPLF two examples provide evidence of continuity between the ML and the ELF. Firstly, the nationalists who were most

---

[27] *Ibid.*
[28] Trevaskis Papers, *Eritrea and Its Future*, p. 5.

closely associated with the cause of independence and who established the external leadership of the ELF in Cairo, Idris Muhammad Adam and Ibrahim Sultan, left Eritrea through what might be called the Khatmiyya underground. When they left Eritrea for Kassala, they initially stayed with Tahir Salim, an Eritrean NCO in the Sudanese army, and then transferred to the house of Hasan al-Mirghani and then to Ali al-Mirghani's house in Khartoum.[29]

Secondly, in the competition between the ELF and the ELM, assistance was sought from powerful religious personalities in western Eritrea. Both the ELF and ELM sought the support of Sayyidna Mustafa of the Add Shaykh, mention of whom has been made. The ELM failed to secure it because of its secularism. Although the ELF portrayed the ELM as communist in ideological inspiration, the subtext of ELF criticism was its irreligiosity. In an account of the early battles and problems of weapons procurement, one early fighter mentioned getting three rifles from Sayyidna Hamid Hamad.[30]

The motivation of Muslim religious figures for this early engagement is obscure, as is their subsequent role. It remains unclear whether they sought to retain a position of religious authority among the tribes, to undermine nationalist organizations opposed to religion in general and Islam in particular and their conception of it, or to remain politically neutral. They do, however, sporadically appear in the early politics of nationalism and the armed struggle. Sayyid Ali Mirghani was head of the Muslim League in the 1940s and, as we have mentioned, nationalist leaders fleeing Eritrea to Sudan and Egypt had their path facilitated by the Sudanese branch of the Khatmiyya and the Mirghani family. In the late 1950s, Sayyidna Mustafa favoured the ELF rather than the ELM. Even the secular ELM sought their support. Many British reports of the period stress the loyalty of the tribes to the Khatmiyya. Two conclusions can be drawn: in the early stages of Eritrean nationalism, the transition from party politics to liberation front formation and the early armed struggle there were links to these religious families, and in establishing the armed struggle in the west the support of these families was considered important.[31]

The ELF was also influenced by the social as well as the cultural context from which it emerged: the pastoralist and recently settled clan

---

[29] *Iritiriya Haditha (EH) (Arabic: Modern Eritrea)* 4/12/1991.

[30] Abu Rijayla interview, *EH*, 4/12/1991.

[31] In 1996, it was reported to me that I had just missed a Khatmiyya celebration in Keren and that people came from all over Muslim Eritrea, and included Tigre, Beja and Sahho, as well as the local Muslim Bileyn population.

and tribal communities of western Eritrea and the environs of Keren. While the ELF founders sought exile in Cairo and were influenced by the Arab nationalism of the Egyptian regime and the Algerian insurrection against French rule, the first fighters came from communities that had strong links to northern Sudan, either through cross-border clan connections or employment and residence. Both the social origins and context of the original ELF made it very difficult to establish an organization that was autonomous of Eritrean society and immune from social conflicts and tensions. In contrast, the EPLF responded to this early history of nationalist division and Eritrean sectarian fragmentation with a secular vision of Eritrean society based on nationalities. The incorporation of Christians in large numbers required that links between privileged rural elites and the church be broken.

The Formation of the ELF

In July 1960, Idris Muhammad Adam announced the foundation of the Eritrean Liberation Front from Cairo. The three-member leadership of the provisional executive committee included him, Idris Osman Galewdewos and Osman Salih Sabbe. In 1962, the executive committee was renamed the revolutionary command (RC), which later became the supreme council. While Idris Muhammad Adam remained titular head and spokesman for the front, Galewdewos took charge of military affairs from Kassala and Sabbe foreign relations and fundraising. A new RC was established in 1965 that lacked the power to influence the three leading personalities or the field commanders of a new zonal structure established at the same time.[32]

The pattern of recruitment into the ELF and its original organizational structure reproduced within the front through the 1960s a variety of Eritrean social, cultural and historic divisions. The first group of fighters were from the Bani Amir and the second batch from Eritreans who served in the Sudanese army, many of whom came from pastoralist backgrounds. A subsequent batch came from the Eritrean police. The armed struggle began in western Eritrea, the homeland of the Bani Amir, and spread gradually to the Keren area. As we have

---

[32] The best account of the emergence and development of the ELF remains J. Markakis, *National and Class Conflict in the Horn of Africa*, CUP, Cambridge, 1987, pp. 109–31. Detailed footnotes provide much information on membership of these committees. Further detail can be found in Muhammad Said al-Amin, *al-Thawra al-Iritiriyya*, Asmara, 1992, Chapter 1.

pointed out, these were the regions of serf agitation. From the very beginnings, nationalist sentiment notwithstanding, the use of clan and tribal linkages became part of the process of recruitment into the armed struggle. Thus Idris Muhammad Adam contacted his Bani Amir kinsman, Idris Muhammad Awate and requests were subsequently relayed from Eritrea to Cairo for arms.[33] In the very early period, there appears to have been limited contact between these first roving bands and growing sympathizers in Sudan and the exile leadership.

The early fighters were very poorly armed and had no resources other than what could be procured locally. The fact that they were largely Bani Amir and Nara produced support among their kinsmen but was counterproductive among the Kunama minority of western Eritrea whose memory of their predatory and cattle-raiding pastoralist neighbours and Nara allies was still fresh. Awate was a Bani Amir section chief who was considered particularly hostile to Kunama villagers. Thus, the initial social basis of the ELF bands initiated a process of exclusion rooted in the historic conflict between the pastoralist and the settled that was to have a deleterious impact on unity.

The demise of the federation in 1958 and the general strike and demonstrations against the lowering of the Eritrean flag in the same year had generated considerable support among Eritreans in the Sudan. In the first few years there were around 80 former Sudanese soldiers in the ELA. As one of the early fighters from the Bani Amir and Sudan army, Abu Rijayleh, recounted: 'I did not know the difference between Eritrea and the Sudan until 1956 when the Sudan became an independent republic.'[34] This comment is indicative of the pastoralist pattern of the Bani Amir sections which crossed the border for grazing and had a shared sense of kinship and common descent with Sudanese Bani Amir clans.

In the 1940s the British officers in the Sudanese Eastern Arab Corps did not discriminate in recruitment policies between Eritrean and Sudanese. According to Glen Balfour-Paul, a former officer in the SDF, it was left to the adjutant whose criterion was not nationality but the potential to be a good soldier.[35] Only after 1941 did the Eastern Arab Corps shift from camels to become mechanized, and up until that date a skill in camel riding had been a prerequisite.

Of the first group of ELF fighters, the bulk were from the Bani

---

[33] See interview with Abu Tayyara, *EH*, 7/3/1992.
[34] Wolde-Yesus Ammar, *Eritrea: Root Causes of War and Refugees*, Baghdad, 1992, Appendix IVb.
[35] Interview, 10/8/1993.

Amir.[36] A key figure in recruitment was the Bani Amir, Tahir Salim. In addition, there were early fighter recruits from the Muslim clans of the Bileyn, the Nara, Sahho and the Marya.[37] There were none from the Christian highlands and few from the Massawa and Dankalia areas in these early years.[38] The force was divided into three operating separately in the Gash, Keren and Haykouta areas, all of which were the domains of the clans and tribes from which the early fighters originated.

As the ELF expanded its operations from the west and recruitment increased, bolstered by Ethiopian reprisals and on some occasions civilian massacres, it took a different organizational form. It became a more advanced military organization and operated with larger force levels than the initial small bands. The new structure, however, increased the penetrability of the ELF by social forces and incorporated long-standing socio-economic conflicts within Eritrean nationalism.

Following the example of the Algeria's Front de Libération Nationale (FLN), a zonal organization was introduced for the ELA. Initially, there were four zones: zone 1 (western Eritrea/Barka province), led by Mahmud Dinai of the Bani Amir; zone 2 (the environs of Keren), led by Umar Azaz of the Bileyn; zone 3 (the highlands), led by Abd al-Karim Ahmad of the Sahho; and zone 4 (Samhar), led by Muhamad Ali Umaru of the Sahho. Subsequently, a zone 5 was created for the Hamasin–Asmara area led by Wolde Kahsai, a Tigrinya Christian. The coordination between the zones was in the hands of the newly created RC based in Kassala. A central training corps was established, and each zone was meant to recruit no more than one-third of its fighters from the zone in which it operated, although this guideline was rarely followed. Each region had a commander originating from the zone to facilitate local recruitment on the grounds that local people would be less likely to inform against a son of the locality.[39]

One consequence of the introduction of the zonal organization based on local society was the continuing process of social exclusion and alienation of groups in historical conflict with the core of fighters in the zone. In zone 4, dominated by those of Sahho origin, settled

[36] There was a proportion from the Bayt Ma'la, a group which had a distinct origin and had become subject to Bani Amir Nabtab.

[37] Ammar, *Eritrea*, Appendix IVa.

[38] Some Dankalia Afar had been recruited into the ELM. Interview, Muhammad Sa'id Nawad, Asmara, April 1993.

[39] Interview with Idris Osman Galewdewos, one of the founders of the ELF and responsible for setting up the zonal system, Asmara, May 1992.

Christian peasants of eastern Akalai Guzai saw the latter not as liberators but as their traditional marauding enemy. A similar process occurred in western Serai province. In both of these cases, as with the Kunama, religious differences overlay the longstanding conflict between pastoralist and peasant. These dual socio-economic and sectarian tensions were sharpened by the ELF practice of procuring supplies from local populations. Where there was a history of support for national independence animal transport and food for fighters were provided in a more voluntary way; in others it was simply taken. A British consular report for 1965 described the process, probably accurately, as follows:

> The shifta [bandits] move on foot across country … they take camels and donkeys from the villages as needed for the transport of e.g. ammunition. They are well disciplined: but in general live off the population. Where this is done in moderation it does not detract from the political support that they receive amongst the Moslem tribesmen such as the Beni Amer and Bileni.[40]

At this period the British estimate was of 500–600 fighters operating in groups of 20 to 60. Procuring food from poor villagers for such large bands obviously inflicted hardship. The only other source of income for the ELA was from armed robberies. Those mentioned in British consular reports concerned Italian plantation and factory owners.[41]

Indicative of the ELF's acceptance of religious separatism was the publication of a proposed political system for Eritrea. The provenance of the proposal and its authenticity cannot properly be judged, but it shares the assumptions underlying the zonal organization. It was given to a British consular employee and outlined a political system not unlike that of Lebanon where positions in the executive and legislature were based on sectarian principles. This proposal reflected a balance between the communities that had emerged in the British period and was sustained to a certain extent during the federation period. It proposed an alternating Muslim–Christian presidency and separate Muslim and Christian congresses to choose candidates from their own community for the highest offices of state.[42]

From the mid-1960s there was an increasing influx of recruits who were more formally educated than the early soldiers from the Sudanese army. They included secondary school graduates and university

---

[40] F.O. 371/18387, VA 1015/30, Situation Report on Eritrea, 25/8/1965
[41] F.O. 371/183840, VA 1015/17, British Embassy, Addis Ababa, 14/4/1965
[42] F.O. 371/183841, VA 1015/24, Appendix 1 to Despatch No. 4, 1965.

students, and an increasing number of highland Christians.[43] Increased Christian recruitment was a function of several factors. In part it replicated a continuity of minority Christian opposition to Ethiopian control represented by the LPP and the Independence Bloc of the 1940s. This strand had been maintained as the ELM spread into the highland towns following the destruction of the federation. Of particular significance was the demise of Tigrinya, through the imposition of the Ethiopian curriculum and the Amharic language and the increase in the numbers of Ethiopian teachers, who were better paid than their Eritrean counterparts.[44]

In 1959 new exchange control regulations hit small importers badly.[45] During the general strike and demonstrations of 1958 the British consul noted that the majority were Christian and that UP members were 'mostly very anti-Ethiopian now'.[46] The 1958 harvest in the highlands was poor and by 1959 peasants to the south of Asmara were selling oxen at very low prices. A combination of economic problems combined with the expansion of Ethiopian control over areas reserved to the federal government from the mid- to late 1950s sparked increasing protest resulting in widespread demonstrations, including Asmara, then inhabited by a majority of Christians.

Ethiopian repression reinforced opposition: 74 were badly injured in Asmara during the general strike and associated demonstrations. The most active participants were secondary school students and workers. It was from these urban strata that many of the first Christian recruits joined the ELF in the mid-1960s.

The new educated recruits, both Muslim and Christian, lacked any military or police background and were sent abroad for training. Batches of those from the Muslim community were sent to Syria to what were then highly politicized military colleges,[47] and a group of 35

---

[43] Throughout 1965 the British consul in Asmara monitored reports of Christian youth of Asmara who had joined the ELF.

[44] F.O. 371/11874, 1956.

[45] F.O. 371/138207, 5/1/1959.

[46] F.O. 371/JA 1016/4, 12/3/1958.

[47] From 1963 onwards, the Syrian army and military training was under the control of the Ba'th party, the ideology of which at this time was a mix of radical nationalism and Marxism. 1963 was the year of the Ba'thist military coup and the first batch of Eritreans going for training. The connection between Osman Salih Sabbe and the Syrian regime was made through a Syrian in Cairo who introduced him to Amin al-Hafiz. For the Ba'thists an Arab was one who spoke Arabic, and since some Eritreans did they were part of the Pan-Arab cause. Included in this first group were Ramadan Muhammad Nur and Muhammad Ali Umaru.

went to China in 1967–8. These new recruits became highly critical of the zonal system, and many of those who demanded the reform of the military and political structure and organization of the ELF became the nucleus of the EPLF. It should be added that others who were in the reformist group, or 'democratic forces' as they called themselves, remained in the ELF, and their critique of the zonal system was not markedly different from that of the founders of the EPLF.[48] Both criticized the absence of unity of the fighters, the debilitating competition between zonal commands compounded by the external leaders' patronage ties to different zonal commanders and the location of the leadership outside the field of combat.[49] The increasing success of the Ethiopian army in dealing with the Eritrean insurgency was also laid at the door of fragmented political and military structures. In the early period of Christian recruitment there were many reports of Christian and Muslims eating separately because of different religiously sanctioned animal slaughter patterns. Ramadan Osman Awlay, later EPLF military commander and central committee member, recalled how in 1966 in his platoon of 40 were three Christians, and how the latter got one goat's head and the other 37 one between them.[50]

Sectarian division congealed with demands for change to further compound the crisis and raised the spectre of the religious polarization of the 1940s. Some of the early Muslim fighters associated Christian highlanders with unionism, and the attempted infiltration of the ELF by Ethiopian military security deepened these suspicions, as did the organization and training by the Israelis of a special commando force raised almost totally from the Christians. The increasingly Marxist and Maoist language of the reformists was very different from the straightforward nationalism of the former Sudan army sergeants and corporals and their kinsmen who had joined the armed struggle. Ironically, the organizational slackness and divisions which the reformists criticized permitted both the emergence of an opposition and a high degree of individual decision-making by ELF military and security commanders and resulted in killings. Two reformists, Kidane Kiflu and Wolde Ghide, were killed in Kassala when, according to the

---

[48] The ELF version can be found in *The National Democratic Revolution versus Ethiopian Expansionism*, ELF, Beirut, 1979.

[49] Most accounts emphasize ethnic ties as the basis of the patronage connections. Markakis mentions Idris Muhammad Adam to the Bani Amir-dominated first zone, Sabbe to the Sahho fourth and Galawdewos to the Bileyn third zone. Galawdewos was not Bileyn but from the Tigre Bayt Juk and grew up in western Sudan.

[50] *EH*, 23/11/1992.

ELF account, there was an attempt to bring them back to Eritrea because they were recruiting fighters to the cause of reform.[51] Both were Christian highlanders. Unmentioned in the reformist ELF account was the killing of other Christian fighters. EPLF sources put the number at 200 in addition to the killing of 50 Christian peasants.[52]

The demand for reform and the attack on the external leadership brought the ELF into a deep crisis and divided it from top to bottom. The attempt to create a more unified and coherent organizational structure and greater leadership accountability further divided both the fighters and the leadership.[53] It resulted in the emergence of what came to be called the Unity of the Three (zones 3, 4 and 5) the leaders of which took a reformist position. To resolve the problem a meeting of all five zones was held. Members of the supreme council took contending positions on unification and the nature of zonal representation at a congress to deal with reform demands. Issues of ideology, organization and power became fused and only partially resolved at the Adobaha congress of 1969, at which a new leadership structure, the Qiyada al-'Ama (general command, GC) emerged. It was a compromise between coalitions of reformists and segments of the leadership that did not satisfy reformists of zones 3, 4 and 5, and it was from these that the EPLF originated.

The political struggles which took place during this period further reproduced communal divisions as leaders and fighters sought to defend their positions through a reliance on relatives, clans and tribes. While the ELF never really recovered and continued splitting from the late 1960s through to its military expulsion from Eritrea by the EPLF at the beginning of the 1980s, the lesson learned by those who split and subsequently formed the EPLF was the necessity to create a disciplined nationalist liberation army impervious to social, ethnic, regional, tribal, religious and ideological divisions. In sum, an autonomous organization which moulded Eritreans rather than one buffeted by Eritrean socio-historic divisions.

The struggle for an autonomous hermetic movement on the part of the leadership of the EPLF involved not only sealing it off from diverse internal social, economic and ideological currents but from external

---

[51] ELF, *National Democratic Revolution*, p. 46.

[52] *Our Struggle*, p.18.

[53] The following relies on Markakis, *National and Clan Conflict*, al-Amin, *al-Thawra*, and interviews with Galawdewos and Hurui Tedla Bairu. A more detailed account of this process remains unwritten. For the purposes of this book, the important point is the impact of the organizational disarray on EPLF founders.

influences, be they through an exile leadership or supportive regional states. From its beginnings, the ELF was a coalition of exile nationalists abroad and fighters recruited locally and from neighbouring Sudan. The zonal organization produced a parallel coalition but was military in form. The actual establishment of the ELF outside was through an alliance of students in Cairo and the leadership of exiled nationalists from an earlier period. The younger generation of students and former students felt that they required 'political names' to establish a credible front.[54] Associating the new front with politicians whose reputation was based on their roles during the period of the BMA and the federation, intentionally or not, incorporated a style of politics based on bargaining, compromise and patron–clientism rife in that period and was a factor in the coalitional character of differential regional groups in the field.

There was a further externality in the foundation of the ELF: the outside leadership was the agency for raising funds, gathering political support from Eritreans abroad and foreign states and securing military training. A key figure in this regard was Osman Salih Sabbe. Through the 1960s, he sought assistance from states which were hostile to Ethiopia because of Ethiopia's links to the US and subsequently Israel. Radical Arab nationalist states and Arab League member Somalia with its irredentist claims against Ethiopia were natural candidates.

The success of Sabbe's diplomacy in the Arab world had two consequences. Firstly, it provided the external leadership with control over considerable funds and quantities of arms to bolster their influence over the field. The resources which the external leadership controlled and the potential influence it brought was a problem for the reformist fighters. Thus, one of their major demands was leadership in the field and the election of a leadership by the fighters. Secondly, it linked the liberation army, which originally consisted wholly of Muslims, to Muslim and Arab states and resulted in an identification of Eritrean nationalism with Islam and Arabism. Thirdly, the external support came from Arab states that had their own agendas and were in constant competition.

Throughout the 1960s, the Arab states were fragmented between a conservative pro-Western camp and a radical nationalist one, and the latter was divided between Nasserist nationalism and the Ba'thist-dominated states of Iraq and Syria. After 1969, Libya with its idiosyncratic foreign policy joined the ranks of the radicals. Links to the Arab

---

[54] Interview, Galewdewos, Asmara, May 1993.

states thus associated the ELF with complex ties to a divided Arab world. In addition, the essential motivation for the involvement of these states, conservative or radical, was foreign policies based on Arab nationalism or Islam, which resulted in an extension of Arab–Israeli competition and inter-Arab rivalries into the Red Sea area. The emergence of the basis of the EPLF from dissident fighters did not resolve the problem of external influence over those in the field, however, as Osman Salih Sabbe broke with the ELF, established a general secretariat and aligned it with the dissidents. Tension between Sabbe and the latter came to a head in 1975.[55]

Conclusion

Much of the ideology and the tactics and strategy of the EPLF were forged in reaction to the sectarian character of the politics of British rule and the continuing identification of Eritrean nationalism with the Muslim parts of Eritrea. Within the ELF there remained some who were deeply suspicious of Christian highlanders because of their historic association with the movement for unification with Ethiopia. *In grosso modo*, these perceptions were accurate. As a consequence, the EPLF portrayed the major divisions (in its Maoist language 'contradictions') as class ones. The use of Marxist and Maoist conceptions rewrote Eritrean history from a different theoretical perspective and thereby divorced Christian highlanders from unionism.

As we shall demonstrate in Chapter 4, implementing policies in the liberated areas based on class analysis had considerable utility for political mobilization. The other theoretical perspective which blurred the connection between Christians and union with Ethiopia was an analysis of Eritrean society partly derived from Stalin. The use of the concept of nationality as the main cultural cleavage between Eritreans also undermined the notion of religion and tribe as significant social entitities. As nationalities were defined by the use of a common language, the linguistic groups of Eritrea were unified by culture, with a consequent downgrading of religion. It also abrogated the perceived connection between Christian Eritreans and the Christian character of the Ethiopian empire.

Of equal importance was the impact of the experience of member-

---

[55] The details of the political manoeuvrings are related cogently by Markakis, *National and Class Conflict*.

ship in the ELF on EPLF founders. We have stressed the permeability of the ELF in two dimensions: the internal and the external. The founders of the EPLF introduced organizational forms and a stress on self-reliance to build a liberation movement which was impervious to historic Eritrean social and political divisions and the influence of actors external to the field command.

II

The Eritrean People's Liberation Front

In the following three chapters we shall examine the formation and structuring of the EPLF, the processes by which it extended its organization outwards and the way it which it adapted to external events. Most notable were its development from small factions of guerrilla fighters to an autonomous state-like organization comprising a liberation army and administration, and its ability to maintain its autonomy from a fragmented and heterogeneous society and the fissiparous influences of regional states. The EPLF has been portrayed in a number of contrasting ways. It has been characterized on the basis of ethnic, regional and religious criteria: as a Christian highland-dominated front and a vehicle for Tigrinya speakers;[1] and as a broad nationalist liberation movement. The question of the ethno-religious character of the EPLF will be addressed in these chapters. It has been characterized by ideology: both as a Marxist-Leninist revolutionary organization[2] and as flexibly pragmatic.[3]

The EPLF's self-characterization has changed over time. From presenting itself as a revolutionary vanguard, the current view of the EPLF-based government in Eritrea is that it was always a broad front reflecting a range of ideological tendencies. Although the policies of the front have changed, there has been a degree of continuity in its practices. In the 1970s, radical egalitarian policies were promoted in the liberated countryside, and these were complemented by policies pursued in the towns that were liberated in 1977–8. By the mid-1980s, a revision of the early programme of the EPLF was introduced at its

---

[1] See Ammar, *Eritrea*; Negash, *Eritrea and Ethiopia*.
[2] Gebre-Medhin, *Peasants and Nationalism*.
[3] Iyob, *Eritrean Struggle*.

second congress in 1987 and this new programme provided a basis for government policies after liberation. With hindsight, then, it might appear fair to characterize the EPLF as a pragmatic movement with limited ideological coherence and lacking ideological continuity. Its strategic goal was always Eritrean independence, and the tactics it used in particular circumstances included militant ideological positions.

The EPLF's outstanding characteristics were strict discipline organized from above combined with space for a degree of creative individualism within that disciplined framework. In Chapter 3 we shall examine its origins and the form the front took. Although the EPLF is considered one of the strongest liberation movements to emerge in Africa, its development into a successful movement that achieved statehood for Eritrea faced considerable obstacles, not the least of which was establishing and retaining such a high level of organizational continuity and coherence. An important part of the explanation of the success of the EPLF was the extension of its internal discipline and organization outwards into key parts of Eritrean society in such a way that the social fragmentation we have dealt with was neither reproduced within the front nor in its associated organizations.

Chapter 4 deals with the process of external expansion. By the middle of the 1970s, the structural shape of the EPLF had been established, enabling it to adapt to its changing political environment and seize political opportunities. These involved: the absorption of Eritreans in flight from the Ethiopian revolution, the recruitment of the peasantry; the competition with the Derg, the Amharic term for the committee that formed the revolutionary government of Ethiopia, for revolutionary authenticity in the Cold War period (the US was unlikely to support a movement which might challenge norms of African diplomacy); and with the ELF which had undergone a regeneration in the 1970s but had not translated it into the same kind of centralized control.

Chapter 5 deals with these key aspects in the liberation struggle in a thematic way rather than through a detailed history of battles. It rests on the argument that after having achieved a mature organizational form in the mid-1970s, the EPLF was able to mobilize and absorb Eritreans and take advantage of events and circumstances as they arose.

The EPLF was, and the government deriving from it remains, a secretive organization. Insights can be gained from assorted eye-witness reports, from EPLF journals and the rare internal document, and from gossip and anecdote from fighters. Some analysis, and the evidential sources for it, has to be taken on trust. Many of those I have spoken to over the years are still unwilling to be named as sources of information. The EPLF has amassed tremendous archives on its politics and on Eritrean society. The quality of its cadres, both those who were educated abroad and those trained in the field, was exceptionally high. In the rear base area in 1977, an anonymous khaki-cloaked figure gave a detailed analysis of the political economy of Keren that would have done credit to a research Ph.D. in rural sociology: an academic in the garb of a guerrilla.

Within the EPLF, individuals have had great significance, as we shall see in the discussion of the dissident problem. For outsiders, however, the particular weight of personality within the front is difficult to assess. The predominance of Issayas Afeworki from the foundation of the EPLF is marked. Given the secrecy, then, there are a fair number of surmises in this analysis of the EPLF and its pivotal role in winning independence. The EPLF is not generous with political information about the detail of the inner workings of the front. Although Maoist self-criticism was institutionalized within the front, it was for individuals and not for the front as a whole, and rarely for its leadership.

Two key documents will be drawn on which illuminate internal processes discussed in Chapters 3 and 4, respectively. The first, *The Destructive Movement*, was translated for me from Tigrinya and deals with the origins of the front and an important internal crisis that took place in its formative period. It was intended for internal distribution and is remarkably frank. The second, *Creating a Popular, Economic, Political and Military Base* (*CPEPMB*), was published by the Research and Information Centre for Eritrea (RICE) in 1982 for a conference on Eritrea in the field attended by foreign observers. It was based on sections of an array of internal documents including the political education of cadres and the guide for land reform used by the mass administration. I have compared the contents of *CPEPMB* with the independent experience and practices of EPLF cadres and can vouch for its general reliability, even though it was produced by the EPLF for an external audience.

A central component of developing the organizational capacity and generating mass support was the structured relationship between EPLF cadres, the mass organizations and the role of political education. A distinction was made between the organized and unorganized and, within the former category, between sympathizers, participants and dedicated members of the mass associations of workers, peasants, women and youth. It was into broader Eritrean social structures and categories that the EPLF penetrated through levels of cadres building institutional and organizational links by means of propaganda and agitation. They were a means of subverting Ethiopian controls and competing with the ELF, which had succeeded in capturing much of the extant organizational membership of the earlier ELM in the 1960s. The ELF had considerable support in many parts of Eritrea, including Asmara, Keren and the small towns of the west. The internal *manqa* crisis, involving the withdrawal of the bulk of EPLF forces to Sahel to defend the leadership, and the civil war were further debilitating experiences for this young organization.

Three

The Formation
& Organization
of the Front

Introduction

We have described the first phase of the break-up of the ELF and now turn to the phoenix. Establishing the EPLF was not without internecine conflicts and the recourse to violence as a means of resolving them. In the following sections we shall examine the process of the formation of the EPLF, the challenge from within and the consolidation of the Maoist model of guerilla organization, with its particular Eritrean characteristics. Most analyses of the EPLF have stressed its attempts to transform Eritrean society. The earlier ELF was established as a guerrilla organization to fight an armed struggle, and it was, in part, problems in achieving this goal that lay behind the splits which brought forth the EPLF. The major goal of the EPLF leadership was to create a unified and centralized military organization to achieve independence. As we shall demonstrate, from the beginning the obstacles to its success were formidable: the unification of the armed factions that had in common only a shared opposition to the ELF; the subsequent civil war with the ELF; and the concurrent emergence of an internal opposition to the early leadership.

From Opposition to Unified Force

The EPLF was formally established at the 1977 organizational congress held in the liberated and sparsely populated Sahel region of northern Eritrea, when the term 'front' replaced 'forces'. It originated from an amalgam of fighter factions which had split from the ELF at an earlier period and had, through a series of mergers, formed a unified front. In

63

the process of its formation, however, it had undergone a set of multi-faceted political, military and ideological crises. The gathering together of the disparate factions occurred simultaneously with increased Ethiopian attacks and a civil war between the ELF and the EPLF factions. The two most important groups of the latter were the Popular Liberation Forces (PLF) and *Selfi Natzinet* (Tigrinya: Liberation Party), also known as the Ala group, which provided the core of cadres and leaders, most of whom originated from the two adjacent strategic regions of Samhar, the east coast province, and the plateau, respectively. We shall also mention some smaller factions the role of which complicated the unification of the dissidents and provided an index of the difficulties in the creation of a unified liberation front and army.

The Popular Liberation Forces

The PLF was an amalgamation of two groups. The first consisted of those who had fled the ELF to Sudan and dissident members of ELF mass organizations. They were contacted initially by Asmarom, the son of Ras Tessema, former president of the nationalist LPP, and Taha Muhammad Nur, a close ally of Sabbe. After registering the names of fighters, they were flown to Aden two weeks later and subsequently crossed the Red Sea to Dankalia. The second group were dissidents from the fourth zonal command of Samhar. The two groups agreed to join forces at a meeting at Sudoha Eyla in southern Dankalia held between 24 June and 2 July 1970, attended by about 100 fighters.[1]

Broad principles rather than a detailed programme were agreed. By the very act of taking on the name of the Eritrean Popular Liberation Forces, referred to by Eritreans as *sha'biyya* (Arabic for popular), a degree of organizational coherence began to emerge. This was under-pinned by the election of a nine-member leadership[2] and a steering

---

[1] *The Destructive Movement (The DM)*. The names of the organizations are sometimes confusing. Later EPLF historical analyses simplified them into PLF I, to refer to the grouping established at Sudoha Eyla and PLF II, to the highland grouping of Ala. At the time, an important point to make for the historical record that continues to be rewritten is that different populations had different names for the groups, whatever they called themselves or whatever they became named in EPLF political education. Although PLF II called itself *Selfi Natzinet*, some Asmarans identified it with Issayas. ELF publications identified this group as the 'Issayas group', distorting its character and locating the split as part of some personalisic politics. Iyob, *The Eritrean Struggle*, p. 115, states that the PLF II/Ala group attended this meeting, although this is not confirmed by this document.

[2] The nine were: Muhamad Ali Umaru, President, Mesfin Hagos, Muhamad Umar

committee for a 'broad-based' organizational congress. Central to their concerns was national unity. The removal of differences based on religion, race, region and descent was asserted as a primary task, and a department of propaganda for raising the political consciousness of fighters was established for this purpose. Arming civilians with the aim of forming a people's militia and attracting ELF rank and file fighters were aimed at bolstering the military capabilities of the PLF. Although links with the former external leadership were not broken, it was emphasized that the connections to personalities like Woldab Wolde-mariam and Osman Salih Sabbe were to be 'ordinary'. It was also agreed to oppose the ELF-GC and the GS and to vet closely any ELF military commanders seeking to join. According to Al-Amin Muham-mad Said, secretary of the post-liberation Popular Front for Democ-racy and Justice (PFDJ), although they were elected by secret ballot, priority was given to the representation of Eritrea's diverse tribal, regional and religious communities rather than to ability and merit.[3]

Initially, then, the PLF was ethnically and tribally coalitional, rather like the ELF. Muhammad Ali Umaru was elected as president, and among the nine were al-Amin and Mesfin Hagos.[4] This coalition of disparate fighters did not last long. One group led by Sudanese army veterans, Muhammad Umar Abdallah (Abu Tayarra) and Umar Damir, both from the Tigre-speaking Marya, went north to Sahel in order to influence the GC in the adjacent Barka area. Mesfin Hagos, the only highland Christian, went to join the group in the highlands. A few Christians from the largely Muslim Tigre-speaking Mensa remained. Another group, consisting of Afar, attempted to establish a separate Afar military grouping.[5]

In al-Amin's account, while the departure of Tigrinya Christian Mesfin Hagos is not discussed,[6] the Marya and Afar are portrayed as

---

[2] (cont.) Abdallah 'Abu Tayyara', al-Amin Muhamad Sa'id, Umar Damir, Mahari Debessai, Muhamad Osman Ahmad, Ma'sho Imbay and Ali Muhamad Osman.

[3] Al-Amin, *al-Thawra*, p. 98.

[4] *Ibid.*, pp. 81–3. Of the leadership and cadres mentioned by al-Amin who were members of the executive council of the PFDJ were Umaru and Ramadan Awlaya. Others included Mahari Debessai. After liberation Mesfin Hagos was chief of staff for a time and subsequently governor of Dubub (South) province.

[5] See M.G. Ashami, 'The Political Economy of the Afar Region of Ethiopia: A Dynamic Periphery', unpublished Ph.D. thesis, Cambridge, 1985.

[6] His departure suggested a Christian–Muslim polarization at the core of the factions splitting from the ELF, which were later to unify. The details remained a topic of private seminar discussion at EPLF cadre school, at which some of those involved eventually taught. A generally accepted account is that Ramadan Muhammad Nur secured his

tribalists, regionalists and practitioners of the 'traditional' armed struggle of home region-based fighters. These early strains within the PLF were a mark of the continuity of problems deriving from ethnic and sectarian solidarities, on the one hand, and the varying connection between the field fighters and the external leadership, on the other.

It was not until September–October 1971 that the Marya-led group in Sahel and the Dankalia group united again at the Ambahara meeting near Hibru, and a new five-man leadership was elected consisting of Ramadan Muhammad Nur, Ahmad Hilal, Abu Bakr Muhammad Hasan, Salih Titu and AbuBakr Muhammad Juma. All were Muslim. The political statement arising from Ambahara combined a radical rhetoric with bland statements about national unity and strongly expressed opposition to the ELF's proposed national congress. Dankalia provided considerable space for regrouping at a distance from the ELF, and its location on the Red Sea allowed access to the outside. Despite its maritime situation, it was an unfavourable place for the new force to develop into Mao's 'fish in the sea' for it was a sparsely populated area of pastoralism and coastal fishing villages. Conditions in the region were extremely harsh. Communications with the external leadership on whom they depended for supplies were particularly difficult, the terrain was arid and the climate very humid and hot with summer temperatures reaching above 50°C. In addition, the Ethiopians began building up their forces along the Red Sea coast as intelligence of the PLF's presence spread.

Most accounts by early fighters present a picture of confusion, poor coordination and vulnerability because of the spasmodic and unreliable supplies from South Yemen.[7] As a consequence, there were high attrition rates among these early fighters. One of the members of this group, Bashay Ghide Ghebremedin Hagos, has described their parlous position. Arriving from Aden, his group was initially involved in a week-long battle at Sodoha Eyla, then moved to Merkato, then back to Sodoha Eyla where the first conference was held, then back to Merkato once more when their supplies from outside were cut. From Beylul, on the coast, they sent three fighters, Abu Tayyara, Umar Damir, and Mahari Debessai, to Aden to make contact with Osman Salih Sabbe. In the absence of the emissaries, local inhabitants warned

---

[6] (cont.) departure and had the aim of creating some spirit of cooperation between dissident ELF factions and, at the same time, averting the primordial suspicions of a highland fighter. Al-Amin's account glosses over the Tigrinya–Tigre tensions and is part of a public rewriting of history.

[7] *EH*, 21/3/1992.

them to leave the area because of the presence of the Ethiopian army. They then moved to Halima where there was more abundant water, and after a month they sent another message to Aden to find out what was going on. Later, they made an arrangement with a boat owner to go themselves to Aden. The boat was defective, and after spending a day trying to fix it they returned to the Eritrean coast. From then on, the group disintegrated, and Bashay and nine others finally surrendered to the Ethiopians in Beylul.[8]

The Obel Group

The Obel group originated from the first zone, the western Barka province. Their leader, Adam Salih of the military committee of the GC, together with Ahmad Adam Umar, Muhammad Ahmad Idris and Osman Ajib, were in disagreement with Salih Hayouti, head of security of the GC. ELF sources portray them as a dissident faction opposed to the holding of the ELF national congress, on the grounds that they would lose their positions to the democratic movement, and concerned to strengthen links to the Arab and Islamic world. Early EPLF sources portray them as opposed to Salih Hayouti's purging and killing of fighters and, as such, a democratic element within the GC. The group was named after the Obel river, where they held their first meeting in November 1970, when they adopted the more respectable name of Eritrean Liberation Forces. Both ELF and EPLF later sources portrayed this group as motivated by opposition to other GC factions and lacking any kind of political programme.

The Ala Group

In contrast to the PLF and Obel, the Ala group was homogeneous and consisted of Christian Tigrinya speakers. It was formed by those who had fled from the west in the spring of 1969 and a group who were part of the fifth zone, the highland region around Asmara. They hid in woodland on the Ala plain of Akalai Guzai province and had little in the way of arms or ammunition. They did, however, receive some minimal support from the local village population. The Ala group contacted the Dankalia group in November 1970 after a long march

[8] He rejoined the PLF in 1974.

from Ala to Simouti in north Dankalia, 'but preferred to stay out for the time being', as one EPLF document phrased it.[9] Prior to this contact the Ala group held a conference at Tekli on the eastern escarpment in August 1971, and elected a leadership consisting of Issayas Afeworki, Mesfin Hagos, Tewolde Eyob, Solomon Woldemariam and Asmerom Gerezgiher.[10]

The Tekli conference resolutions reasserted opposition to the ELF–GC and its proposed congress, railed against religious and tribal divisions and attacked the triumvirate of imperialism, Zionism and Ethiopian colonialism. The Ala group, by way of self-advertisement, issued *Our Struggle and its Goals*. Although it had the imprint of the group, it was probably written by Issayas Afeworki in late 1971. It provided an analysis of Eritrean society, justification for the group's separation from the ELF and the bare outline of a programme. Embedded in the pamphlet was a stress on the unity of the Eritrean nation and the necessity for a 'revolutionary organization with a revolutionary line' to forge unity. The ELF was attacked for mobilizing support through stressing the Christian character of the Ethiopian empire, and thus implicitly on the basis of Islam, rather than on a broad and positive Eritrean nationalism. The ELF leadership was also blamed for discriminating against Christian highlanders in order to retain power, for killing reformist Christian members of the leadership and Christian peasant and worker recruits. The stress on the ELF's discrimination against Christians and its emphasis on Islam was followed by the argument that although the group was Christian its coherence was based not on religion but persecution, and that the split from the ELF derived from the lack of any alternative course of action. The concerns of the pamphlet, then, focused on issues which were of greater import for Christian Tigrinyans than other Eritrean communities.

While recognizing that there were 'ethnic ties' between Arabs and Eritreans, *Our Struggle* stressed the 'alien' nature of the Arabic language and the need to develop 'our languages'. This line of argument raised ethnic and cultural issues. As has been pointed out, many of the Muslim communities traced their ancestral origins to marriages between indigenous peoples and migrants from Arabia. Tigre- and Sahho-speaking literates used Arabic, and the *lingua franca* for Muslim Nara and Tigre

---

[9] *The DM.*

[10] The first two and the last retain post-liberation positions. Tewolde Eyob was associated with the *manqa* and was executed. Solomon Woldemariam had continuing tensions with the EPLF leadership and is thought to have been imprisoned after fleeing to the Sudan and executed.

speakers in the west, for example, was frequently Arabic. Along with Tigrinya, Arabic had been an official language during the BMA. By making such a sharp distinction between indigenous languages and Arabic the intention was to negate the portrayal by a section of the ELF leadership of Eritreans as being closely connected to Arab and Islamic culture. Although Eritreans could not be considered Arab, there were strong links between Eritrean Islam and Arabism, and particularly between some Eritrean communities and the northern Arabic-speaking Sudan. Not only did the former ELF leadership emphasize such connections but so did the PLF's external ally Osman Salih Sabbe; both used them to gain financial and military support from Arab states. The strong links between Ethiopia and Israel also facilitated an Eritrean approach to both radical and conservative Arab states. From the late 1960s onwards, radical pan-Arabist Ba'th governments had come to power in Iraq and Syria and, given that their main objective criterion of Arabness was speaking Arabic, Eritrean liberation fronts which portrayed Eritrea as culturally linked to the Arab world were well placed for aid and assistance from them. Osman Salih Sabbe was particularly adept at cultivating Arab governments whatever their ideological orientation and, when he was removed from the leadership of the ELF, took his contacts with him when he formed the general secretariat.

Our Struggle called for developing indigenous Eritrean languages and introduced more broadly into Eritrean political language the conception of nationalities. Tigre, the spoken language of the majority of Muslims, was far less developed than Tigrinya, and Tigre speakers, consequently, less well placed to make their language equal to Tigrinya. While recognizing the educational and cultural links to the Arab world, the pamphlet stated starkly that 'to insist that our people learn, speak and study an alien language … undermines our national identity and negates the spirit of our liberation struggle. Therefore, we totally reject it.'[11] This position taken by the Ala group was more likely to appeal to Eritreans of Christian background and, to a certain extent, to secularists from the Muslim communities. Despite the cogency of developing the cultural basis of an Eritrean nationalism, in the minds of some it reinforced the perception that the Ala group, while not necessarily 'prophets of Christianity', were sectarian and narrowly regionalist. In the longer run, this early and crude position was eroded as EPLF publications appeared in both Arabic and Tigrinya, although

[11] *Our Struggle*, p. 22.

as we shall show a Tigrinyanization of the front took place. The language issue remained a divisive one even after independence.

The Civil War and Unification

Through the whole course of the liberation struggle sustained efforts were made to overcome problems arising from cultural, religious and linguistic divisions within Eritrean society. As we have noted, their impact on Eritrean politics began in the 1940s and took an even more serious course as they became entangled in the conflict between the different liberation organizations. When the conflict erupted into the first civil war, it was yet another scarring of Eritrean nationalism. It provided a bloody impetus for the unification of the former ELF groups and an obstacle to the later unification of the ELF and EPLF because of the bloodshed and deep distrust. The civil war is an important part of the historical record of Eritrean nationalism, and although it is impossible to verify the accounts of its beginnings, both ELF and EPLF attribute blame to the other for the turn to violence.

The civil war decision was ostensibly taken at the ELF November conference in November 1972, and endorsed at its first national congress in March 1973 on the grounds that the 'Eritrean field cannot bear more than one organization and one leadership'. The actual beginning of the civil war is conventionally dated as February 1972. Al-Amin Muhammad Said, however, argues that there was an informal meeting of leading ELF cadres to discuss the problem of the opposition. It was attended by some members of the general command, with Abdallah Idris[12] at their head, in June 1970, together with some members of the military units in the Kolontabay area in Barka province in western Eritrea. It was here that the decision was taken to liquidate the opposition forces, with Abdallah Idris and Osman Azaz taking military and financial responsibility for the project, respectively.[13]

Taking men and arms from a unit in Akalai Guzai province, Abdallah Idris set out to attack a PLF force moving from southern Dankalia to the Simouti area, west of Mersa Fatma. Apparently, the

---

[12] Abdallah Idris was from the Bani Amir and, according to documents produced by the EPLF, his group began conspiring with Ethiopian officials prior to independence. See appendices, al-Amin, *al-Thawra*. After independence, he took to armed opposition to the new Eritrean government, and those that know him depict an overwhelming personal hatred of Issayas Afeworki.

[13] Al-Amin, *al-Thawra*, p. 122.

attack was stopped by a group of ELF fighters. A second attempt to initiate fighting was made in November 1970 in the Dabat area. On this occasion, opposition to an attack was led by ELF fighters, and a dialogue committee was formed from them to discuss problems with PLF forces. A major source for al-Amin's account of these incidents was Muhammad Sa'id Barih, one of the ELF fighters at the Dabat meeting, and from the Tigre-speaking Muslims, who opposed the ELF's recourse to military means.[14]

The ELF's account of the origins of the civil war differs from that of the EPLF. It traces its beginnings to 'provocations' by the PLF and Obel. It is nigh impossible to disentangle what actually happened. Given the ELF leadership's early determination to brook no opposition, as indicated by its attack on the armed wing of the ELM in 1965 at Ela Tzada, the eventual outbreak of a full-blooded civil war at the end of February 1972 came as no surprise. Although ELF official sources state that the meeting between the three breakaway factions and Sabbe in Beirut was only 'later revealed', it is unlikely that ELF leaders were unaware of the meeting and the potential military and financial backing for the dissidents that would ensue.

The calculation of the ELF leadership was that it would be a short campaign and focused on defeating the separate forces of PLF and Obel and leaving the Ala group alone.[15] On 29 February, two of the ex-GC Obel leaders and their forces surrendered when they were surrounded. Full-scale military operations against the PLF began on 16 March 1972 in the She'b area. After another battle toward the end of March at Hahout some of the survivors of Obel and the PLF withdrew to northern Sahel. The Ala group, though not initially attacked, was determined not to return to the ELF and was inevitably drawn into the fighting.

The beginnings of the civil car and the need to acquire arms from Sabbe's general secretariat were catalysts in forging a national front between the dissident fighter groups and Sabbe's external faction. The Beirut meetings from 3 to 12 February 1972 between them and Sabbe went some way to clarifying the relationship between an external

---

[14] He was subsequently elected to the EPLF political bureau in 1977.

[15] The ELF version is that 'Sabbe's PLF faction' and the Obelites attacked ELF fighters and stores. Although the Ala group, or the 'Essayas faction' as they called it, was vilified, the ELF did not blame it and purposely did not attack it. That the group was wholly highland Christian was the main factor. *Eritrea: The National Democratic Revolution versus Ethiopian Expansionism*, 1979.

71

leadership with access to arms, ammunition and money and the field commanders and fighters. From mid- to late October 1972 a meeting of all three factions of the opposition concluded with a set of political, administrative and military decisions aimed at creating a united front.

Given the drift to civil war and the Obel group's links to Sabbe, the opposition factions were keen to ensure a regular flow of arms and finance from outside Eritrea and gain control of the field. The meeting in Beirut attempted to regulate the relationship between the field fighters and the general secretariat, renamed the foreign mission (FM), and resulted in further discussions on unifying the fronts. A committee was formed to distribute weapons and money fairly among the groups, to enhance political education and provide literacy training for the fighters, to organize civilian Eritreans and provide assistance to refugees and the families of martyrs. It was also agreed that a conference would be held within a year.

The agreement also proposed a dual autonomy for the field and the FM on the basis of mutual non-interference, and an attempt was made to make the latter accountable through regular monthly reports and statements of expenditure. Three-quarters of the money raised was to be spent in the field and the remainder outside. The FM was to expand its activities outside the Middle East and establish ties with progressive Ethiopian forces. The agreement was essentially a compromise. For the FM, it provided links with an armed force in the field and thereby furnished it, and Sabbe in particular, with political and military credibility vis-a-vis the ELF and Arab governments. For the fighters it was a means of securing money and arms and diminishing the influence of external political leaders and, through them, regional states, particularly Arab Muslim states. It was a step on the way to creating an autonomous organization impermeable by external forces.

For the three armed factions the linkage brought access to money and arms. For the PLF, the link provided continuity: a significant number of PLF fighters came from Samhar province, particularly the Massawa-Harqiqo area, and had links with Osman Salih Sabbe. He had been a schoolteacher in Harqiqo, an active nationalist and recruiter of students into the ELF. Among others he taught or recruited were Al-Amin Muhammad Said, Ramadan Muhammad Nur and Ramadan Awlaya, a heavy artillery commander through the 1980s. The Samhar command, the fourth zone led by Muhammad Ali Umaru, had been relatively privileged given its easier access to arms which Sabbe shipped across the Red Sea.

The centrality of Sabbe's role in this area has been recounted by Ahmad Shaykh Ibrahim Faras, a ship captain. In the early 1960s, he acted as a conduit of arms and ammunition from the Arabian peninsular to the Eritrean coast. He recalled how, in 1965 when the zonal system had been established, he met Sabbe in Italy and the latter asked him to contact Muhammad Umaru, commander of the Samhar zone, to find out what he needed. A meeting with Umaru was arranged in Harqiqo, and the latter requested a radio, binoculars, ammunition, grenades, photographic equipment and, more mundanely, underwear. After getting a radio and binoculars from Asmara, Ahmad went to Jiddah to meet Sabbe and passed on the requests. The secret Massawa network was part of the conduit and included Massawa police, customs officials and boat owners. The Massawa area had provided a significant contribution to the armed struggle: at the beginning of 1962 30 policemen had fled with their arms to join the ELF, a significant addition to the small number of fighters at that time.

For the Obel group, a shared pragmatic nationalism made for closer cooperation with the FM than it did with the young radical ideologues of the PLF and the Ala group. The latter were rather uneasy in their relationship with Sabbe. Not only had he always argued for links to the Arab world, he had been remarkably successful in building them. The introduction to his book, *The History of Eritrea*, written originally in Arabic, begins:

> My motive in writing it is not only my wish to fill the gap in the Arabic library about ... the past of this country which enjoys historical, geographical and cultural ties with the Arab world,[16]

and adds that he will stress the closeness 'bypassing any sensibilities, domestic or external, that could be provoked'.[17] Written in 1974, the domestic sensibilities referred to were those of the Ala group. In marked contrast to the line propounded in *Our Struggle*, Sabbe asserted that 'Arabic has been the language of culture for Muslims ... [and] its propagation enhances the promotion of culture in Eritrea and the unification of the people who speak various dialects'.[18]

Such differences in approach to Eritrean culture were a combustible ingredient in the relationship between the FM and the Ala group leader Issayas Afeworki, although it took some years to ignite. A major beneficiary of the agreement, however, was the Ala group, isolated

---

[16] O.S. Sabby [Sabbe] The History of Eritrea [English translation from Arabic] Bierst 1974.
[17] *Ibid.*, p. 14.
[18] *Ibid.*, p. 260.

from the inactive highland peasantry and opposed to the Arabist position of the FM. It was supplied with arms even before the complete unification with the PLF.

In spite of the pressures of the civil war, unification remained a slow process. The three groups met in October 1972 and announced a set of measures aimed at enhancing coordination. They agreed to issue a joint monthly publication, *Vanguard*, to publicize common policies and influence ELF rank and file, to organize seminars among fighters with the goal of developing a unified consciousness. A more integrated administrative structure was established with a joint leadership known as the Gehteb executive, after the place where the meeting was held. The highest authority was a 57-member committee (21 from PLF, 25 from Ala and 11 from Obel)[19] with an administrative committee of nine playing a day-to-day leadership role.

The administrative committee was 'above all bodies, supervises administrative matters, issues directives, receives reports and reviews and implements policy'.[20] It was essentially a Marxist–Leninist structure with democratic centralism as the operative principle and thus considerable powers for this latter committee. It prefigured the establishment of the central committee–political bureau structure which emerged from the EPLF congress of 1977. Members of the administrative committee headed various departments: information and political education, finance and supply, health, military and intelligence. A tribunal was also established drawn from personnel in the administration and the administrative committee, and a military judge was included. It was agreed to establish a base area in Sahel and concentrate forces there to defend the bases against the ELF and to continue classical guerrilla war by smaller bands against the Ethiopian army. As a step towards full military integration, it was also agreed to establish a common military and political code for all three forces. A further organizational congress was proposed six months on when a leadership would be formally elected. It was at the Gehteb meeting that agreement was reached on the essential principles of the national democratic revolution, which were debated and ratified five years later at the first national congress of the EPLF.

[19] The greater number from the Ala group is a mark of the expansion in numbers of the Christians. According to some accounts, a significant number of Asmara high school and University of Addis Ababa students were recruited through a written appeal from Issayas Afeworki. According to Ammar, *Eritrea*, pp. 91–2, the appeal was to highlanders to join to 'defend their dignity'. There was a general 'buzz' about the 'Issayas group' among young nationalist Asmaran Tigrinyans in the early 1970s, according to many of my informants.
[20] *The DM.*

At the end of April 1973 the administrative committee, or 'Gehteb executive', met at Tegeh to review conditions for the integration of the three forces. No progress was made and the guerrilla forces remained under separate commands. One major problem was relations with the Obel faction and Abu Tayyara, a veteran ELF fighter and former Sudan army NCO who led a small Marya group. He had initially taken them into the PLF, taken them out again and then linked up with the Obel group. Eventually, the Obel group refused to participate without consulting with the FM, and the PLF and the Ala group proceeded to negotiate a merger independent of it.

At the end of June 1973, the administrative committee, reduced to seven members after the withdrawal of Obel, and a committee of the military units pressed for unification with the Ala group, calling for a unified administration and a unified military force and mass organizations.

In August 1973, the two leaderships met to discuss problems and study the obstacles to full unity. At this meeting it was decided to mix up the fighters of the groups as individuals rather than as units. One obvious problem was that of language: the PLF spoke Tigre and used Arabic for written reports while the highland group used Tigrinya. It was decided that the best solution was to let it emerge in a spontaneous way through the daily mixing together of the fighters. No decision was taken on language policy, indicative of the sensitivity of the issue.[21] It was a decision which left language issues in the market place. Over time, Tigrinya emerged as the language for military training and for the front as a whole as increasing numbers of highlanders joined.[22]

Creating a unified administration was left to the leadership of the separate forces. Establishing an organizational programme was placed with a committee of studies to report within twenty days. The committee of studies completed its task on 29 August 1973. In the process of unification, a more defined political and organizational structure of the front emerged based on democratic centralism and obedience to the agreed line, dissidence against which was punishable, and political education for the fighters along with training in military and literacy skills. The style of unification had been one of caution based on studious preparation, in part a function of mutual suspicions. An agreed political programme and unity of the rank-and-file fighters became a prerequisite for unifying the groups, a procedure on which the EPLF

[21] Al-Amin, *al-Thawra*, p.91.
[22] ELF military codes and communications remained in Arabic.

insisted in later unity discussions with the ELF. It was diametrically opposed to the line of the latter, which favoured unity of organizations.

Manqa: The Internal Crisis

The institional framework for attaining full unification provided a forum for a root-and-branch criticism of the nascent political organization. The major focus of the critics was the undemocratic nature of the front, the lack of rights of fighters and the failings of the leadership in a wide range of areas: administration, supply, health and military. At the heart of the opposition were university- and secondary school-educated who had joined the Ala group after a conscious recruitment campaign aimed at them by the Ala leadership.[23] Much of the criticism of the leadership was concentrated on Issayas Afeworki, and pulled into the opposition orbit two of the original members of the Ala group: Solomon Woldemariam and Tewolde Eyob.[24] It is a mark of the sensitivity of this challenge to the leadership that the episode has never been publicly acknowledged. While many have used the internal challenge as a means of criticizing the EPLF, an account of it is important because of its impact on the organizational development of the front and, in particular, in enhancing the solidarity of the leadership.

The opposition force was called the *manqa*, after the Tigrinya word for bat, and derived from the opposition's habit of mobilizing support through discussions and propaganda conducted with fighters at night. *The Destructive Movement* portrayed the campaign graphically:

> On every occasion, in every valley and hill-top, at the highest pitch of their voices they began spreading news that there was no democracy and the rights of the freedom fighters were violated.

In October 1973, two leading dissidents, Mussie Tesfaimikael and Afeworki Kiflu, issued a statement. The former took the opportunity of the meeting held on 3 October, and called by the committee of studies established in April 1973 to examine administrative integration,

---

[23] See Ammar, *Eritrea*.

[24] It has been argued that the motivation of these two early leaders was an Akalai Guzai regionalism opposed to the power of those from Hamasin. See Iyob, *The Eritrean Struggle*, p. 117. Although Akalai Guzai regionalism seems rather far-fetched and a leadership struggle between founders of the Ala group makes more sense, this split has been characterized as a 'rightist' challenge to Afeworki's position. *The DM* mentions 'a person called Solomon'.

76

to raise a wide-ranging attack on the leadership. The resolution of the crisis in favour of the latter was a formative influence in shaping the nature of the relationship between the leadership and the fighters. In this regard, it was a victory of a centralist conception of democracy rather than a populist one. It was a victory for the approach advocated by Issayas Afeworki and his allies in the PLF. It also set the tone for the way in which Eritrean society was mobilized by the leadership both during the armed struggle and after liberation. In the short term, it enhanced the power of the ELF in the plateau as the PLF withdrew its forces there, allowing the ELF to extend its secret organizations in Asmara and the other towns. Together with the civil war between the ELF and the PLF, this deep and divisive crisis strengthened the military position of the Ethiopian army in Eritrea, which only the fall of the imperial regime in 1974 undermined.

The Destructive Movement, the official EPLF account of the crisis, although in some ways self-serving, provides a fascinating insight into the early nature of the EPLF which, a decade later, was in control of much of Eritrea. It also provides a clear portrayal of Issayas Afeworki's early conception of democracy. He was a major target of the opposition attack and a defender of the leadership. A useful supplement to this document, al-Amin's account covers rather similar ground. Al-Amin was a leading cadre of the PLF and on the committee to investigate the criticisms made by the *manqa*. Oddly, but perhaps unsurprisingly, Al-Amin names Mussie, Yohannes Sebhatu and Afeworki Kiflu as the most prominent members of the dissidents, but leaves Tewolde Eyob and Solomon Woldemariam, founder leaders of the Ala group, unnamed.

Although the later EPLF gained the admiration of many foreign observers for its efficiency and the egalitarian relations between the fighters, the criticisms made by the *manqa* directly attacked both. In the military sphere, criticism was made of poor coordination and intelligence, resulting in PLF forces attacking each other; of inadaquacies of supply to units in the highlands and on battle fronts in the north; and of the organization and coordination of movements of men and supplies from the base areas to the highlands. The style of leadership, particularly that of Afeworki, was heavily criticized. The opposition argued that physical force was used against fighters who voiced criticism of the leadership and against the civilian population. Surprisingly, and in contrast to other documents, statements and pamphlets issued later by the EPLF, individuals were named. From a contemporary standpoint, it must be an embarrassment that leading members of the post-independence government were accused of assault and that members of the PFDJ central committee were hit. This kind of rumbustious brawling, as some of it turned out to be, was later corrected by a more forceful internal policing. The *manqa* crisis, then, ultimately created a stronger framework of control over internal dissidence and Ethiopian and ELF infiltration.

The accusations of beatings and hittings were generally proven and admitted. The 'mistakes' admitted in the military sphere were 'subsequently corrected'. The argument of principle about the nature of democracy was won by Afeworki through a combination of alliance politics with the PLF leadership, the regard for Issayas on the part of the highland units and a general disregard for democratic accountability in the context of the battle against the ELF and the Ethiopians. In particular, the PLF leadership was either scornful of the ideological debate or sympathetic to Afeworki and mobilized key cadres against the *manqa*. Markakis, in his otherwise authoritative account of the EPLF, was partly inaccurate when he wrote of illiterate PLF fighters having no taste for obscure Marxist–Leninist theory. As the EPLF official account makes clear, the *manqa* opposition forces had garnered some support from PLF fighters.

The *manqa* argued that the rectification of mistakes was best achieved through increasing the democratic accountability of the leadership and power-sharing. Their solution was to establish a 'people's administration' through the establishment of a 'supervisory body'. In essence, it called for an institutional check of a permanent nature. In his response, Issayas Afeworki stressed the necessity of a guiding role for the leadership and controlled participation through discussion:

> The duty of the leadership is to try to understand the real and potential problems of the people it leads and find lasting solutions for them. Any leadership must be very careful not to make hasty decisions. Decisions made by the leadership should then be conveyed to the lower strata of society. Here, the decisions are debated and finally approved or rejected. The leadership would be informed of the results of the process and make necessary amendments ... Popular administration does not mean that all the people will administer. Leadership of the people means representing the wish of the people.

This paragraph is again resonant with the language of Mao and the Chinese Communist party (of learning from the people, of solving the problems of the people[25]), but like the criticism it was couched in very practical terms.

[25] In an interview with *Eritrea Now*, January 1980, Afeworki made clear that he had little taste

Afeworki went on to list the attributes of 'a democratic system of administration in a revolutionary organization'. These included an elected legal organ, which established political doctrines and administrative structures, instructed the departments and supervised departmental relations. The leadership would appoint department heads and take decisions on which the departments could express their views, to which the leadership would then react. Individuals could only claim rights to participate, express opinions, vote and stand for election on the basis of their acceptance of five basic principles: the organization is above the individual, majority decision-making, the existence of differences in ranks, the subordination of departments to the leadership, and a common leadership but separate areas of responsibility. Accountability of the leadership was confined to critical comments by departments arising from implementing policies. The leadership, however, formulated policy and made appointments to departments. The criticism levelled at the internal dissidents and challengers to the authority of the leadership is again similar in language to the writings of Mao in *On Correcting Mistaken Ideas in the Party*, with its attack on ultra-democracy, petty-bourgeois individualism and subjectivism.[26]

This internal struggle within the EPLF was a protracted one, beginning in September 1973 and only resolved with the appointment of a jury at the end of May 1974 and the approval of the verdict of execution in August of the same year. One account lists those executed as Yohannes Sebhatu,[27] director of publications and information; Mussie Tesfamikael, political commissar and unit commander; Habte-Selassie Kidane, political commissar; Haile Hahtsun, doctor; Afeworki Kiflu and six other fighters.[28] The intensity of the internal agitation was such that older members of the leadership took sides, both trained

---

[25] (cont.) for then contemporary Chinese leaders. 'We content ourselves with what other Chinese have taught us in making their revolution.'

[26] *Selected Works of Mao Tsetung*, Vol. I, Peking, 1975.

[27] Sebhatu had been a leading student agitator at Haile Selassie University in Addis Ababa and founder member of the Marxist Crocodile Society. He was expelled from the university in 1965 and suspended indefinitely in 1969. R.R. Balsvik, *Haile Selassie's Students: The Intellectual and Social Background to Revolution 1952–1977* (African Studies Center, Michigan State University, Michigan, 1985), pp. 118, 154, 258.

[28] The other fighters named were Hberash Melke, Dehab Tesfatzion, Workuha, Hebrahtu Woldu, Alazar TesfaMichael, Michael Russom, Abieto Tazaz and Semere Guadad. 'Unita Nazionale e Nazionalismo Eritreo', *Africa*, no. 4/5, Sept–Oct. 1977, p. 153. Haile Hahtsun is presumably Haile Mahtsoun, who was not executed but imprisoned for some time. Opposition sources give higher figures for those executed. Considerable numbers were disciplined and imprisoned.

political cadres and new recruits were mobilized and the PLF had to pull its forces out of the highlands to the Sahel base area. The defeat of the populist line was organized through a set of committees. By this time all wings of the EPLF were committed to fighter committees elected and selected by the leadership of the PLF and the Ala group, and both were so committed to unity that they could not brook further internal dissension. Their main task was to restore the military and political capacity of the new unified front, the Eritrean Peoples Liberation Forces, to deal with the ongoing civil war against the ELF and to confront the Ethiopian army, a series of developments we shall examine in Chapter 5 on the military expansion of the EPLF from the Ethiopian revolution to liberation. Here we shall retain a focus on the establishment of administrative and control structures of the EPLF. Without these it would have been impossible to maintain the dynamics of its development as it responded to changes in its external environment beyond its control.

It is clear from the section of the report written by Issayas that a major impetus to developing the PLF into the successful military organization that it became was the criticisms raised by the *manqa*. Implicit in the defence and vindication of the leadership and the detailed criticisms lay the plan for the organizational future. Much of it was implemented and laid the basis for the political, administrative and military strategies for the following years. The special edition of *Vanguard*, reviewing the developments of 1975, makes a clear, if somewhat indirect, reference to the means by which the internal opposition was quelled. The major stress was placed on rigorous political education for the 'mass' of the fighters, on democratic centralism and criticism and self-criticism as means of rectifying past mistakes from which 'anarchistic elements' and 'opportunistic agents' benefited.[29] With the large civilian flight from the vengeful Ethiopian regime in the mid-1970s, the absorption of new recruits had to be managed in a 'more controlled and supervised fashion'.[30] No doubt the kernel of these strategies was there, laid by the training period in China. To expand activities in the highland areas a clear set of goals was established. These included recruiting new men, organizing in the towns, particularly among the students, establishing an information department and intensifying propaganda activities, politicizing and organizing the peasantry and mobilizing the different Eritrean nationalities, in particular the Sahho and Dankali Afar.

[29] *al-Tali'a* (Arabic for *Vanguard*), 13 January 1976, pp. 2–3.
[30] *Ibid.*

The report also proposed reducing dependence on supplies coming through Sudan by a strategy of self-reliance based on developing closer relations with rural producers, enhancing food storage and beginning to farm. In order to improve military skills, it was proposed to establish military camps for new trainees, upgrade political education and translate political education material into Arabic. In aiming to politicize the rural population, priority was given to those closest to the EPLF's military positions through providing them with health care and education. Specific forces based on Chinese and Vietnamese experiences, armed propaganda squads and barefoot doctors, were to be allocated these tasks. Priority was also given to the tens of thousands of Eritrean refugees in the Sudan.

This comprehensive strategic framework aimed at increasing the number of fighters, developing links with the civilian population and enhancing its military capacity enabled the front to absorb the large numbers which joined it between 1974 and 1978. During these four years the EPLF took advantage of a series of dramatic events: the Ethiopian revolution, the joint EPLF–ELF assault on Asmara and the bloody Ethiopian reprisals, the liberation of the towns and the 'strategic' withdrawal from them in 1977–8. Organizing the towns and expanding the network of secret cells there both facilitated urban military operations and provided a conduit for civilians and supplies into the EPLF. Providing health care for peasants and pastoralists in areas which had no medical facilities generated significant rural support, in a way that politicization through political education with its unfamiliar Marxist/Maoist class analysis did not. In addition, it insulated the growing numbers in the base areas from local epidemics. Similarly, the expansion of veterinary care for the animals of the rural population enhanced the popularity of the front. For both pastoralist and peasant their camels, oxen, sheep and goats were critical for their livlihoods. Such welfare provision also provided ease of entry into both the pastoralist camps and the villages. We shall return in the following two chapters to this crucial period between 1974 and 1978.

Only in 1973 were joint administrative departments established and the health centres and hospitals of the three forces combined. Administrative functions and responsibilities were not clearly defined: the discharge of the sick and wounded from hospital was shared between Issayas Afeworki, leader of the Ala group, and Ahmad Hilal of the PLF, the secretary of the executive and also the head of the health department. Supplies for both the highlands and Sahel were not easy to come by. They were affected by meagre financial resources as well as by restrictions placed on them by the Sudanese government and interruptions caused by Ethiopian army and the ELF attacks. In the highlands, although money was provided to purchase supplies from the towns and the local population, the poverty of the latter was a serious constraint. The front, at that period, was also subject to infiltration because it lacked a sohisticated intelligence department and had only a handful of secret cells through which fighters could be recruited and assisted to Sahel.

Mishandling civilians was admitted but the *manqa* accusation of compulsion and mistreatment was disavowed. The organization of Eritrean civil society both in the villages and the towns was not far advanced. As Issayas Afeworki put it in the *Destructive Movement*: 'the situation of civil war is so unideal that we can hardly leave our positions to enjoy a bit of peace. Those civilians within our reach are taught of our objectives but for the moment we cannot organize them.' Extending outwards into Eritrean society (the theme of the following chapter) was a function of its internal organizational coherence and autonomy that was based on three characteristics: the continuity of leadership cadres, the ideological framework for absorbing recruits into the front and the internal system of discipline and controls.

Leadership and the Expansion of the Second Tier

A strict democratic centralism was the core organizing principle of the front. Within the EPLF, personalities have great significance, as we have seen in the discussion of the dissident problem. For outsiders, however, the particular weight of individuals within the political bureau is hard to assess. The predominance of Issayas Afeworki from the foundation of the EPLF is marked. Other than those martyred during the armed struggle, the leaders elected at the unification meeting of the Ala and PLF groups remained more or less intact until the first congress of the EPLF in 1977. The two key figures in the unification process were Ramadan Muhammad Nur and Issayas Afeworki. They had been part of a small study circle in the mid-1960s in Kassala, which also included Haile Woldetensai, Ali Sayyid Abdallah and Al-Amin Muhammad Said.[31] Both Ramadan and Issayas had been part of the ELF batch trained in China in 1967 and

---

[31] Connell, *Against All Odds* pp. 79, 287.

had returned as political commissars, respectively, for the fourth and fifth zones, from which they were elected to attend the Aradib meeting representing the reformist position against the ELF leadership. Both again were elected to the provisional leadership of the three dissident zones in 1968.[32] Ramadan's politico-military origins in the fourth zone, his role as one of the founders of the PLF, together with his admiration of the Chinese and Vietnamese guerrilla strategies shared with Issayas, were important factors in facilitating unity. Ramadan had also been elected at the Ambahara meeting of the PLF to the leadership, which sought agreement on coordination with the Ala group. His influence was a decisive factor in providing the latter with arms received from Sabbe. He was also reported to have played a key role in the departure of Mesfin Hagos from the PLF to the Ala group. As well as being radical, educated and politically formed, he was from the Muslim Tigre and, thus, a fine complement to Issayas Afeworki's Ala group, which was systematically portrayed by the ELF as Christian highland chauvinists.

The formal establishment of the EPLF took place at its first congress in January 1977, and democratic centralism was institutionalized in the selection of delegates and election of leadership. Ramadan Muhammad Nur was elected secretary-general and Issayas Afeworki assistant secretary-general. The national democratic programme was also adopted although it had been formulated much earlier.[33] Units of the EPLF and the mass organizations elected 315 members to attend the congress, with one-third from the mass organizations. Congress elected a central committee of 37 with six alternates, and its members had to have had two years' experience in the armed struggle. The central committee elected the political bureau of 13, the qualification for which was five years in the armed struggle. The specification of numbers of years fighting distinguished between two political generations of recruits. For the central committee, there was provision for those who had joined before the mass influx following the Ethiopian army response to the EPLF/ELF attack on Asmara in January 1975, and for the political bureau those who had joined before January 1972. These latter were founder fighters of the PLF and the Ala group or those who joined in the first one and a half years after the split from the ELF, a period of considerable hardship.

PB members were Issayas Afeworki, Haile Woldetensai, Mesfin Hagos, Petros Solomon, Sebhat Ephraim, Berhane Gerezgiher, Okba

---

[32] Al-Amin, *al-Thawra*, pp. 22–3.
[33] As stated explicitly in *The DM*, published in 1974.

Abraha, Ramadan Muhammad Nur, Mahmud Sharifo, Ali Sayyid Abdallah, Ibrahim Afa, Al-Amin Muhammad Said and Sa'id Barre. Most had backgroumds as university and secondary school students[34] followed by military training in Syria, China and Cuba. All but three had left from the ELF. Petros Solomon and Sebhat Ephraim were involved in the *manqa* agitation, illustrative of the capacity of the older core leadership to absorb the second generation radicals. Of different social and political backgrounds and educational and cultural experiences, they had more or less absorbed some combination of radical socialist nationalism, Marxist–Leninism and classical guerrilla war tactics and strategy. They were a contrast to the early ELF leaders of the nationalist struggle who had found their political language in Egypt, their tactics in Algeria and their skills in the Eritrean police or the Sudanese army.

The leadership of the EPLF, in internal discussions or negotiations with the ELF, generally combined a limited number of people. There were those around Ramadan Muhammad Nur from the Massawa–Harqiqo area, mixed Tigre and sections of the Sahho, and those around Issayas Afeworki. They were bonded together through victory over the *manqa*, complex relations within Osman Salih Sabbe, cosmo-politan military training in guerrilla war and opposition to the unreconstructed ELF, and a presence, if at times temporary, in the highlands and proximity to supply routes across the Red Sea. The determined Afeworki had in his circle Haile Woldetensai and Mesfin Hagos of the 'old' fighters, and Petros Solomon and Sebhat Ephraim of the post-1973 but pre-1975 fighters. From the PLF fighters were Ramadan Muhammad Nur, Ali Sayyid, Ibrahim Afa, and Al-Amin Muhammad Said. Not all of those who had field commands had had any kind of overseas military training: Petros Solomon and Sebhat Ephraim gained their military training in the field. Others like PLF cadre Ramadan Awlaya had military training in Syria and continued in the EPLA; he became a successful commander of heavy artillery units in battles through the 1980s. Veteran fighters like Al-Amin and Sa'id Barre moved to responsibilities for foreign affairs, particularly with Arab governments in the Gulf.

[34] Ties of friendship and shared political activism prior to joining the struggle linked several of these together. Issayas and Haile Woldetensai were student organizers in the Prince Makonnen Secondary School at Asmara in the mid-1960s, students together at university in Addis Ababa and joined the ELF at the end of 1966. Sibhat Ephraim and Berhane Gerezgiher were students in Addis and left together to join the EPLF in 1972, as did Okba Abraha and Petros Solomon.

The main administrative command structures under the PB were committees for military and political affairs and departments of economics, health, social welfare and mass administration. A group of four from the PB constituted the standing committee which was responsible for day-to-day decision-making and included the secretary-general and assistant and the secretaries of the military and political committees. Many of the PB acted as military commanders through to liberation, and some shifted between political and military work. After the 1977 congress Sebhat Ephraim was responsible for mass adminis-tration, a crucial instrument in the expansion of the organization of and control over Eritrean society in the liberated, semi-liberated and occupied areas. After the second congress he was responsible for military affairs and led the army into Asmara in 1991. Petros Solomon was in charge of the eastern front in 1977–8 and later was in charge of security. Ali Sayyid and Ibrahim Afa[35] were front commanders and Mesfin Hagos was commander of one of the four divisions on liberation.

There was a greater degree of continuity of PLF founder members, whereas of the original founders of the Ala group only Issayas and Haile Woldetensai were elected to the PB. In the second tier of the leadership, the central committee, were other PLF founder members: Al-Amin Sarraj, Ramadan Osman Awlaya and Musa Rabi'a. Of the early members of the Ala group were Asmarom Gerezgiher and Adhanom Gebremariam. There would appear to have been a marked bonding within the leadership between those who made the transition from the PLF and Ala into the EPLF and those who joined during the process of merger and the period of civil war.

There is one qualification to the rosy picture of a dominant leader-ship after the defeat of the *manqa,* and it arises from the emergence of a grouping identified as the *yamin* or rightist opposition. Mention has to be made of this group because, like the *manqa,* it was an opposition movement that remained publicly sensitive after independence. No clear account of it has been given and yet all fighters know about it to

---

[35] Ibrahim Afa died in 1985. His death has become a matter of controversy. ELF sources imply a power struggle between him and Issayas Afeworki. Other explanations include an organizational difference over the role of the military committee, of which he was the head, to be abolished at the 1987 congress, while the reader of a draft of this book suggests an additional disagreement over military strategy. Controversy and suspicion arise from the two-year gap between Ibrahim's death and its announcement. The detail involved in assessing the circuitous interpretations of Ibrahim Afa's death will be left to an Eritrean Agatha Christie.

one degree or another. The motivation and membership of this grouping is more shrouded in mystery than the former. It has been portrayed as regionally particularist, rooted in an Akalai Guzai sub-highland regionalism, by one well-informed Eritrean writer who has linked it to Solomon Woldemariam's attempt to take advantage of the *manqa* disturbance.[36]

The present author's sources suggest that it was not a coordinated opposition and could not be accurately characterized as a movement. The tag of 'rightist' was an obscurantist device to cover a motley of educated critics who were in key positions but who were not associated with the *manqa*. It was a collection of individuals from different highland provinces, some of whom were frontline fighters while others were from the internal security organization. The dissent began in 1976, and a dozen or more were executed in 1980. The great majority were imprisoned and subsequently reincorporated into the front. Some of those involved were exposed in public criticism sessions and accused of criticizing the leadership of the front for neglecting areas from which they originated and attempting to recruit others on a particularistic basis. Several of the individuals who have been identified with this rightist tendency and were imprisoned were from Hamasin province.

Whatever the highland province origin, that these networks of opposition emerged on some claimed form of highland particularism provided a further impetus for centralization and organizational and ideological discipline based on open, public criticism and self-criticism sessions. Solomon Woldemariam, a non-ideological opponent of Issayas, was at the centre of one ineffective network of opposition, and despite that was forgiven and somewhat protected, unlike Tewolde Eyob, until his individualistic activities proved too much. He was captured fleeing to Sudan in 1980 and some years later executed. The devil of early Eritrean nationalist division had been one of Muslim against Christian Tigrinya, and divisions between Tigrinyans on the basis of provincial primordialism was a horrific spectre for the leadership and had to be quashed. Although this challenge did not mobilize on anything like the scale of the *manqa* it was the last challenge to the consolidated leadership of the EPLF.

At the EPLF's second congress in 1987, the PB was reduced to nine

---

[36] See Iyob, *The Eritrean Struggle*, pp. 116–17. The author is related by marriage to a former EPLF internal security and central committee member and, one assumes, well-connected. Yet the paragraphs on these pages and the explanatory endnotes, particularly no. 34, are obfuscating in the extreme. Given the sensitivity of internal dissent issues, perhaps the obscure prose is intentional.

members[37] and the position of assistant secretary-general was abolished. The secretary-general gained more formal powers over day-to-day decisions and appointments assisted by a secretariat. A general staff was also created under the secretary-general, who acted as commander-in-chief. Issayas Afeworki replaced Ramadan Muhammad Nur as secretary-general and it was to him that these extensive powers accrued. PB members retained considerable spheres for individual initiatives within their areas of responsibility.

The central committee was expanded to 71, with seven alternates, and the congress to above a thousand. There was, then, a shrinking core of the top leadership and an expansion of the second tier. This restructuring reflected the increasing responsibilities of Issayas Afeworki, the marginalization of Ramadan Muhammad Nur, a narrowing of the numbers at the apex of the EPLF and an expansion of the second tier into a number which reflected the expanding functions and members of the front. The broader leadership of 71 became an unwieldy body for decision-making and more one of ratification of the decisions of the core leadership. A combination of leadership dominance, collective decision-making and scope for individual initiative within front guidelines was a salient characteristic of the EPLF mirrored at all levels of the front.

The 1987 congress also marked the incorporation of the ELF central leadership, or Sagem group. Although most of the Sagem fighters were highlanders, and thus augmented the already dominant fighters from the Tigrinya speakers, associated with them was Ibrahim Totil, a veteran ELF leader from the Nara community of southwestern Eritrea. The Nara community had long been linked to the ELF, and the inclusion of Totil and other ex-ELF Nara fighters was of symbolic value for the EPLF in the eyes of Eritreans who made ethnic calculations.

The Ideological Framework:
Nationalities and Classes[38]

The twin pillars of the ideological framework established by the EPLF were derived from a conception that the major cleavages in Eritrea

---

[37] Ibrahim Afa was killed by Ethiopian artillery (and not at the behest of Issayas Afeworki, as a false but continuing ELF-inspired rumour has it) and Mesfin Hagos, Berhane Gerezgiher, Okba Abraha and Sa'id Barre were not elected.

[38] The following summary is derived from the NDP of 1977 and the EPLF *Memorandum* of April 1978.

were those of nationalities and classes. These informed the basic political education text, *General Political Education for Fighters*. Eritrean political history was an important part of political education. The Eritrean question was a colonial one, in that the 'nation' was created by Italian colonialism, and the anti-colonial character of the struggle was maintained through continuing Ethiopian occupation. The Eritrean nation was multi-national with nine nationalities defined by language and residence in defined geographic territories. Eritrea's right to self-determination was not based on the right of self-deter-mination of a 'nation' but of colonized peoples. The territory of Eritrea was defined as the area created by Italian colonial boundaries in the late nineteenth century. The national democratic programme (NDP) asserted the equality of rights for all nationalities, the preservation of their spoken and written languages and their cultures and traditions, and the necessity of strengthening their unity and fraternity. There was also an element of social engineering with an explicit commitment to have all nationalities represented within the front and to train cadres from them in various fields to assure 'common progress'.

The only significant change to the 1977 NDP in the revised version of 1987 was the provision that each nationality could establish its own democratic administrative organs compatible with its specific condi-tions. This approach was not pursued. While emphasizing freedom of religion and belief, religion was separated from state and politics and from education.

A socialist society was to be created by the revolutionary forces (the EPLF) leading the class struggles of 'workers, peasants, revolutionary intellectuals and other oppressed masses'. The major alliance was between the workers, the poor peasantry and the revolutionary intel-lectuals. In the following chapter we shall examine the specific modalities of political organization and the EPLF's class analysis. It is worth mentioning that agro-pastoralists in both the 1977 and 1987 NDPs were to be encouraged through various mechanisms to follow settled lives. In a 1972 EPLF publication, which defined the social base of the ELF, agro-pastoralists were defined as the 'backward part of the peasantry in transition from nomadism to settled agriculture'.

An important part of the ideological framework of the EPLF was the mobilization of women, part of 'other oppressed masses', into the front and its mass associations. In the conclusion to the 1971 *Our Struggle and its Goals*, one of the stated objectives of the new front was the creation of a united national front 'with no distinction as to religion, ethnic affiliation or sex'. The 1977 NDP had a separate section under social rights dealing with women's issues, including full rights of equality in politics, economy and social life. Women were targets of recruitment into the front and of the EPLF's programme of social transformation.

The character of the nationalities of Eritrea and the nature of Eritrean class structure were a fundamental component of EPLF political education and provided the basis for socializing members into the front. It was a form of social control through the provision of a shared vision of the past based on a set of ideological precepts which demonized religion and tribe. Insofar as Eritrean contemporary history had been considered by most Eritreans to be one of sectarian division it swept away this perceived past with two straightforward conceptual devices. These shared concepts provided an integrative process for the many young Eritreans who joined the front in the 1970s in that they explained the behaviour of the past generation without reference to religion. For example, the sons and daughters of Christian unionists became revolutionary intellectuals of the Tigrinya nationality, a nationality which they shared with Muslim Jiberti.

This shared vision of Eritrea was an organizational one, and acceptance of it became a mark of a corporate sense of identity and belonging to the EPLF. For the most it marked them off from the ELF: in the history of the armed struggle sections of the political education programme the latter was presented as a reactionary force whose leadership was given over to the manipulation of religion, regionalism and tribalism. Songs were also used to mark the diffences between the two fronts: an infamous one in which the new EPLF recruit was coached stressed the effeminacy of the ELF fighter.

It should be emphasized that the brief account of political education given here refers to the very basic level of the subject. The higher the educational and intellectual level of the member or the position he/she occupied in the organizational hierarchy, the more sophisticated the education given and greater the debate that occurred. At the top level was the political education provided by the cadre school. Of major importance was the fusion of political education, involving acceptance of the revolutionary line as expounded by the leadership, with organizational unity based on acceptance of the principle of democratic centralism, the character of which we have treated in the citation from Issayas Afeworki. The coherence of the political education programme combined with the continuity of the leadership at the centre of this democratic centralism was an important component of the survival of organizational unity. Cross-cutting the centralized structure of the front were organizations of internal control and discipline that only came together at the apex of the EPLF.

Internal Structures of Control and Discipline

There was a high degree of secrecy about the nature of internal controls, a fundamental component of enhancing front autonomy both in the sense of minimizing outsiders' knowledge of the front and of containing internal dissent. With the constant and large-scale fighting from the mid-1970s onwards, while there may have been individual disgruntlements, there were no serious internal political problems. One issue on which the author found extensive criticism of the leadership from the the rank and file originated from its refusal to publicly condemn the Soviet Union's political and military support for the government of Ethiopia. Another arose from the 1978 strategic retreat when some brigades were reluctant to withdraw from the Massawa area.

There were at least three structures involved in internal controls: the party, the cadres, and the security and intelligence organizations. While security and intelligence are usually areas of clandestine activity and the role and operations of political cadres are somewhat more open, the revelation of the existence of a secret party within the EPLF surprised many. In addition to these three structures, there were EPLF laws and internal disciplinary rules and codes. Until the late 1980s when a department of justice was established, security and intelligence cadres from the investigation and prison department had the function of internal policing and punishment.

There were levels of discipline. Basic misdemeanours, like negligence in fulfilling ascribed duties, were dealt with at the level of the unit or team through a process of criticism by unit members and self-criticism by the miscreant. As well as producing cooperative behaviour, this was intended to create a sense of individual responsibility for the larger collective of comrades. Continued failure to perform duties was dealt with through a series of official warnings and, if these were not properly heeded, a set of punishments would follow. These might include imprisonment or hard labour. One place for the latter was the salt pans of the Red Sea coast, where the punishment was excavating blocks of salt. Discussion of punishments as well as prisons and their location was forbidden and the code used by fighters for the latter was 'that place'.

The three structures of internal control usually erred on the side of caution when dealing with possibilities of external penetration. On occasion, fighters were arrested simply by vague association with someone suspected of being an Ethiopian infiltrator. Once a member of the front it was nigh impossible to leave Eritrea save with the sanction of the political bureau. In addition, there were a set of procedures for disciplinary problems arising from relations between fighters and the civilian population. These were within the orbit of the department of mass administration, and will be dealt with in the following chapter.

Reinforcing democratic centralism and the authority of the leadership, then, were the cadres, security and the clandestine party. Members of all three structures were selected by the leadership, and there was a degree of overlapping membership and similarity of function between them in the sense that all three combined together security and political and ideological control. Not all members of the security organization were party members. Nor were all cadres. Some members of the central committee and longstanding military commanders did not join the party or attend cadre school until a few years before liberation.

The Eritrean People's Socialist Party[39]

The party was a shadowy organization, with even its name remaining obscure. Some writers have it named as the Eritrean People's Forces Party and some the Eritrean People's Revolutionary Party.[40] It was called the Eritrean People's Socialist Party, with 'socialist' replacing the earlier 'communist' name as the USSR backed Ethiopia. Members were sworn to secrecy. Its existence was only publicly acknowledged in 1994, five years after its supposed dissolution in 1989. According to a senior PFDJ official, the idea of a clandestine vanguard party was first mooted by Idris Galewdewos in the mid-1960s as a means of securing

---

[39] Much of the very little that is known about the party derives from anonymous sources. The existence of a party was rumoured for many years and various of Osman Salih Sabbe's publications pointed to its existence. Most EPLF members discounted the rumours as an ELF smear.

[40] R. Iyob, 'The Eritrean Experiment: A Cautious Pragmatism', *Journal of Modern African Studies* Vol. 35, No. 4, 1997, p. 660. Sabbe called it the People's Democratic Party, *Judhur al-Khilafat al-Irititiriyya wa Turuq Ma'alijatiha* (Arabic: The Roots of Eritrean Differences and Means of Treating Them), 1978, p. 46.

support from the communist states.[41] Issayas Afeworki and Ramadan Muhammad Nur were charged with establishing it, but nothing emerged, in part, because the ELF leadership was not serious about it and, in part, because of the internal conflicts within the ELF in the late 1960s. The idea was carried by these two leading ELF dissidents into the new organization and it began its formalization between 1970 and 1972. Given the subsequent role of these two, one can assume that it was an important instrument in unifying the PLF and the Ala group, and its early members provided a crucial cement in the difficult process of unification.

The structure of the party mirrored the democratic centralist structure of the EPLF. At the apex of the party was Issayas who was party chairman, a position which facilitated the increasing centralization of power in his hands. PB member, head of the political department and of the cadre school Haile Woldetensai was a key organizer. While political bureau and central committee members of the EPLF and party were the same in the 1970s, by 1987 not all EPLF Central Committee members were in the party. Members were recruited from those who were the 'most committed, active and ideologically sound'. Some were recruited from cadre school while others were first recruited and then sent to it. Potential members were usually approached by a high-standing party member of their military and adminstrative unit. Recruitment into the party was broadly based and included fighters from a range of different social backgrounds as well as members of the mass associations and secret cells. The membership reached down into the military and administrative units of the EPLF and outward into its mass organizations.

Party meetings were held in secret from unit comrades. The cover for such meetings was provided by the widely accepted practice of fighters being 'called for duty' without questioning. The practice of criticism and self-criticism provided the opportunity for party members to exert influence and take initiatives in expounding the leadership line within units. It provided a continuity between the early core of members and those recruited from the massive influx between 1975 and 1978 and subsequently. Even so some key military commanders and longstanding EPLF members did not join until the late 1980s. Individuals like these had considerable weight within the front without

---

[41] Interview, March 1996. In the following account there is a degree of speculative interpretation based on this interview and other anonymous ones that provided the factual bare bones. Many long-time observers of the EPLF, including myself, had also assumed that there was a party drawn from the graduates of the cadre school.

the status of party membership. Estimates of members range from 2,000 to 10,000, although a figure in between the two seems more likely.

The party played a role similar to that of the vanguard communist parties of China and Vietnam, which operated within broader nationalist struggles. In the first place, it promoted leadership positions as a 'mass line', campaigned for policies at congresses and was a force in the elections to congresses and the highest bodies of the front. Party congresses were held before the first and second EPLF congresses. After the revelation of the party, some fighters recalled to me the heightened activism of certain cadres in their units in the debates and selection of representatives leading up to the 1977 and 1987 congresses. It would be reasonable to assume that there was some agreed list of those put forward for election to the central committee and that the upper echelons of the leadership shared a consensus on candidates for the political bureau. According to one authoritative source, the party was dissolved as the ideological gap between party members and ordinary EPLF members disappeared, a consequence of the modifications to the NDP at the 1987 congress. As party members remain sworn to secrecy about the party even after its dissolution in 1989, announced in 1994, it might be some time before an authoritative internal account emerges. Some informed EPLF members remain convinced that the party was not dissolved or at least not in 1989. The party was probably the most important of the three instruments of internal controls as it was both secret and deeply embedded through all front structures.

Cadres

Cadres were distinct from party members in that their status was openly known. Cadres were those who had been sent for advanced ideological training at the cadre school. They were distributed among the different branches of the front. One of their major functions was political organizing and supervising political education. This will be treated at greater length in the following chapter. Selection to attend the cadre school was considered something of an honour. Political education there was given at a higher theoretical level and discussions of the history of Eritrea, the armed struggle and the EPLF took place in more detail. Classic texts of Marxism–Leninism, Stalin and Mao translated into Tigrinya were used. There was usually a teacher who was able to discuss topics from Arabic translations.

The courses for cadres were usually three months in duration with numbers attending the course at times very large (sometimes reaching 500), but broken into smaller groups for discussions. Although there was no secrecy about who was a cadre, there was a degree of secrecy about the cadre school insofar as the topics of lectures and discussions were supposed not to be passed on to those outside the cadres. Key cadres were often drafted in for special tasks, like the political education of the waves of ELF deserters in the 1970s. After graduation from cadre school, cadres had political and organizational roles separate from the EPLF's administrative hierarchy. They might, for example, organize and lead meetings at which their administrative and departmental unit heads were simple attenders. By the mid-1980s, however, most unit and department heads were cadres and long-serving fighters considered akin to cadres.

Security

There were several sections of the department of security. The internal security organization was known as the *halewa sawra* (defence of the revolution). Unsurprisingy, little has surfaced on this organization but it functioned against both the Ethiopian regime and the ELF as well as playing a role as military police overseeing internal discipline. It was a feared organization within the front, and like the party, it is an organization about which Eritreans are loath to speak. According to ELF sources, more reliable on facts than interpretation, members were recruited from units to the *ma'askar hibu'an* (camp of hidden ghosts) where they had special military training. Senior members of the EPLF associated with its direction were political bureau member Petros Solomon and central committee member Musa Rabi'a, an early PLF fighter. It ran the investigation and prisons department, and the latter was responsible for internal political dissidents as well as ELF captured prisoners and senior ELF fighters who had left the ELF in the transition to their integration into the EPLF. It underwent considerable expansion from the mid-1970s onwards as it had responsibility for guarding the thousands of Ethiopian prisoners of war.

A separate security organization that also had specialist training operated outside of Eritrea, particularly in Sudan where there was a strong ELF organizational infrastructure and thousands of supporters. One of the tasks of security was the infiltration and subversion of the ELF. Indeed, many ELF leaders and sympathizers assert that the disintegration of the ELF was partly a function of the high level of EPLF penetration. This is an exaggeration, however, as its major role was within Ethiopia and behind enemy lines in Eritrea where it operated secret cells and had networks of informants, some of whom had access to highly sensitive political and military information.

Secrecy

We have already mentioned the culture of secrecy, an inevitable outcome of a protracted military struggle and a defence against Ethiopian and ELF infiltration. Although 'knowledge is power' is a cliché with a grain of truth, secrecy is a means of controlling knowledge. Within the organization of the EPLF there were both hierarchical and horizontal levels of secrets. Notionally, political discussions in the political bureau were secret from central committee members, and the latter's discussions similarly secret. While some have argued that secrecy was one cultural manifestation of an oppressed peasant society in states geared to taxing them, and that this would provide a basis on which a movement like the EPLF could draw for military purposes, the continuation of secrecy after independence seems disproportionate.[42]

Women

We have mentioned above the stress placed on gender equality in early EPLF pamphlets. While the EPLF position on women's rights to equality was a principled one, it had greater resonance for young women with some education and was of practical strategic value for the front. Women made up half of the Eritrean population, and their recruitment into the front provided a valuable human resource for the expansion of both its military and administrative capacities. An index of the successful incorporation of women is provided by EPLF sources: from a handful in 1973 they constituted 30 per cent of front members and 13 per cent of frontline fighters by 1979.[43] By 1989, the latter figure had reached 23 per cent, a figure perhaps exaggerated by the

---

[42] See the discussion of the 'cult of secrecy' in Iyob, 'The Eritrean Experiment', pp. 658–9.

[43] Much of the following draws on *Women and Revolution in Eritrea*, Eritrean Womens Association, June 1979, and W.W. Selassie, 'The Changing Position of Eritrean Women: An Overview of Women's Participation in the EPLF' in M. Doornbos and L. Cliffe (eds), *Beyond Conflict in the Horn*, Institute of Social Studies, the Hague, with James Currey, London, 1991.

movement between administrative and military units during the 1980s.[44] Women also provided significant percentages of personnel in administration (35 per cent), industry (29 per cent), transport (25 per cent) and health (55 per cent). These proportions are demonstrative of the high level of participation of women and the reliance on the mobilization of women into the front for carrying out many of the essential tasks in administering the base and liberated areas and the operation of military support units.

The incorporation of women wrought changes in the character of the front and in the prevailing relationship between men and women in the EPLF. Both of these had the effect of reinforcing the organizational solidarity of members. Most Eritrean women, Christian and Muslim, were subordinated by a combination of traditional practices and the customary laws of their communities.[45] Civil law codes have had only a limited impact even in the urban areas. In both *sharia* and highland Christian customary law, with some limited exceptions, inheritance of property is for the male descendants. In the customary law of Showat Anseba, it is stated that a husband may beat his wife below the neck as long as it is not damaging. If a bride is found not to be a virgin, then she would be returned to her parents. Female genital mutilation – cliterodectomy and infibulation – is practised in the Christian and Muslim communities, respectively. Child betrothal arranged by the men of the family was the usual pattern.

A revolutionary change occurred within the EPLF in stark contrast to gender relations and marriage practices in broader Eritrean society. Until 1977 celibacy was strictly enforced. The prolonged nature of the struggle and the large increase in women members brought about reform.[46] The EPLF marriage law of 1977 was pivotal in introducing the radical changes which drew a clear line between the sexual practices of EPLF members and those outside the organization. Fighters were permitted to have sexual relations prior to marriage as long as their relationship was registered. In the event that marriage did not ensue from a relationship premarital sex was effectively sanctioned in principle. The EPLF supervised the process of courtship and marriage

---

[44] Selassie, 'Changing Position', p. 69.

[45] Information on customary law is drawn from Khadija Naib, 'Women's Rights and their Challenging Struggle', in *Images of African Women: The Gender Problematic*, Occasional Paper 3, Centre of Commonwealth Studies, University of Stirling, pp. 73–84.

[46] The best account can be found in Trish Silkin, 'Changes in the Negotiation of Marriage in Those Areas of Eritrea Controlled by the EPLF', unpublished M.Phil. thesis 1989, Goldsmith's College, University of London, 1989.

through the head of the administrative department or military unit, who would provide a note to the medical department for contraception. As to marriage, it was to be based on the 'absolute will of the two partners', and ages of 20 for men and 18 for women were specified as well as two years of experience in the armed struggle.[47] Permission for marriage came from the department of social affairs three months after a relationship had been registered. A detailed questionnaire had to be answered and submitted separately by the couple to the department of social affairs to ensure that there was no pressure or coercion. The EPLF also supervised divorce and, in the case of a divorce contested by one of the partners where mediation had not resolved the problem, the case could be referred to the political bureau, which acted as a court of appeal.

The stress on equality of gender within the front was reflected in the provisions of equality in the marriage law as a whole: a 'new democratic marriage law based on the free choice of both partners, monogamy, the equal rights of both sexes and the legal guarantees of the interests of women and children'. The EPLF appropriated the roles which had been associated with fathers and male family members. In extending the law to marriages of civilians in the liberated areas, there was a degree of flexibility and sensitivity to traditional values. Despite the modernity of much of the provisions of the law, there was an absolute prohibition against abortion, which the EPLF stuck to in an extremely rigid fashion through the 1970s, even in the cruellest of circumstances like rape by Ethiopian soldiers. This prohibition against abortion was reversed in the 1980s[48] but was reimposed in 1990, one year before liberation, on the grounds that it went against Eritrean religious and popular sentiments. Despite the radical egalitarian changes initiated by the EPLF, the changing position on abortion indicated a trend whereby the treatment of women was something of a political weathervane.

From 1977 onwards there were increasing numbers of marriages between fighters, and by the end of the war the figure was in the thousands. As a consequence 'EPLF married couples' gave way to 'EPLF families' with the birth of what were called the 'Sahel babies' born in the base areas. The social, organizational and legal role of the

---

[47] The text of the law can be found in Silkin, 'Changes' and A. Wilson, *Women and the Eritrean Revolution*, Red Sea Press, Trenton, NJ, 1991, Appendix 6a.

[48] Several informants have attributed the change to the increased incident of pregnancies of women involved in relations with the leadership.

EPLF in marriage and divorce was symbolic of the state-like character of the front, which was reinforced as it introduced changes to customary practices in liberated and semi-liberated areas.

The Infrastructure of Absorption

Given the vagaries of external support, as experienced in the changing relationship with Middle Eastern states, the stress on self-reliance was an important part of the strategy of creating organizational autonomy. The early dependence on South Yemen as a source of supplies ended in 1976 when under Soviet pressure it shifted to support the Ethiopian regime. The Libyan government followed suit. The severance of ties with Sabbe's foreign mission in 1975 also encouraged the leadership of the front to organize the Eritreans who had fled to Europe, the US and the Middle East and they became a significant source of fund-raising, as we shall point out in Chapter 5. The principle of self-reliance was intrinsically linked to the internal infrastructural development of the EPLF.

By the mid-1970s the organization the new EPLF recruit joined was very different from that of five years earlier. It had formulated a political programme and had clear internal structures and regulations. Projects for manufacturing and modifying captured equipment had also begun. Most of the large base infrastructure was established or significantly expanded in 1974–5. All recruits would fill in a long form providing extensive information on social, ethnic and religious background. Male recruits would undergo six months of political and military training and women and boys nine months. By the 1980s, this introductory training had been reduced to three and six months, respectively.

In 1976–7 the training group comprised about 60 to 70 members, to which two teachers, one military and one political, were attached. The training was rigorous, with both military and political exams taken at the end, and a repetition of the course on failure. Literacy classes were supplementary and also involved an exam. Literacy classes were given to the 30 per cent proportion of illiterates, a figure reflecting not only the peasant base of the EPLF and but also the sizable 70 per cent from the highland towns, Massawa and the nearby villages with access to educational institutions. Training groups were divided into teams with team leaders. This basic unit would share cooking, cleaning and tasks like gathering firewood. The free day was usually spent on social and cultural activities, the latter including the music, songs and poetry of the nationalities. All personal property would be handed over to the stores. Watches, for example, would be reallocated to those already serving in active military units. Clothing, a significant discriminating mark between those of peasant background and the more sophisticated urbanite, usually referred to as a 'bourgeois', would also be handed over.

Adaptation to life in the Sahel training areas was more difficult for the urban recruit. There was a lack of variety in food, with lentils a staple. Washing of clothes was allowed very infrequently. Like other fighters in the base area, the new recruit slept with a blanket on the ground and had one pair of trousers made from coarse cloth. Life was communal, with little privacy. The rocky and stony terrain played havoc with those used to pavements and roads. Shoes were exchanged for black plastic sandals, like the Kalashnikov, a mark of the fighter. Great stress was placed on looking after the property of the front. In the 1970s, there was a general equality of hardship. In the early 1980s, however, small signs of inequality made an appearance as some of the leaders added private kitchens to their dwellings and had extra allowances of sugar. After fighter complaints a 'campaign against excesses' was mounted, but to limited effect.

At the lowest level, discipline would be enforced and reinforced through criticism and self-criticism within the team. Warnings would be given to those who failed in their tasks, were recalcitrant in going about their duties or careless with front property. The whole process of incorporation was intended to inculcate discipline and both individual and group responsibility. Children below the age of 15 would enter the revolution school and those above 15 the vanguard school, which was established in 1975. In both, political and some military education was given. About half of the new recruits to the vanguards came through the EPLF's mass organizations. In October 1977, at the time of the occupation of the cities, there were about 1,100 attending vanguard school classes, with about 300 waiting to enter. Obviously, teaching and training resources were stretched very thinly at this time, and were to become even more so with the withdrawal from the cities and the flight of villagers and townspeople with the Ethiopian reoccupation in 1978. Prior to this expansion in numbers, there was already a shortage of exercise books and pens. In 1977, there were six lecturers and the size of lecture/discussion groups varied between 50 and 70.

The programme of political and military education was demanding.

A typical day would begin at 4 a.m. with two hours of physical education, followed by an hour of military education and then breakfast. After breakfast and until 4 p.m., there would be literacy classes and language training and rest. At four in the afternoon two hours of political education were given. Based on *General Political Education for Fighters*, instruction placed much emphasis on Eritrean history and dealt with Ethiopian colonialism and the EPLF's version of the armed struggle. In addition, a class analysis of Eritrean society was provided. Songs had a distinctly old-fashioned Chinese communist ring to them: 'Rise up, workers and peasants'; as did verses like: 'As a revolutionary party you point your gun, with an internal problem you solve it democratically. I will struggle saying: victory to the masses.'

The level of sophistication of the political education classes depended on the social composition of the group. One cadre stated that educating those of peasant background into the mores and discipline of the front was particularly difficult. Teaching was conducted in Tigrinya. Although Arabic was not mentioned, the author observed some fighters teaching others Arabic and the Arabic script. This was not a general phenomonon and was curtailed.

After initial training, the new fighter was assigned to different sections of the front. Before the civil war ended, after training most recruits were assigned to military duties. By the mid-1970s, the EPLF was undertaking a considerably varied number of functions and had developed into a large and complex organization. In the base area was an array of administrative departments, workshops and medical facilities. From the front's training establishments came the frontline units, the 'barefoot doctors' who would range far and wide, the armed propaganda squads operating in the villages, the guards for Ethiopian prisoners of war, the engineering teams constructing rough roads from Sahel through the highlands, and the mass administration responsible for activities ranging from political education to land reform, agricultural activities and veterinary advice for pastoralists. There were a range of production units in the base area manufacturing or modifying equipment for the frontline fighters.

In every area of front activity to which the new recruits were assigned, political education was continuous. Those in frontline units had two hours weekly and others two hours daily. As we have strongly emphasized, it was the essential means of socializing EPLF members into the front and communicating the leadership line. Although literacy was also ongoing, only team and unit leaders had to write reports on the activities of their groups, and thus had their literacy reinforced in a practical way. Assignment to departments and frontline units was decided by the political bureau and, indicative of the greater attention to detail before 1978, the PB member responsible for that department would personally read out and explain the assignments. Most graduates expressed a wish to be assigned to military units. In general, pre-EPLF formal education and literacy levels were a factor in the deployment of graduates of the programme. For example, a degree of formal education and literacy was a prerequisite for an assignment to the medical and information departments, whereas this was less important for assignment to frontline units.

The large-scale expansion in terms of numbers and the area under its control placed severe strains on the administrative capacities of the front, one mark of which was the reduction of the age limit below 18 before assignment. Two interviewed in Keren were aged 16 and were responsible for giving political education to peasants and police duties. Giving their youth such positions of authority in Keren and its conservative surrounds was both a symbol of the EPLF's reliance on the young and the practical strains of administering the captured cities simultaneously with laying siege to Asmara and Massawa.

The infrastructure of health was a microcosm of the practices of the EPLF, with a focus on enhancing the military capacities of the front and providing health care for peasants and pastoralists. In addition to 'normal' medical activities there was a stress on training and teaching staff as more territory was liberated and increasing numbers of Eritreans brought under the authority of the front. A frontline system of medical provision was implemented at the beginning of 1976. Medical teams comprising surgeons, doctors and nurses were attached to frontline fighting units and provided emergency operations on the spot. These procedures saved lives, decreased the incidence of sepsis and gangrene and were important for fighter morale.

At the platoon level there was a field-trained squad paramedic, and at the battalion level field-trained doctors and nurses. Frontline medical units were backed up by regional hospitals to which the wounded were released for further surgery and recuperation. The regional hospitals had X-ray machinery and laboratories. In addition, there was a network of clinics which were the bases for the mobile teams and the barefoot doctors, the personnel of which were interchangeable. Based on the Chinese model, the latter were given basic training in the treatment of common diseases in the region, like TB and dysentery. They would range over a relatively wide area carrying penicillin, vitamins, chloroquin and basic equipment like syringes. A particular concern of these barefoot doctors was local communicable diseases in the Sahel area to limit the impact of any epidemic on the forces concentrated there.

Given the general lack of education among the pastoralist and semi-pastoralist population in the north and the great mobility of both fighters and the civilian population in flight from battles, protecting the health of EPLA military units was symbiotic with delivering health care to the rural population. The latter was an important part of generating support from a rural population inhabiting areas far from any Ethiopian health provision. The mobile units that would go into villages and conduct propaganda campaigns and initiate village land reform would also have field-trained paramedics with them.

At the centre of the system was the general hospital to which the chronically-ill civilian and the recuperating fighter would be sent. It had operating theatres, wards, X-ray equipment and associated laboratories and the general pharmacy. Some of the equipment was captured, some brought from abroad and some transported from the towns captured in 1977. The hospital also provided elementary medical training for the squad and barefoot doctors, more advanced training for clinical staff and battalion doctors, as well as education in laboratory techniques, radiology and anaesthesia. Already trained and qualified personnel oversaw the upgrading of nurses and former medical students into doctors. In addition, more complex operations and rehabilitation programmes for wounded fighters were sometimes provided abroad.

Similarly, the small-scale workshops scattered around the base area fed into the military and social activities of the front, their raw materials procured through urban raids or windfalls from liberated territory. The metal workshop, which in the early days of its activities spent about 70 per cent of its production activities in maintaining existing equipment, began manufacturing simple agricultural tools, sterilizing trays for doctors, and making parts for grenades and replacement triggers for captured Doshka guns in 1976–7. A metal cutter was brought from the agricultural estate at Elaborat after its capture in 1977.

As in other base area enterprises, on-the-job training was an important component of small-scale repair and manufacturing activities. Between 1976 and 1977 about 30 apprentices were trained by the more experienced workers, some of whom were graduates of the higher technical school in Asmara. All available material was used: the metal from the traditional peasant swords captured in the Ethiopian peasant march was used for making an assortment of metal parts. Many of the tools used for hammering were made in the woodwork shop. In the tailoring shop, established in 1975 and using machines captured in 1976 and other machines brought in from abroad, four different sizes of shirts and shorts were made from textiles liberated from a textile factory in Asmara, as well as overalls and heavier jackets for forces operating in the cooler highlands. In 1975, the capture of a large amount of leather initiated the establishment of a leather factory which produced 11,000 bullet pouches, as well as watchstraps and belts. The workshop was staffed by eight experienced leather workers and in 1977 10 were undergoing training.

The large intake of urban Eritreans in 1974–8 not only swelled the manpower of the front but also the numbers of educated and skilled workers whose abilities were harnessed for military and broader training purposes. There was a tremendous benefit to the front from the incorporation of urban highlanders from Asmara as well as those living in Addis Ababa. The detailed files kept by the EPLF enabled them to shift personnel when and as circumstances and captured matériel became available.

The structure of the organization was able to absorb recruits, socialize them into the ways of the front and distribute them into its expanding activities. Eritreans of more educated backgrounds, particularly those from Addis Ababa and abroad, were particularly scrutinized for their involvement in secret cells, welcomed but frequently given a hard time by the older fighters. Educated and new recruits to the front who lacked long secret cell involvement or marked devotion to the front in London, Brussels or Washington, unless they had particular skills, were treated with a degree of suspicion. Even though the core of the leadership of the EPLF were almost all of university background, after the *manqa* the selection process of the educated was monitored by party members and cadres. Reports were made on the performance and behaviour of unit members and members of the secret organizations. In a society where clan ties counted (as marked in the highlands as in the more traditional clan-based economy of the the lowlands) loyalty to the front as guardian and liberator of the nation cut against family connections. As far as I know, relatives of the leadership were equally subject to the discipline of the front.

Conclusion

The formative impulses in shaping the EPLF were its reaction against the historic fragmentation of both Eritrean society and nationalist political movements, in addition to its early fragility as exposed in the political challenge of the *manqa* movement. The Maoist and Vietnamese ideological and organizational models provided a framework for the establishment of an ordered and disciplined movement. A cluster of factors facilitated their adaptation to the Eritrean experience. These included the cultural and educational background of the leadership and the connection of the two component parts of the early EPLF to the two regions of Eritrea with relatively high levels of urbanization, literacy and education (academic, technical and skilled). These were areas where modern middle and working classes had developed. Both the highlands and the Massawa area had been historically located within ordered state/imperial administrative systems and the social organization of the countryside long penetrated by these systems. It was most marked in highland rural society, with its closely organized village structures. From the Sahel base areas, through a mix of land reform, popular mobilization and strategic skills the EPLF incorporated the mass of Eritreans in these areas. To land reform, popular mobilization and the organizational extension of the EPLF we now turn.

Four

Organizing
the Masses

Introduction

Awat Nahafash (Victory to the Masses) was the signature slogan of the
EPLF and a slogan put seriously into practice. Establishing clear lines
of internal organization and discipline within the front were symbiotic
with a rigorous programme of political education to root the EPLF's
version of Eritrean history and society firmly in the minds of members.
In conjunction with this stress on internal organization were the
political and military imperatives of expanding the EPLF's structures
into broader Eritrean society. The organizational outreach of the
EPLF resembled that of the Chinese communist guerrilla practice of
constructing a 'frame of steel' so that when the frame moved so did the
people.[1]

The major targets to be bonded to the frame were the peasantry,
youth, women, the small urban working class and Eritrean refugees
and political exiles across the globe. Extending organizational structures
into the civilian population brought the latter under EPLF rules and
regulations. Political education classes were a major instrument of
incorporating and organizing the different social groups of Eritrea and
connecting Eritrean society to the front. As we have pointed out,
political education was compulsory for all fighters and so it was for the
membership of the mass organizations and secret cells in villages and
towns. It functioned as a means of ideological and social control.
Acceptance of the EPLF's version of history and its class analysis

---

[1] T. Kataoka, *Resistance and Revolution in North China* cited in K. Hartford, 'Repression and
Communist Success', in K. Hartford & S. Goldstein, *Single Sparks: China's Rural Revolutions*,
M.E. Sharpe, New York 1989.

became an emblem of membership and commitment to the cause. It also had the purpose of linking together the social transformation of Eritrea and the military struggle. Before describing the structural and institutional links between the EPLF and the Eritrean people, it is necessary to underline again the prominence given to political education and its connection to organizational expansion.

Before dealing with EPLF organizational activities in the rural and urban areas from the mid-1970s to the early 1980s, a peak period of expansion, it should be emphasized that the underlying pattern was one of centralized control and guidance balanced by considerable scope for initiative on the part of EPLF cadres. Eritrea was divided into six zones in addition to a special zone for Asmara and its suburbs. A zonal leader appointed by the PB headed a zonal committee comprised of zonal department heads. At the grass roots level cadres from the mass administration would operate guided by handbooks on land reform and the means of establishing popular organizations. Although these handbooks were very detailed, the means of achieving the goals set out in the handbooks were not subject to strict central controls. Once a specified organizational level had been reached members of departments would take responsibility for functional activities, like education or health care. Problems between civilians and cadres or between cadres of different departments would be resolved at the zonal level. The extension of EPLF political organization marched hand in hand with recruitment into the EPLF, the EPLA and the linked zonal armies. Much emphasis has been given to the social transformation of Eritrea undertaken by the EPLF. It is important to note that it was primarily established to liberate Eritrea through military means and sustaining the armed struggle required recruiting fighters.

In the following sections we shall examine the methods of EPLF expansion in different rural locations, in liberated towns of 1977–8 and in different military contexts. The most fertile recruiting grounds were the highlands and, for reasons we shall show, not because of its ethnic affinity with one section of the leadership.

The Highlands

The highlands and the highland peasantry were of particular significance, and not simply because of the Maoist blueprint for fighting a protracted armed struggle based on mobilizing the peasantry. They were of strategic and tactical military value, as well as of political and historic importance for the EPLF. The highlands made up half of the population of Eritrea, were densely concentrated and practised settled agriculture. The settled village-based communities were ideal recruiting grounds for fighters. Although in many harvest years there was little surplus, it was a potential source of supplies for small guerrilla bands.[2] For historic reasons capturing the hearts and minds of the highland peasantry had great political symbolism: the highlands had been at the core of the UP, were a main recruiting ground for the commandos[3] and, in several districts,[4] provided recruits for local militias armed by the Ethiopian government. Whether imperial or people's socialist republic, Ethiopian governments had to hold on to the loyalty of this region, for the loyalty and sympathy of the peoples of western Eritrea had long been lost. While a successful expansion into the highlands would undermine Ethiopian legitimacy to rule Eritrea, this was also an area which the EPLF had to penetrate to compete successfully with the ELF, which had an earlier, if patchy, presence across the region. The greater the presence, the greater the capacity to recruit from highlanders.

Ethiopia's major garrison centres were in the highlands (Asmara, Decamhare), and it was from there that ground troops could most easily reinforce the outlying garrison at Keren, the gateway to the west and north. The major road link from Massawa to inland Eritrea and northern Ethiopia rose from the Samhar coastal plain to Asmara. The main road infrastructure in Eritrea was also in the highlands.

The highland villages around the urban centres, particularly those around Asmara, were useful sources of information about Ethiopian troop movements and provided meeting points for EPLF cadres and secret cell members, and thereby access to urban society. Prior to the running down of manufacturing, some villagers worked in Asmara factories. The villages functioned as contact points in a further way: most of the urban inhabitants of Eritrea would have retained contact with their village of origin in one way or another. Many of *restenyat* background would collect their share of the harvest from their village. There were, then, important conduits from the villages into the highland urban centres, not the least of which were the establishment and coordination of urban secret cells from the villages.

---

[2] The EPLF highland fighters were under strict instructions to pay for supplies or at least provide services.

[3] A military organization trained by the Israelis for counter-insurgency warfare.

[4] Tsenedegle in Akalai Guzai and parts of Carneshim in Hamasin province.

The Highland Peasantry

We have mentioned already the strategic significance of the highlands and, in our discussion of highland society, the unequal access to land in the highland villages. One of the major programmes of the EPLF was the introduction of land reform, which went along with the organizational penetration of highland society through the establishment of EPLF institutions.[5] Linked to this was a programme of developing 'elementary cooperatives' drawing on traditional and existing forms of mutual assistance.[6] Ideology, organization and reform all worked together, albeit sequentially.

The EPLF identified the major inequalities in the countryside as arising from differential access to land in the different forms of land tenure. In *diesa* (communal village ownership with periodic redistribution of plots), 'feudal lords and rich farmers' were able to block land redistribution. In *tsilmi* ownership, 'poor families' did not acquire sufficient land for subsistence. In *demeniale* (state land where estates and plantations were established), 'lower peasants' were pushed off the land or it reverted to a form of *tsilmi* in that 'feudal lords and sheikhs' controlled it. In the latter case, feudal relations were strengthened. In addition, land rights were denied to *makalai ailat* (the largely poor and landless peasantry), women and the unmarried young. One further area of rural social problems arising from the land system was that of land disputes between villagers and between villages. A political concomitant of that was the flow of cash to those who operated the mediatory and judicial system through bribes and fees.

In late 1975, the EPLF began its land reform based on its national democratic programme (NDP), even though the latter was only formally ratified at the EPLF's first organizational congress in 1977.[7] The sections of the NDP which dealt with agriculture were a hybrid of socialism and developmentalism. Big plantations (already nationalized by the Derg in 1975[8]) were to become state farms, 'feudal land relations' were to be abolished and an equitable land distribution carried out, and

---

[5] Much of the following is based on the RICE publication, *CPEPMB*.

[6] 'Collective Activities and Mutual Aids', Part III of *CPEPMB*.

[7] The EPLF programme is available in the EPLF *Memorandum* as well as in a bowdlerilized version in L. Cliffe and B. Davidson, *The Long Struggle of Eritrea for Independence and Constructive Peace* (Trenton, NJ: Red Sea Press, 1988), Appendix.

[8] See following chapter for section on the Ethiopian revolution.

cooperative farms set up. Services and finance were to be provided for nomads 'to enable them to lead settled lives'. In addition, the programme called for an association that would 'organize, politicize and arm the peasants with a clear revolutionary outlook'. Before examining the specific modalities of political organization and its links to the EPLF's class analysis, it is worth mentioning that agro-pastoralists were to be encouraged through various mechanisms to follow settled lives in both the 1977 and 1987 NDPs. In an earlier EPLF document of 1972, which defined the social base of the ELF, agro-pastoralists were defined as the backward part of the peasantry in transition from nomadism to settled agriculture. Reform, then, was essentially focused on an idealized highland peasant system.

Although demands for changes within the systems of land tenure were voiced by the peasantry, the kinds of demands made fell short of the programme of the EPLF in that they called for the reform of existing systems rather than their 'qualitative and radical' transformation.[9] In *diesa*, they involved shortening the period when land was redistributed, reforming tenure relations and solving boundary disputes; in *tsilmi*, the removal of absentee owners and the reform of sharecropping agreements;[10] in *demeniale*, the return of land from foreigners and the redistribution of land controlled by 'feudal lords and sheikhs'. Although the EPLF recognized these popular demands as 'democratic', they still excluded the *makalai ailat*, youth and women. The EPLF goal was to redistribute land that benefited the poor and middle farmers. By its own estimate, this group comprised almost half of the peasantry.[11] Land redistribution was not only socially just and democratic (in line with the national democratic revolution), it linked the EPLF to the majority in the villages, an important ingredient for the penetration and organization of the highland village communities.

The stated policy of the EPLF was very ambitious. In the first place, it envisaged the 'abolition' of the *enda*, the extended family unit based on common descent from a shared ancestor, and its replacement by class solidarities. Basic to this long-term goal was propaganda and ideological struggle to bring about an understanding of the alliance of poor and middle peasants and the nature of class struggle. The political

[9] *CPEPMB*, p. 30.

[10] At this period in 1975, the EPLF had only limited areas of *tsilmi* under its control, a reflection of the greater ELF presence in Serai province. See *Eritrea 1991: A Needs Assessment Survey* (Leeds University, 1992) p. 94.

[11] The general line of the EPLF was that it differed from the ELF in that the latter favoured the rich peasants. Interviews, November 1977.

instrument of achieving this goal was to 'establish the dominant position of the democratic line, the political base [organized in cells] … and the arming of the masses'.[12] In order to do this, separate associations were established for rich, middle and poor peasants.

The initial implementation of the land reform was rather more modest than the ultimate goal of social revolution. It emphasized the return to a purified system of *diesa* tenure. There was still the exclusion of the unmarried, with some exceptions. However, *makalai ailat* were given rights of land use, as were widows and divorced women. Absentee villagers would be 'considered' for the allocation of a plot of land. The dependent families of fighters were to have rights to land, whereas any villagers serving in the Ethiopian army lost their rights to land – both a strong sanction against them and a pressure to desert.

A committee representing the proportions of the different strata of the village was responsible for the implementation of the land reform, under the detailed guidelines set out by the EPLF. By the mid-1980s, the EPLF claimed that land reform had been instituted in 138 villages (all *diesa*) and 24 in *demeniale*.[13]

The mode of entry to the village was as follows: the EPLA would go in and help with the harvest, followed by the armed propaganda squads of about 15 fighters and then the medical teams.[14] Detailed studies of village social and political structure were undertaken. Information was gathered by way of a formal survey on family size, amount of land and means of labour, as well as on kinds of agricultural produce. In addition, a section of the survey form included comments on political orientation: whether the person was anti-EPLF in inclination or sympathetic to the enemy.[15] Poor peasants were approached individually and secret cells were set up. The inclusion of rich peasants occurred if they held 'progressive ideas'. A village meeting would be arranged at which EPLF cadres and secret cell members would call for land reform. Two committees would be elected: one of nine members to direct the land reform and another of 12 to direct village affairs. The EPLF cadres played a role in directing the debate and insisted that the committees did not include former chiefs or rich peasants.[16]

---

[12] *CPEPMB*, p. 33.

[13] *Ibid.*, p. 29.

[14] Interview with Sibhat Efraim, PB member responsible for mass administration, Keren, November 1977.

[15] The form is included in *CPEPMB*.

[16] Jean-Louis Peninou, 'La Réforme Agraire à Azim' [For Azim read Azen] in *Revolution in Eritrea: Eyewitness Reports*, Research and Information Centre on Eritrea, Belgium, 1979.

The Cases of Zagir and Azen[17]

Zagir has frequently been used by supporters of the EPLF to illustrate the EPLF's radical approach to land reform. Dan Connell provides a graphic first-hand account of land reform in what he calls the EPLF's 'model village'.[18] It lies west of the Asmara–Keren road in north Carneshim district of Hamasin province.[19] Symbolic of the historic feudalism of the highlands, Carneshim means 'good for a chief'. Of particular interest is the EPLF's account of the land redistribution process there which illuminates the way in which propaganda and education campaigns were combined with establishing EPLF organizational structures in the highland villages around Asmara.

By the early 1940s, the periodic land redistribution had shifted from the ideal seven years to 16, heralding the collapse of the communal *diesa* system and the movement towards a form of individual ownership.[20] There were three *endas*: Arai, Teklai and Enghede. All claimed common descent from the priestly Levi tribe. The Enghede owned land in *tsilmi*, but within that system it was redistributed between *enda* families, a micro form of *diesa*. In the early 1940s the population was 1,800 and by the mid-1970s around 3,000, an extremely low population increase and an indication of migration out of the village to Asmara. The EPLF came to the Zagir area in 1974, the year it returned to the highlands in numbers, when the civil war was being fought in the area and the Ethiopian revolution was in its first throes. Following the usual EPLF practice, meetings and discussions were held with the villagers. A prerequisite of instituting reform and establishing organization was a transitional period of political struggle to undermine the dominant landholding clans. Initially, secret cells concentrated on organizing youth, women and poor and middle peasants, and these became the vanguard for raising the land question.

Detailed studies of village economic and social structure were carried out. It was indicative of the cautious approach of the EPLF, in

[17] Zagir was a village where the three main *endas* all claimed descent from ancestors from Tigray who founded the village. Trevaskis Papers, *Hamasein*.

[18] Connell, *Against All Odds*, Chapter 7, 'A Model Village'. The following account is based on this chapter, supplemented by my own notes and a brief section in *Hamasein*, Trevaskis Papers. There are descriptions of similar processes in two other Hamasin villages, Azen and Medre-Zen, in *Eritrea in Struggle*, Vol. II, No. 7, April 1978.

[19] The author visited the village for several days in autumn 1977 at a time when the the the first cooperative had been set up.

[20] Trevaskis Papers, *Hamasein*. Connell reported that the land had not been redistributed since the 1930s.

part a reaction to the strength of clan solidarity, which cut across differences in landholding, that limited reforms were introduced: only 40 of the 120 landless received land. To deepen the process, the EPLF removed the old administration formed of village dignitaries who represented the dominant clans, and replaced it with a people's committee. Simultaneously, it set up secret cells within *endas*, thereby working within the heart of village social structure and attempting to create a loyalty to the EPLF's peasant association. In addition, the small people's militia was considerably expanded, although the quality of the weapons was poor.

The organizational activity culminated in the election of a people's assembly in 1977, the year when many of the highland towns were liberated. Reflecting the EPLF's goal of creating a democratic sytem of control based on the majority of poor and middle peasants, the assembly of 37 consisted of 22 peasants (14 poor, six middle and two rich), eight youth, seven housewives, four cadres and nine militia. Of the 37, nine were women. It should be noted that within the assembly 20 were considered 'committed' to the EPLF, and at their core were the 13 cadres and militia members, while 17 were considered 'participants'. A political web was thereby created, with the EPLF organizers at the centre, extending outwards through cadres and militia to assembly members and then to villagers. There were, then, three pillars of EPLF organization reaching into Zagir: EPLF fighters–political organizers; village members of EPLF organizational structures who had undergone a course of political education; and the semi-autonomous village assembly. The latter incorporated three target groups: poor and middle peasants, women and youth. The former constituted a majority in much of the highlands and, through land reform and peoples' assemblies in the villages, the EPLF built institutions and implemented policies that connected it to that majority. In addition to the vertical links to local EPLF cadres, horizontal links were created to the peasant association.

The organizational thrust of the EPLF in Zagir was replicated in other highland villages, and thus brought in the skein of EPLF organizations and institutions and firmly embedded them in this area of concentrated peasantry. In the village of Azen (from Add Zien, descendants of Zien),[21] it has been estimated that 95 per cent of the inhabitants were poor and middle peasants, and that communal land, by custom redistributed every seven years, had not been redistributed

---

[21] The descendants of Zien have *endas* in many villages of the Carneshim district of Hamasin and traced their origin to the Solomonic dynasty. Trevaskis Papers, *Hamasein*.

since 1922.[22] As a consequence there were 600 families without land, almost as many as the 800 with land. An EPLF survey of 14 *diesa* villages in 1979 provided a similar picture: 90 per cent were poor and middle peasants, and they owned 65 per cent of the oxen. Within these two categories, 60 per cent were poor peasants, who owned 20 per cent of the oxen. The latter produced 36 quintals of grain, while the 10 per cent of rich peasants and 'feudal chiefs' produced 20 quintals.

Neither the EPLF's nor Connell's account of Zagir mentions church land, but Peninou discusses it briefly in Azen. There, it was established that no priest could have more land than a peasant, and that priests had to cultivate their land themselves. In Azen, a village of 5,000, Peninou was informed that there were 50 priests. Given the size of the poor and rich peasants and the inequalities, land reform and the institutional ties associated with it reinforced the mobilizational capacity of the front.

The political and military advantages of building a large peasant base are obvious. Certain disadvantages arose from alienating those who derived privilege from the status quo: rich peasants and absentees. The former provided the traditional political leadership and were accustomed to public speaking in village forums, handled local disputes through mediation and were versed in customary law. The opposition of the rich peasants in Zagir was based on a set of objections to EPLF programmes. These were, firstly, that the EPLF was taking the land of villagers of Zagir origin resident in towns. Since rich peasants had the money and the oxen to farm their land, they were a major beneficiary of absentee landholders, usually from the same descent group. Secondly, the move to cooperative farming was initially criticized on the grounds that the EPLF was taking land for the benefit of the front and not the villagers. The establishment of cooperative farming through 'mutual aid teams' again cut into the privilege of the richer peasants.

In recognizing that rich peasants could be both nationalists and subversive of the 'democratic struggle' the EPLF tactic was twofold. Only the land which had been acquired unfairly was taken from the rich peasants for redistribution.[23] As to absentees, a flexible approach was adopted. Land was allocated to married youth and to those who 'fulfil their duties and responsibilities'. This latter proviso allowed absentees to retain land if they contributed in cash or kind to the cause.

---

[22] *Eritrea in Struggle*, Vol. II, No. 3, December 1977, and the account by Peninou, 'La Réforme Agraire à Azim' [sic] in *Revolution in Eritrea*. The figure of 95 per cent appears very high.

[23] In Zagir elders of leading clans had been allocated state land during the Italian period, and this was given a different status, called *kolkol*. It was meant to have been distributed, but the elders retained it.

The EPLF made a distinction between implementing land reform in liberated and semi-liberated areas. The determinants were the length of time under the EPLF, the depth of organization and the particular politico-military context. For example, Addi Hawasha village to the south of Asmara had an open EPLF presence only in 1977 and was categorized as semi-liberated.[24] The village was used as a meeting place for cadres and Asmara secret cell members and, as some villagers worked in Asmara factories where they organized clandestine cells, their land was not redistributed. The process in Zagir and other highland villages came to an end with the return of the Ethiopian army in 1978 after the strategic retreat. As in other villages where the EPLF had had a strong presence, many of the villagers were pulled out with the EPLF and many of the young became fighters.

The Highland Periphery

Below we shall examine land reform in two areas where, in contrast to the highland peasantry, the population was Muslim and agro-pastoralists who cultivated their land seasonally. Details of the land reform in these areas are derived from two different military contexts: the Wadi Labka reforms were undertaken at a time of full liberation whereas the Akalai Guzai reforms were implemented in a semi-liberated or contested zone, which had been under ELF control.

The Case of Wadi Labka

Wadi Labka is an area in the eastern plains of Sahel province around the seasonal Labka stream, which has its sources in the northern highlands and flows into the Red Sea. Cultivation is done by the construction of dams and irrigation works to collect the water from the spate floods and the silt carried with them. The inhabitants, around 10,000, are agro-pastoralists, moving between Wadi Labka and the Afabat area, and Muslim. Afabat developed some of the characteristics of a market town. The EPLF liberated it in 1977 but had had a long presence in Sahel, the location of its base areas.[25] It was an area which had been part of the societies based on master–serf relations. Although

---

[24] The following is based on an interview with an EPLF mass administration cadre operating out of the village. November 1977.

[25] The author visited Afabat in October 1977. EPLF policy in the area was one of encouraging agro-pastoralists to settle by developing education.

the chiefs were weakened in the 1940s during the serf rebellion and the British reconstructed the tribes, it is apparent from EPLF studies that the economic relations between former serfs and their masters were changed but not significantly transformed. The irrigated land in Wadi Labka was retained by the chiefs of the Add Tamariam through their control of *demeniale*. The Add Tamariam were part of the feudal Bayt Asghede, like the Habab and the Add Takles.

As in other areas of Sahel, the EPLF expanded its influence through the provision of services, particularly medical and veterinary. The whole area was little touched by the Ethiopian state. The EPLF established a clinic in Afabat and from there medical teams, the 'barefoot doctors', would roam the region. Most of the former serfs were agro-pastoralists but worked the land as sharecroppers and rural labourers, receiving a share of the harvest for working it with animals and/or labour.[26] Trevaskis gave the number of Bayt Asghede, the feudal clan, of the Add Tamariam as 904.[27] Although the British reorganized the *tigre* tribes a more capitalist form of relationship emerged based not on feudal dues and obligations but on landlord–tenant relations.

The EPLF allowed the inhabitants of the Atombosso area to till the land unconstrained by the sharecropping agreements.[28] According to the EPLF, the opposition of the landlords was based on tribalism and religion encapsulated in the following slogans: 'There are two organizations in Eritrea [the ELF & EPLF], we Add Tamariam will organize our tribe and set up a third' and 'Taking land that is another person's property is condemned by religion, it is blasphemy.'

Given the strength of opposition and its religious character, the EPLF took the land under its own control[29] and announced that it would consider the case if the owner of the land in Atombosso came personally. The compromise contained the opposition and the EPLF began constructing secret cells and a militia among the sharecroppers. The EPLF's position was enhanced by the fall of Afabat in April 1977 and the establishment of a people's assembly and mass organizations. In May, demonstrators again raised religious slogans against the literacy classes for women: 'Our women are subject to Quranic laws and they shall not attend schools' and 'May those not joining us be denied access to heaven.'

---

[26] A detailed account of sharecropping arrangements is given in *CPEPMB*.

[27] Trevaskis Papers, *A Report on the Tribal Reorganisation of the Western Province*.

[28] Most of the information on Wadi Labka is based on *CPEPMB*.

[29] This method of dealing with a difficult land problem could be viewed as a precursor of the post-independence land law where all land became state land. This topic will be treated in the last chapter.

Secure in military victory, the EPLF organized a series of meetings and arrested six landlords who had planned the demonstration. Subsequently, the land reform was implemented, but in two stages. In the first, land of landlords was redistributed and the rich peasants were left untouched. In the second, rich peasants' land was redistributed. In all, just less than 2,000 tenants and poor and middle peasants received land. In a revolutionary step for this undeveloped traditional Muslim area, 75 women received land.

Eastern Akalai Guzai

A similar pattern of social structure, inequality and reform can be found in the Muslim Sahho area of the eastern escarpment of Akalai Guzai, but here local circumstances required a different approach. The EPLF administration came into the area after the demise of the ELF in the early 1980s. It was behind enemy lines and thus a contested area where a challenge committee rather than a people's assembly was established. A team was drafted in from the front, the majority of whom had some ethnic or linguistic links to the area.

There were two different spheres of intervention, both of which involved land issues, only one of which could be considered land reform proper. In the first sphere, in the area between Arafale and Bure, the seasonal grazing pastures of the Gaasu tribe of the Miniferi and the Hazu had long been disputed, with the effect that it had not been cultivated for some 25 years. Both claimed that the Italians had granted seasonal cultivation rights to the other. The ELF had attempted to deal with the problem without success. The EPLF dealt with it through a process of mediation.

In the other area, there were two land problems. The first was one where one agro-pastoralist group of Sahho had two different areas of seasonal cultivation. They spent half the year in the Hadish area and half in the Addi Qayyih/Senafe area. The EPLF land reform involved their choosing land in one of the areas only. The second was one of unequal access to land, and a situation similar to that of Wadi Labka. Some detail is provided on this case because it illustrates the local particularity and complexity of implementing land reform faced by the responsible cadres, and provides an example of the space for initiative.

There was one individual, Mahmud, the *shumanya* of the Sahho Assalisan, who owned a large area of land. The population was divided between the Assalisan, a sub-tribe of the Assaorta, the Hazu and a few Afar. The mass administration team set up a land reform committee comprised of four elders and three youths, the former for their knowledge of local circumstances and the latter for their greater flexibility and sympathy for the EPLF. The *shumanya's* land was taken from him and distributed in equal parcels of fertile and arid land through the committee. A great deal of persuasion was required because the local inhabitants had knowledge of EPLF land reform in the Zula area, where the land reform was based on proximity to the household, and thus did not differentiate between fertile and arid. Gender issues also were involved. The basis of redistribution was the household. Since beneficiary households had to choose land in one of their grazing areas problems arose for polygamous households. The EPLF insisted that the husband had to choose membership of one. To ensure non-evasion wives were incorporated into the proceess: they had to sign the document acknowledging receipt of the parcels of land.

The process of land redistribution took three years, starting in 1983 when the ELF left the area. Because of the proximity of the Ethiopian army and the lengthy presence of the ELF, the organization was through a resistance committee. Opposition came from the *shumanya* who had been an adherent of the ELF. In line with general mass administration guidelines that 'strict disciplinary measures' be taken against the abuse of power, he was imprisoned for three weeks. His imprisonment, however, was on the grounds that he held a gun unlicensed by the EPLF rather than on the grounds that he opposed the reform, in contrast to the disciplinary measures taken in the Wadi Labka area where a strong EPLF presence averted such subtlety. The process of reform was further complicated by the presence in the area of an ELF battalion leader from the local Assalisan who, after the demise of the ELF, had joined the Ethiopians. He would on occasion return to the area, and the *shumanya* used him as a threat to blackmail the bulk of the people. Through clandestine contacts with sections of the youth seven men were identified as central to the implementation of reform. They were imprisoned for a day while the cadres attempted to convince the mass of people to side with them.

A Note on Religion and Reform

It is interesting to note that in the EPLF account of the process of reform in Zagir no particular mention was made of the church and the priests. However, all the cadres involved in the land reform were Tigrinya speakers and thus identifiably of Christian background.

Given the religiosity of the peasantry, it would be unlikely that ethno-religious affinities eased the path of the EPLF cadres. In the other extensively EPLF-documented case of land reform, religion did become involved and was used by landowners to preserve their privileges. In Wadi Labka, however, the population was Muslim. Similarly, in eastern Akalai Guzai, cadres made reference to Quranic verses which emphasized social justice.

It was an ironic reversal of historical processes that while in the 1940s and 1950s the church and priesthood were defenders of privilege and key actors in undermining the trajectory to national independence and that the early Eritrean national independence movement was strongest in Muslim areas, it was in Muslim areas liberated by the EPLF that Islam was used by reformers and resisters. Much of the opposition was presented in Islamic terms and the cadres quoted pieces of the Quran justifying the changes.

Organization

We shall describe process of setting up organization in the villages and argue that although the ultimate goal was to establish relatively autonomous functioning popular institutions and administration, these functioned as an extension of the EPLF and EPLF control. They implemented the policy directives of EPLF departments and mass organizations, were subject to mass administration controls and were auxiliaries of the EPLA. Detailed guidelines were issued for the performance and behaviour of front institutions, including regular reports on action taken.

In order to connect the peasantry administratively to the EPLF, it was initially necessary to remove the existing village administration, whereby village chiefs and committees of elders maintained law and order and collected tax for the Ethiopian central government. Insofar as these traditional leaders and institutions were connecting points between Eritreans and the Ethiopian government, inserting the EPLF's administrative structures into the village not only aimed at transforming internal village social, economic and political relations but also at breaking the connection to the Ethiopian state.

In analysing the connection between the peasantry, land reform and the EPLF, great emphasis was placed on the necessity of organization. Indeed, in EPLF Arabic publications the front is referred to as *al-tanzim*: the organization. After the strategic retreat of 1978 organizing was subordinated to the military fight-back, and many of the personnel involved in mass administration returned to military duties during the 1980s.

The stress on organization was derivative of the Chinese experience.[30] It was a means of both mobilization and control. The nature of organizational structures among the peasantry varied with different contexts: the depth and length of liberation, the level of political consciousness, and the military balance of forces between the EPLF and both the Ethiopian army and the ELF. Even after 1981–2, when the ELF had been defeated, the sympathy of the local population toward the ELF was taken into account. In the same way that the theory of people's war developed in stages, so did organizational development. The form of the latter was determined by the social and strategic context, with different types in the rural and urban areas.

The first stage involved the establishment of people's committees, which were of two kinds. The first functioned as replacements of the traditional leaders and as institutions transitional to the establishment of people's assemblies. The second type were organizations operative after the establishment of the latter and which continued functioning clandestinely after the strategic retreat. In the second stage, people's assemblies were established whereby the EPLF was in full control, and where a 'relatively adequate level of consciousness and organization in the form of political bases had been reached'.[31] These emerged in 1977 as the EPLF liberated large parts of Eritrea. In the third stage, resistance committees were formed. These were largely aimed at inserting EPLF administrative structures into the large areas which the ELF had controlled completely or partially, and were developed in 1981.

The *Guidelines for the Formation, Constitution and Operation of People's Administration* issued by the EPLF give a clear picture of the administrative linkages between front and people. The different social forces (rich, middle and poor peasants), women and youth elected their representatives proportionally to the people's assembly (PA). The latter reported to the general village meeting which 'takes instructions from the district Mass Administration Office'.[32] In villages with average populations, the PA had to be not less than 45. Although this relatively large number was aimed at reducing the powers of the handful of traditional clan leaders, it also associated a large core of villagers directly with EPLF administrative structures. The PA elected an

---

[30] 'Fourteen Great Achievements' *Mao, Selected Works*, Vol. 1.
[31] *CPEPMB*, p. 80.
[32] *Ibid.*, p. 84.

executive committee, which met twice a week. Links to the EPLF were reinforced through the role of mass administration (MA) cadres in establishing and attending PA meetings until 'enough initial experience is gained',[33] and through the PA's executive committee. The latter had between 10 and 15 members, including a chairman, and they were responsible for departments ranging from animal wealth to security. The functioning of the departments is indicative of the supervisory role of the EPLF, its role in implementing at the grass roots level policies formulated by the EPLF and its associated mass organizations, like the peasants' association.

For example, the judiciary committee resolved village disputes which had traditionally been in the hands of the village heads but more serious disputes were handled by the MA district office. Social affairs and health care, forestry, mining and water resources took instructions from the EPLF department of social affairs and the central committee of the peasant association, respectively. The executive committee member responsible for security came from the people's militia and was elected by all village militia members and had security, police, quasi-military and intelligence gathering functions. In addition, to ensure the continuation of the armed struggle, he 'prepared youth who would join the People's Army'.[34]

The Towns

In the course of 1977, the EPLF captured many towns and cities beginning with Qarora[35] and culminating in the liberation of Keren and Decamhare[36]. Following the 1977 first EPLF congress a separate department of MA had been established under PB member Sebhat Efraim, and this department organized the establishment of the people's assemblies in the towns under a set of regulations distinct from those for the rural areas. The nucleus of this department was already in existence. The EPLF was, however, not beginning from scratch as it already had secret cells in towns like Decamhare and Keren, although they were not as extensive in the latter, a town whose

---

[33] *Ibid*, p. 86.

[34] *Ibid.*, p. 89.

[35] Other than an Ethiopian army post, it was a deserted settlement on the northern border with Sudan. Most of the inhabitants had uprooted to the Qarora on the Sudanese side of the border.

[36] The author spent a week in both in October and November 1977.

population had historically stronger sympathies toward the ELF.[37]

The two towns were also socially and economically different. Keren was a market town with considerable merchant influence, and the major urban centre of the Bileyn minority. Decamhare was in the Tigrinya-speaking highlands and, although a vibrant small industrial town by the 1970s, was very run down. Both had big Ethiopian garrisons, and Decamhare was the training centre for the Eritrean commandos.

The organization of the cities was based on zones, and the assemblies were elected from zonal congresses. Utilizing the zone as the basis of administration followed on from the Ethiopian government's organization of the towns on *kebeles*, urban dwellers' associations. Delegates of each organized 'social force' sent delegates to the zonal congress and also elected the people's assembly. The process was, then, distinct from rural organization where the whole village congress elected the people's assembly. Urban social forces were delineated as: workers, housewives, youth, professionals (upper, middle and lower) and semi-workers. In addition, provision was made for peasant representation.[38] As in the rural areas, the EPLF regulations called for large people's assemblies. MA cadres attended the monthly meetings of the PAs. In other respects, the administrative departments of the executive committee of the people's assemblies were connected to the EPLF in a form similar to that described for the villages. Similarly, the EPLF established economic institutions like people's shops, comparable in concept to the attempt to introduce cooperatives in liberated villages. In the towns, however, such innovations would bring them into competition with the merchants.

In examining the process of organizing the towns I shall look at Decamhare and Keren in rather different ways: the first is based on an EPLF case study[39] supplemented by personal observation, and the second wholly on personal observation and interviews.

Decamhare

The first step of the EPLF was to dismantle the *kebele* system and this was followed by organizing the different social forces, a process which

---

[37] In Keren, I was able to have a greater degree of freedom from the department of protocol guide as many of the inhabitants spoke Arabic. At the time, I had assumed that the irritation of my guide at my frequent escapes from him was to ensure control. After liberation, he informed me that his worry was that I might run into trouble because of the clandestine ELF presence. There was no similar problem in Decamhare.

[38] *CPEPMB*, p. 90. EPLF cadres used Marxist terms like petty-bourgeoisie.

[39] *CPEPMB*, pp. 98–101.

occurred together with intensive political education classes. Subsequently, the town was divided into two zones and people's assemblies were formed for each. The assemblies had 22 and 29 members and, according to EPLF figures which do not tally, combined, were constituted of 16 professionals, 15 workers, 11 women and 10 youths. New elections were held after six months, and the 72 members displayed a change in the proportions of social forces represented: 15 workers, 18 professionals, 21 women and 18 youths, marking a significant increase in the latter two categories. Indicative of the role of leading EPLF civilian members, seven of the new people's assembly had attended cadre school.

The assemblies, working under the guidance of the MA, organized political education and were responsible for grain marketing and distribution through people's shops and forming a militia. In addition, they administered the issuing of EPLF identity cards to all Decamhare inhabitants. The militia consisted of 61 men and seven women. The judiciary committees treated legal problems in two ways: through 'criticism and self-criticism' and through judicial examination. In line with the EPLF's policy of bringing swift justice in contrast to the expensive and protracted nature of the Ethiopian-controlled judicial process, in six months more than 1,400 cases were dealt with.

The economic committees worked as administrative auxiliaries of the EPLF economic department. Two important areas they administered were house rents and prices. The EPLF did not reverse the nationalization of urban properties over and above one residence introduced by the Derg, and continued to collect rent from those nationalized. In addition, it controlled prices to prevent merchant profiteering and the inflow and outflow of goods. Because supplies in the people's shops were inadequate, merchants were allowed to import from Sudan and provided with transport by the EPLF for that purpose.

Of the 72 members of the PAs, 39 left with the EPLF and joined the EPLA. Although there are no figures for members of the mass organizations who also left with the EPLF, they were considerable. For, if the frame of steel connected the urban inhabitants to the front, the front had also developed an infrastructure for the absorption of new recruits and for the protection of civilians fearing Ethiopian reprisals and revenge in the base areas of Sahel. In addition, during the strategic withdrawal, the people's assemblies helped organize the withdrawal of the EPLF and both its equipment and machinery found in Decamhare that could be utilized in the base areas.

Keren

We have mentioned above the differences between Keren and Decamhare and the rather different sources drawn on. Keren was also distinct from Decamhare in that it had a large Muslim community and, as a consequence, a female population which was accustomed to conforming to strict codes of personal behaviour. At one political education-cum-literacy class I attended, many of the women were very heavily veiled. Keren was a more difficult proposition than Decamhare, where some ground had been prepared by the secret cells. Those in Keren, however, were rather limited. Similarly, Keren was a major market town for the surrounding area as well as a city which was a major link between the highlands and, in 1977, the ELF-controlled west. The ELF had a presence around the town and controlled the western half of the large, formerly Italian-owned plantation at Elaborad, to the south of the town.

In Keren, it was more possible to observe at first hand the radical policies of the EPLF. Indeed, some of the local population nicknamed the EPLF 'the Eritrean derg', in part a reflection of its mercantile culture and the EPLF's socialist reputation. According to EPLF research, 15 big merchants controlled trade worth about \$E200,000.[40] Their wealth derived from the ownership of lorries, shops, mills and bakeries. The EPLF introduced controls over profits and supplies. After its liberation, retail and wholesale merchants were restricted to a 10 per cent profit and, in addition, paid the EPLF for the costs of transporting goods from Sudan. Trade between Asmara and Keren was also controlled to ensure that merchants did not profit excessively from the sale of goods from Keren and its hinterland to Asmara, on the one hand, and the sale of consumer items brought from Asmara in exchange, on the other. I was informed that merchants had tried to transport large supplies of onions bought at 75c per kilo for sale at \$3E per kilo in Asmara. On their return they would bring out luxury consumer items like soap. The EPLF placed controls over these trade exchanges between the liberated areas and those under Ethiopian control.[41]

The EPLF retained the Ethiopian policy of nationalized houses, but introduced a sliding scale of rent decreases, with the largest benefiting the poorest tenants. Rents below \$E25 were cut by a half. The rent for

[40] D. Pool, *Establishing Movement Hegemony*, Manchester Papers in Politics, 1992, p. 15.
[41] A similar kind of combination of assistance and controls took place in Afabat, where merchants were allowed a profit of 10–12 per cent on the sale of tea and sugar. The EPLF ran one lorry a day from there to Keren and four to Qarora.

one of the pharmacies was reduced from $E30 to $E18. Although merchants did not complain about the removal of the Ethiopians, they did point out that much of their retail trade had been dependent on the purchasing power of the 3,000 soldiers of the Ethiopian garrison.

In Keren market, price controls were placed on fruit and vegetables and grain. The EPLF brought down the price of dura, a staple grain, and placed a very low profit margin of 10c on transactions in the fruit and vegetable market. For the peasant hinterland of Keren, two important cash crops were peanuts and reed for the weaving of mats and baskets. The EPLF increased the wages of the casual workers who sorted these.

The EPLF also introduced changes in pay scales for workers, most of whom were employed by the municipality and electricity supply, and government employees. The salaries of the higher paid were reduced and the wages of the lowest paid increased. A wage of $E30 was raised to $E50. Day labourers' wages were increased from 60c to $E1. In addition, the EPLF established a people's shop selling sugar, coffee and seeds.

For the different social forces and mass organizations political education, along with literacy classes for some, was in full swing in autumn 1977. Political education consisting of two two-hour sessions per week was compulsory for the mass organizations. Indicative of the importance attached to political education, 50 courses were held in one week![42] At a teacher's meeting of around 40, one cadre was explaining primitive communism, feudalism, capitalism and the role of the bourgeoisie. In others, the history of the armed struggle was expounded, with emphasis on the reactionary nature of the ELF. It was a theme of some importance for the EPLF in 1977 as a unity agreement between the two fronts was in the process of negotiation and was announced at mass meetings the following week. The secret organizations held separate meetings, and the one I attended included a merchant. Most of the meetings were repetitive and the attenders seemed not to have totally absorbed the EPLF line. At the teachers' meeting, one stated that even the bourgeoisie was pleased with liberation. They had expected the EPLF to be like the Derg, but it was not because their property and riches were preserved.

The EPLF placed great stress on the provision of services. Keren hospital, badly damaged during the fighting, was repaired and reopened. An EPLF clinic with an EPLF doctor was attached to the hospital and medical supplies were brought from the central pharmacy.

---

[42] *Eritrea in Struggle*, Vol II, No. 5, February 1978.

Increasingly, rural people with serious conditions were referred to Keren hospital by squad doctors operating in the surrounding areas. Schools were reopened and continued to function despite the fact that teachers' salaries were not coming through from Asmara.

The EPLF succeeded to the array of local taxes and levies collected by the Ethiopian government: rent from nationalized properties, charges for veterinary checks on animals brought for sale in the market, for example. Ethiopian taxes were diverted for the provision of goods and services.

In line with EPLF policy of mobilizing and recruiting core groups of support, a special emphasis was placed on youth. The PB member responsible for MA stressed that 'youth were a bridge' between different sections of Eritrean society. They were not delineated on the basis of class and comprised both genders between the ages of 16 and 28.[43] The tasks set for youth in Keren largely involved menial tasks but gave an introduction to and taste of EPLF discipline. Squads from the youth organization in the different zones were set to work cleaning and repairing the infrastructure of the different zones. In the fifth zone, the poorest part of Keren, major tasks were weeding and clearing tracks; in the third zone, largely inhabited by salaried officials, the youth squads cleaned the hospital compound.

Indicative of EPLF policy, and in part a function of the demands on the EPLA in simultaneously laying siege to Asmara and Massawa, policing Keren was in the hands of the Vanguards. In an extensive interview with two of them, a 16-year-old boy and girl, they emphasized the role of youth, repeating the EPLF line that youth were the revolutionary generation and best fitted to transmit the revolutionary culture. Plans for the establishment of a club for youth were also justified on cultural grounds, but with a strong moral twist: the youth club would be a means of building a new culture and eradicating decadent behaviour introduced under Ethiopian rule: dancing, drinking, prostitution and the use of hashish. Like many urban centres which were also garrison towns, Keren had scores of bars from where prostitutes plied their trade. The EPLF had stopped the prostitution and, I was informed, was re-educating prostitutes. The EPLF took a strong moral stand on these issues and generally blamed them on Ethiopian rule and immigrant Ethiopians.[44]

---

[43] EPLF publications usually give 28 as the upper age limit.

[44] A similar view was strongly expressed by many EPLF officials after the liberation of Asmara. There was a particular disgust at the decadence of discos and the morally corrosive nature of such places on urban youth.

The liberation of Keren also provided the opportunity and the setting for organizational expansion and the demonstration of EPLF power. The people's militia of Sahel and Senheit province held a conference there and a military parade in August 1977, and in May 1978 the first congress of the Association of Eritrean Students was held. It included participants from Eritrea and abroad. In March, 1978, the first congress of the Association of Eritrean Peasants met under the slogan of 'Consolidate the worker–peasant alliance'. In all three conferences, central committees for these mass organizations were elected. The holding of these congresses was indicative of the expanding organizational control and outreach of the EPLF as it brought together members of the branches established across Eritrea, as well as Eritreans abroad.

Agitation and propaganda were given special emphasis as part of the policy of incorporation of different classes and strata.[45] Political education classes were expanded recruiting cadres from the people's assemblies who were given special training. These individuals were 'dedicated members' who were

> the backbone of the organization. These should be people with wide-ranging experience and should be of such iron discipline as would not budge from the political line of the EPLF. As full time revolutionaries, they should master the art of fighting against the enemy and should be ready to suffer honourable death ... Only through intensive ideological training can dedicated members of associations persevere through difficult conditions without losing their bearings. Armed with such knowledge, they will be able to recruit new members, strengthen the link between the EPLF and the people and carry the lofty revolutionary qualities demanded by their position. This is a matter of principle.

For these advanced members ideological topics were fused with organizational ones. All active members were given ideological training of two to three weeks on topics like the national democratic programme, elementary analysis of classes in Eritrean society and 'revolutionary morality' as well as on the principles and guidelines of the mass organizations.

From the active and trained members of the mass organizations some were selected to attend a month and a half course at the cadre school run by the department of mass administration. Topics studied were more broadly ideological (dialectical and historical materialism),

---

[45] Most of the following is based on 'General Political Activities' in *CPEPMB*.

historical (the history of the Eritrean revolution and of the EPLF), practical (land redistribution and cooperatives) and organizational. As well as providing an organizational link between the front and the rest of Eritrean society, these cadres together with the youth were a key source of front fighters. The occupation of and subsequent withdrawal from the towns witnessed an increase in fighter recruitment on a scale similar to that of 1974–5. The increase in recruits between 1974 and 1978 also saw the large-scale incorporation of women into the front.

Women

The role of women in the EPLF and the general culture of equality within the field has been mentioned above and have been hailed by many observers.[46] The EPLF pursued policies in the liberated zones that also changed the traditional roles of women, most markedly in the shift from the private to the public sphere. Women were elected to people's assemblies on the basis of a 15 per cent quota, encouraged to attend political education and literacy classes and given rights to land. The increased participation of women and their greater visibility in public spaces was in marked contrast to traditional social behaviour in and norms of broader Eritrean society, as reflected in Tigrinya proverbs and sayings: 'Just as there is no donkey with horns, so there is no woman with brains' and 'Where is the gain if one marries a woman to give birth to a woman?'

The introduction of EPLF reforms in this sensitive area of women's rights and public roles was not without reaction from men. After the establishment of the local assembly gave women representation in the conservative town of Afabat, protesters meeting at the local mosque complained: 'As if Afabat has no men, 24 women now sit in the people's assembly. Abomination! It is against the *sharia* for women to talk in public, to open their veils, to leave their families and go to work alone.'[47] Women were also oppressed in the Christian communities of Eritrea. In the highlands, they worked the fields like the men and were solely responsible for the arduous tasks of collecting water from distant wells and gathering firewood. A common sight in rural Eritrea is that of a young girl or old woman bent almost double with daunting loads of brushwood on their backs. Both *sharia* and customary law codes in

---

[46] See Wilson, *The Challenge Road: Women and the Eritrean Revolution*.

[47] Eritrean Womens Association, *Women and Revolution in Eritrea*, June 1979.

the Christian areas enshrined inequalities. In both communities female genital mutilation was widespread with the most extreme form in Muslim communities. The EPLF campaigned against these practices in the liberated areas and approached the issue through literacy classes, health education and propaganda campaigns.

Concurrent with the EPLF marriage law of 1977 permitting fighters to marry,[48] the EPLF began modifying customary laws in areas under its control. One unpublished account of marriage argued that the influence of the EPLF law on shaping marriage practices outside the front varied from area to area and with the presence of the Ethiopian military. The very great difficulty of changing local practices, even in areas of longstanding EPLF presence, was evidenced in the local opposition to EPLF modifications to customary practice in Muslim Sahel, when a clause opposing infibulation was inserted in new customary law.[49] Balancing progressive change while maintaining popular support was more difficult where women's position was associated with religion and culture.

In line with the changed roles and positions of women within the EPLF, the front introduced changes in gender roles in liberated areas. It took a consistent stand on the participation of women and rights to land and provided for the representation of women in the people's assemblies through the women's associations. In almost all villages a strictly consistent proportional representation was not introduced because of cultural constraints. However, all EPLF popular assemblies at all levels had some form of representation, ranging from 15 to 30 per cent. Organizing older women was particularly difficult. With the increasing numbers of young women in the EPLF, greater use was made of female cadres to involve rural women through informal discussions, often in their homes. Such an approach was important in expanding female literacy into the older generation as well as breaking taboos against female education for their daughters. In some semi-liberated conservative Muslim areas, cadres had first to deal with the men. One of the strategies for breaking down older gender barriers was through organizing on an age-specific basis through the mixed-sex youth association.

---

[48] See Silkin, 'Changes in the Negotiation of Marriage'.

[49] For an account of women and customary laws see Naib, 'Women's Rights and their Challenging Struggle'.

Youth

For long EPLF leaders had stressed the political treachery of the older generation and focused on youth as the vanguard for developing a revolutionary culture. Along with women, youth was the only non-class category targeted for mobilization into EPLF para-front organizations. The organization for youth, in both the rural areas and the towns liberated in the 1970s, comprised both men and women from 18 to 28 years and they were represented in people's assemblies. It provided the largest proportion of all the EPLF's associations for cadre training. By the mid-1970s, for many young civilians their icons were Kalashnikov-carrying fighters. The young were more amenable to new ideas, and a large proportion of them suffered adult discrimination in access to land and marriage arrangements. Both the EPLF land reform and the marriage law were appealing. For the EPLF, they were ideal recruits for the EPLA and supporters of the social, economic and political reforms. The great waves of new members from the mid-1970s onwards came from this social category and provided the bulk of the frontline fighters.

Refugees and Émigrés

The organizational outreach of the EPLF was not limited to Eritreans within Eritrea. An important source of political and financial support and recruitment was Eritreans who had fled Eritrea. These included the refugees in Sudan, Eritreans who had moved to Ethiopia and the Eritrean communities in the US and Europe. The Eritrean refugees were the largest community outside of Eritrea, and although the proportions changed over time, the great majority were from Muslim communities. Sudan was the main transit to other continents and the majority of those who left for them were from the highlands. On liberation, there were about 500,000 in Sudan.

An index of adult Eritreans outside the country can be gained from voting figures for the 1993 referendum: Sudan 153,806; Ethiopia 58,466; elsewhere 82,598. Of the latter the wealthiest communities were 14,000 in North America, 7,000 in Germany, 6,000 in Sweden, 37,000 in Saudi Arabia and 5,000 in Italy. Refugees in the Sudan were an important recruiting ground for the EPLF, which had a strong team of organizing cadres operating from its offices there. Sudan provided

an opportunity to compete with the ELF among communities traditionally associated with it in a context where there was no ELF military
presence. The Eritrean émigré community in Ethiopia provided
recruits into the front and was an important source of funding and
information through the EPLF secret cells.

The EPLF organizations were particularly strong in northern
Europe and North America, and the Eritrean communities there had
been socially and educationally upwardly mobile. After the foundation
of the EPLF, many of these, particularly from North America, came to
the field, and by the mid-1980s were in key secondary positions as
economists, doctors, departmental administrators and political organizers, with several elected to the central committee. Most of those
overseas would pay a proportion of their income to the EPLF and were
active in street collections and other forms of fund-raising. Meetings of
EPLF organizations outside provided a considerable source of income:
regular attendance, participation in political education classes and
payments at meetings were a mark of EPLF membership. The price of
not fulfilling these obligations was a form of social exclusion from the
community.

Of considerable importance were the connections and networks
built by EPLF organizers from offices across Europe and the US.
Initially, they established mass organizations replicating those in Eritrea
and members had to attend the weekly political education classes and
obey organizational rules of attendance and behaviour. These organizations and cadres then created a network of local support committees.
A parallel activity was the establishment of foreign sympathizers in the
media, universities, churches and aid agencies.

Several of the latter were of particular importance in funding
projects in Eritrea in conjunction with the Eritrean Relief Association
(ERA). ERA was an extension of the EPLF, dealing with fund-raising
for the welfare and relief of refugees, famine victims and the internally
displaced. Its officers in Europe and the US were EPLF external
organizers. As the majority of Eritreans in Europe and the US were
Christian, as well as being qualified and highly educated, links to
religious aid organizations like Christian Aid and Norwegian Church
Relief were more easily facilitated.

In sum, a package of benefits accrued to the EPLF from its external
organizational efforts and activities. The efficiency of both ERA and
the EPLF in delivering services to the needy in Eritrea was a further
factor in bolstering its external support. The EPLF performance in
these areas was widely publicized thanks in part to the networking of

EPLF and ERA cadres in media circles and favourable newspaper reporting by journalists.

Conclusion

The strength of the internal organization of the EPLF and its organizational outreach were salient factors in the success of the EPLF in mobilizing support from the different strata of Eritrea, generating resources and maintaining and sustaining the front. Of great significance was the development of the infrastructure of the base areas and the incorporation of the personnel to run it. These components enabled the EPLF to continue the armed struggle and mobilize fighters against tremendous odds.

In this and the previous chapter we have emphasized social and political factors internal to Eritrea and Eritrean society drawn largely from the late 1970s, by which time the EPLF had attained a peak of political and organizational maturity. Although these factors were important in sustaining the front through the long years of combat, without significant peaks of military success from its foundation in 1970, victory would not have been attainable in 1991 and independence in 1993. In the following chapter we examine some key episodes in the path to military victory, illustrating how even in the face of military reversals the leadership and cadres turned setbacks into advantages by seizing opportunities. Without the framework which we have described, however, it would have been extremely difficult to turn the tide against Ethiopia.

Five

The Roads to Liberation
From Sahel to State

Introduction

In this chapter the focus is on aspects of the liberation process which
do not neatly fit into analyses of the character of the EPLF or its
relationship to Eritrean society. I have so far argued that the successful
outcome was built on the unification of the armed groups into the
EPLF, the ideological and organizational framework and the physical
infrastructure that was put in place. These characteristics provided the
basis for the EPLF's capacity to sustain itself and to grow in military
strength. The author cannot pretend to any strategic expertise but of
necessity will deal here with some key turning points on the way to
independence.[1] In addition, mention must be made of developments
which contributed to the expansion of the EPLF and eventual military
victory. These include the Ethiopian revolution and the ultimate disintegration of the revolutionary regime, the tactical alliance with
Ethiopian opposition forces, the second civil war and the expulsion of
the ELF from Eritrea, the increasing international recognition of the
front through military victories and the appropriation of internationally
recognized status through its management of famine in the 1980s.

Some of these developments that were significant contributory factors
to the success of the EPLF may seem incidental to the explanatory and
analytic focus of the previous two chapters. There are two ways in
which the topics of this chapter are directly related to the earlier
analysis. Firstly, the EPLF partly or wholly influenced developments in
Ethiopia and, secondly, the autonomy and cohesion of the organization

[1] A more detailed account can be found in R. Pateman, *Even the Stones are Burning*, Red Sea
Press, Trenton, NJ, 1990.

and leadership enabled it to take advantage of developments external to it. The focus of this chapter, then, is how the EPLF seized both military and political opportunities and turned them to its advantage even in the direst of circumstances. To illustrate the rapidity with which the EPLF grew, we shall provide a portrait of the front prior to the Ethiopian revolution, a process which boosted the fortunes of the EPLF in both human and military terms. As we shall also show, from the late 1970s the EPLF became the sole representative of Eritrean nationalism as the ELF was marginalized. We shall begin with a portrait of the EPLF in the early 1970s.

The Military Position of the EPLF on the Eve of the Ethiopian Revolution

With the resolution of the *manqa* crisis the major constraint on the expansion of the EPLF was the conflict with the ELF. Most of the early battles between the fronts took place in Sahel and ranged from occasional skirmishes to several days of trench warfare fighting. An internal EPLF account of the early stages of the civil war is remarkable in that EPLF battle casualties were given. The EPLF's later practice was to give only enemy casualties. The detailed figures for the early fighting were produced as part of the leadership's internal response to *manqa* criticism of military mistakes, and can be considered accurate. Battles which occurred during 1972 lasted two or three days, and the better performance of the EPLF suggests the success of its tactics of beginning the shift from thinly spread to concentrated forces. Derivative of Maoist military strategy, it was to become a permanent feature of the EPLF's battle preparations, although in the 1980s a mix of fixed positional and mobile guerrilla warfare was adopted.

The *manqa* critics had attacked the leadership on the grounds of its lack of accountability but linked its criticism to failures in the military sphere. *The Destructive Movement* provides an analysis of the military position and relative strengths of the EPLF and ELF and the Ethiopian forces in the years just prior to the fall of the imperial order in 1974.[2] The fragile position of the EPLF in 1972–3 was an unlikely springboard for the heady victories of 1977 when the EPLF captured the towns of Keren, Decamhare and Segeneiti, laid siege to Massawa and encircled

---

[2] Although the dating of Issayas's report is October 1973, mention is made of a battle in January 1974.

Asmara. Together with the ELF, which liberated Tessenei, Agordat and Mendefera, the liberation fronts controlled most of Eritrea only four years after the *manqa* problem and the merger of the EPLF factions. The shift in the military balance between the fronts and the Ethiopian army was in part a consequence of the bloody power struggles of the Ethiopian revolution and the ensuing military conflict between Ethiopia and Somalia after the latter's invasion of the Ogaden area in southeast Ethiopia.

Dealing with the *manqa* and combining the administrations and military units of the EPLF and the Ala group, provided a solid basis for the resurgence of the EPLF and the confrontation with the ELF. The EPLF's portrayal of its position through 1972 was a bleak one. During the fighting with the ELF, EPLF forces frequently attacked each other. As well as being unfamiliar with the Sahel area they lacked the technical equipment to provide communications between units, particularly after dark, and generally suffered from a lack of military skills, a consequence of poor training.[3] The EPLF had not, at this period, a dress or weaponry distinct from the ELF.[4]

Problems of this kind produced setbacks for the new front at the battle of Ayett in May 1972. At the battle of Terekruk, the following month, a complete lack of radio communications hampered EPLF units. In February 1973, EPLF forces mistakenly attacked forces under the command of Abu Tayyara, a consequence of the separate commands. Throughout 1973 the EPLF also fought battles against the Ethiopian army until the front line units in the highlands were withdrawn to the Sahel base area to deal with the *manqa* threat. The ELF had about 300–500 fighters in northern Sahel with about 100 concentrated at Belikat, the ELF's main base area. South of the Asmara–Massawa road there were forces drawn from the Sahho people, as there were small pockets of forces in the northeastern part of the highlands stretching from She'b through the Mensa area. In Barka, the core area of the ELF, it was estimated that there were above 700. Supplies for ELF Sahel forces came from Sudan, through Qarora, with their main ammunition store around the Anseba outside Keren.

The report pointed out that the ELF forces were not as well equipped as the EPLF, a legacy of the importance of Osman Salih Sabbe, the *bête noire* of the EPLF radicals, in providing arms. With the EPLF's subsequent push southwards and its commitment to a strategy of

---

[3] *The DM.*

[4] Subsequently, EPLF fighters put on distinctive arm bands when going to the highlands where there were ELF units.

reestablishing its highland forces and linking them to the Sahel base, clashes between the two fronts shifted southward into the plateau. Several attempts to end the civil war had been made but had proved unsuccessful.

Both the ELF and the EPLF were concerned to maintain their positions. The EPLF had to make a mark in the highlands: a significant part of its leadership came from there and it was where there was a concentration of settled peasantry and big towns. The ELF wanted to retain its presence in most parts of Eritrea and insisted on the EPLF returning to the positions it held in Sahel when the civil war started. Ending the civil war entailed complex and divisive questions of cooperation and unity and, on the latter, the positions of the fronts were fixed. The EPLF's stance was based on the procedures followed by the early unification of the factions which came to constitute the PLF.

The intensity of the conflict between the two fronts decreased as a process of protests, rebellions and mutinies evolved into the Ethiopian revolution. The first civil war formally came to an end after the popular intervention of villagers to the north of Asmara and delegates from the capital brought a truce between the two fronts in November 1974, one month after the deposition of Emperor Haile Selassie. As to the balance of forces prior to the Ethiopian revolution of 1974, the report gives some figures for the Ethiopians but more comprehensive ones for the ELF. At the end of 1973, there were interlinked Ethiopian camps in Sahel, stretching from Afabat through Naqfa to Qarora on the Sudanese border, comprising about 1,000 ground forces. There were about 800 in the highland 'frontline' in places like She'b and Zagir north of the Asmara–Massawa road. There was a large garrison at Keren and others along the Asmara–Massawa road: at Nefasit, Embatkalla, Ginda, Dongolo and Dogali. In areas like Carneshim and Tsenedagle there were local people organized into militias by the Ethiopians. In the short term, military planning for the highlands was modest: the frontline would consist of 180 guerrillas, 60 of whom would be engineering units. A team of only 15 would monitor lines between Sahel and the frontline. Of concern were communications between the Sahel forces and the frontline: these again involved low-level courier links.

The emphasis was on keeping weapons in the Sahel area to a minimum and building up weapons in the highlands. Connecting the northern base areas to the plateau along the eastern escarpment was facilitated by the regional origins of the two major components of the EPLF and was the fulcrum of the 'eastern' military strategy. It linked

135

the Sahel base and training areas to the major urban centres and the core of the peasantry. The highland origin of the Ala group and the concentration of Ethiopian forces in Asmara, the limited involvement of the highland peasantry and townspeople with the liberation movements, and the importance of the Massawa–Asmara supply route were all factors in the strategy of rebuilding the highland forces after their withdrawal to defeat the *manqa*. Fully incorporating the highlands into the arena of liberation struggle joined together the Maoist strategy of confronting the enemy and gaining access to a peasantry which would provide the backbone and mass of a large liberation army. Developments in Ethiopia provided new opportunities for both fronts.

The Ethiopian Revolution[5]

The process of revolution initially involved the weakening of Ethiopian central administration and was followed by the consolidation and centralization of power under Major Mengistu Haile Mariam. Like other revolutions the consolidation of the new regime was facilitated by a nationalist appeal against an external threat. In the Ethiopian case the latter took the form of an insurgency in the Somali-speaking Ogaden province of Ethiopia supported by the Somali army. The new regime's nationalist appeal, under the slogan of *Etiopia tikdem* (Ethiopia first), took a narrower slant when it was directed at mobilizing against the insurgency in Eritrea. The loosening of central power and subsequent centralization boosted the activities and appeal of the liberation fronts. Taking advantage of the vacuum in Addis Ababa, a degree of cooperation emerged between them as the impact of the events there affected both the army and the administration in Eritrea, and in Asmara in particular where the Ethiopian army Second Division and the Eritrean police played an active role in protests against the centre. The increased presence of the fronts in the highlands and greater freedom of movement gave a further impetus to the recruitment of new members by both fronts, as did specific incidents and policies introduced by the Derg while consolidating its grip on the state.

Aman Andom, prime minister, minister of defence, chairman of the Derg and of Eritrean origin, though essentially a figurehead with

---

[5] A. Tiruneh, *The Ethiopian Revolution 1974–1987*, CUP, Cambridge, 1993 has a detailed account of the unfolding process, and C. Clapham, *Transformation and Continuity in Revolutionary Ethiopia*, CUP, Cambridge, 1988 presents a more analytic account. Neither foresaw the possibility of Eritrean independence.

limited authority over Derg members, resigned at the beginning of November 1974 and was killed at the end of the month. His death symbolized the end of any possibility of reconciliation with Eritrean nationalists. It was unlikely, in any case, that the weak and vague autonomy proposals he made would have been accepted by the liberation fronts, particularly as the power of the centre appeared to be crumbling.

Subsequently, the re-emergence of an autocratic central authority pursuing repressive policies based on a simple appeal to Ethiopian nationalism and unity further bolstered the fronts. As the Derg confronted civilian opposition political organizations in the bloody 'Red Terror' period in the urban centres, the latter turned to rural guerrilla strategies and sought alliances with the Eritrean liberation fronts.

Part of the new government's strategy of undermining the student base of the civilian opposition in the towns was the *zemacha*, a combined rural literacy and propaganda campaign, announced in the middle of 1974 and initiated at the end of that year. It conscripted students and dispatched them to the countryside. Many of the young Eritreans caught up in this campaign viewed it as a cynical political manoeuvre by the military government and joined the fronts directly or after a period as refugees in Sudan.

In the Eritrean context, this dual process of disintegration and consolidation of the imperial centre had a significant impact on the political and military fortunes of the front. Of particular significance was the Ethiopian response to the combined, but little coordinated, attack on Ethiopian military centres in Asmara, and the attack by the fronts on the prison to release political prisoners in late 1974 and early 1975. The attack was met with savage and indiscriminate reprisals on civilians in the Eritrean capital. Dawit Wolde Giorgis, an army officer, a high level official and administrator who served in Eritrea, described 1975 thus: 'it was indiscriminate death, it was either to stay and die or flee to fight'.[6] Giorgis also pointed out the permanancy of Ethiopian terror: 'I knew that between 1975 and 1978 terrible crimes had been committed by the security forces against civilians. Even junior army officers and security officials had licence to drag people out of their beds or offices ... and either execute them or put them in jail. There were no files, no records.'[7]

[6] Dawit Wolde Giorgis, *Red Tears: War, Famine and Revolution in Ethiopia* (Trenton, NJ: Red Sea Press, 1989), p. 90.

[7] *Ibid.*, p. 100. An interesting personal account of this period can be found in A. Tesfagiorgis, *A Painful Season and a Stubborn Hope*, Red Sea Press, Trenton, NJ, 1992.

As a consequence of the violence in the Eritrean cities as 1974 turned to 1975, thousands flocked to the fronts. Classically, repression played into the hands of the rebels. Subsequently, the emergence of a sinister unit from within Ethiopian military intelligence, called *afanyi guad*, struck fear into the heart of many clandestine supporters of the front. Its technique was to strangle with piano wire Eritreans suspected of nationalist sympathies. This unit was still operational as late as 1978 and many young Asmarans fled for the security of the liberated areas. In addition, university students from Addis Ababa and abroad joined the front, as the regime crumbled and bloody internal conflicts erupted between Derg factions and between the Derg and civilian political movements, at the forefront of which was the Ethiopian Peoples Revolutionary Party (EPRP).

1975 also brought with it increased military activities by the EPLF, involving both front fighters and its urban guerrilla forces, the *fidayin*. This increased activity in the urban areas and in the highlands raised the profile of the EPLF and, allied with increased Ethiopian repression, enhanced recruitment there. In 1975, when the EPLF had about 500 fighters in the highlands, it claimed responsibility for 110 operations in the principal cities. The focus was on Asmara with attacks on the airport, the post office, the trade bank, Asmara's electricity-generating station at Belaza and the Melotti beer factory, as well as against Kagnew station, the former American base and command centre of the Ethiopian army in Eritrea. The assassination of Derg supporters was also organized, the most spectacular taking place at the Ginda bar in the centre of Asmara.

Providing food and military equipment for the increased numbers of recruits flooding into the base areas, capturing food, weapons, ammunition and means of transport were also given priority. Although it is difficult to assess the scale of each of the different military operations, the detail of the quantities and types of weaponry and transport provided in EPLF internal communiqués is an indicator of its success in pursuing a strategy of supplying and training new recruits from Ethiopian army stocks. By the spring of 1975, the capture of military vehicles had begun to transform the logistics of the front. Motorized vehicles began to take over from long treks on foot and supplies transported by camel. Stores were constructed in the base areas for more permanent supply depots.

The success of the urban raids was largely based on detailed information from networks of secret cells about the location of Ethiopian goods and troops, about the drinking habits of Ethiopian officials and officers and the location of equipment required for stocking the infrastructure and myriad activities of the base areas. While urban raids had a certain utility they were nothing compared to the scale of the military successes of 1977.

Taking the Towns, 1977

The victories of 1977–8 were a reflection of the increased military capabilities of the EPLF and served to expand those capacities. They had an impact on the growth of the EPLF in three ways: the capture of large amounts of new military equipment; direct access to the urban population of Eritrea, particularly in the highlands; and increasing international publicity and prestige.

At the beginning of 1977, the EPLF took a string of Ethiopian garrisons and towns stretching southward from Qarora on the northern Sudan–Eritrea border through Naqfa and Afabat in Sahel province, to Keren in the semi-lowlands and Decamhare, Segeneiti and Digsa in Akalai Guzai province. Massawa and Asmara were effectively put under siege, with subsequent military successes following along the Asmara-Massawa road. The ELF had comparable success as it liberated Umm Hajar, Tessenei and Agordat in the west and Mendefera and Addi Quala in Serai province. The fronts shared certain areas. For example, the ELF controlled the western part of the agro-industrial complex of Elaborat and the EPLF the western part. Transiting around the rural areas to the west of Asmara, the author noted a greater degree of carefulness on the part of EPLF guides in the large village of Himbirte than at the frontline trenches facing the Ethiopian forces around Zolot village to the south of Asmara. There was an uneasy cooperation between the fronts in this period despite the announcement of a unity agreement between them in autumn 1977.

The military developments of 1977 were based largely on the EPLF's eastern strategy, which involved linking the Sahel base areas to the highlands along the eastern escarpment. The capture of Keren provided an important bridgehead from Naqfa and Afabat into the highlands, enabling them to control the gateway to the north and to the ELF's heartland in the west. Their control over the eastern escarpment down to the hills overlooking Massawa was a development of the track used originally by small guerrilla groups as their entry point into Hamasin from around She'b. From this area the EPLF was able to put Massawa under siege, closing the supply lines from Eritrea's main port.

139

The Ethiopian forces and the civilian population of Asmara could only be supplied by air. In January 1978, the EPLF liberated the string of small towns along the Asmara–Massawa road: Dongolo, the Ethiopian naval training centre, Ginda with its fruit plantations, Embatkalla and Nefasit. With the liberation of Mai Habar the EPLF encircled Asmara from the east to Decamhare to the south.

The eastern strategy, more successfully replicated between 1990 and 1991, provided considerable military and political benefits for the front. Large quantities of military material were captured from the defeated Ethiopian garrisons: Soviet and US tanks and heavy and light weapons, ammunition and various forms of transport including jeeps, trucks and oil tankers. Large amounts of cash were also taken. The extensive control over the rural highlands and the urban centres brought the EPLF considerable authority over a large number of people and placed it in a position to establish governmental and administrative structures. Connecting a large mass of Eritreans to the front was an important component in the provision of future human resources for the reproduction of man and woman power to sustain the armed struggle through the following decade and a half.

Eritrean Unity and Disunity

Between the disintegrative consequences of the Ethiopian revolution and the consolidation of the new regime, the ELF underwent a further internal crisis which turned to the benefit of the EPLF. The extent to which the EPLF security apparatus played a role in the crisis is unclear but the position the EPLF took on unity after the Ethiopian revolution was a factor in intra-Eritrean conflicts and increased the human resources of the EPLF.

To explain how this took place, it is necessary to return to the strange alliance between the fighters in the field and the external leadership. Between September and November 1975, a split occurred between the external foreign mission of Osman Salih Sabbe and fighters in the field over the question of unity with the ELF. Over and above the method of unification of the Eritrean fronts and ideology, the dispute was over representation. Osman Salih Sabbe viewed the FM as the political leadership and the unified administrative committee in the field as 'the temporary military leadership'.[8] The EPLF's need for external finance

---

[8] Sabbe, *Our Efforts for Unity* (Arabic) ,1978, p. 49. This short book reproduces letters from

and arms from the FM had been reduced as they captured Ethiopian arms and developed close relations with the Marxist government of South Yemen.

The precise details of the failure to unite have been obfuscated despite the publication of a series of letters by Sabbe implying an initial agreement on the part of the EPLF to attend unity meetings. In any case, Sabbe went ahead with unification discussions, meeting the ELF leadership in Sudan. The result was the dissolution of what had been an uneasy alliance and the formation of a third front, the Eritrean Liberation Front–Popular Liberation Forces (ELF–PLF) led by Sabbe. It would seem that the ELF calculated that the association with Sabbe would provide some advantages, not the least of which would derive from popularity within Eritrea deriving from its acceptance of unifying all nationalist forces. The coalitional nature of the ELF made it easier to enter discussions with Sabbe rather than refuse. It is probable that the agreement with Sabbe was conceived as a means of dividing the EPLF and as an opportunity to access Sabbe's connections with Arab states.

Whatever the calculations, the agreement between Sabbe and the ELF had deleterious consequences on the latter. The EPLF at a meeting in the field in March 1976 announced that after studying the Khartoum agreement it had concluded that the FM no longer represented it, and called on the ELF to cease dealing with Sabbe. It stressed the necessity of any unity dialogue being based on unity of thought through a unification of fighters in an internal process.[9] During 1976 and early 1977, the ELF provided areas for the ELF–PLF in western Eritrea in and around the Agordat area. The denationalization of houses in Agordat allowed the EPLF to more deeply etch the portrait of the ELF as reactionary and proclaim its own revolutionary credentials. Denationalization allowed the ELF to distance itself from the policies of the Ethiopian regime and to caricature the EPLF as similar in political character to the Derg. If the ELF's association with Sabbe was also a negotiating gambit in the later 1977 unity discussions with the EPLF, it went badly awry and was an index of the continuing turmoil resulting from the coalitional politics of the ELF.

There had been a large-scale influx of new fighters into the ELF in the 1974–5 period, similar to that of the EPLF. Many of these were highlanders and students. Despite the EPLF's claim to hold the mantle

---

[8] (cont.) the foreign mission to the field fighters.

[9] Al-Amin, *al-Thawra*, pp. 135–7. The EPLF did later participate in unity discussions outside Eritrea.

of revolution and radicalism, many of these recruits saw little difference between the two organizations.[10] While the EPLF had developed a highly organized process of incorporation based on its political education programme and an array of disciplinary controls, the ELF remained a far looser organization. Many of the recruits into the ELF of the post-1974 period identified themselves as the 'democratic movement' and the loose organization of the ELF permitted more open internal debate and criticism than occurred within the EPLF. The ELF leadership identified this new dissident movement as *fallul* (Tigrinya for anarchists), a term which the EPLF initially used for it. Armed conflict broke out between elements of the ELF leadership and the dissidents resulting in a breakaway group of about 2,000 joining the EPLF in the middle of 1977.[11] In interviews with a selection of these in autumn 1977, just after they had arrived in the EPLF base areas and were undergoing political education and constructing shelters, several attributed their dissent to the ELF unity agreement with Sabbe.

Self-Reliance After Sabbe

The EPLF victories of 1977 brought to the EPLF the then intangible factor of international recognition as a major player in Eritrean and Ethiopian politics by Western Europe and the US. Within EPLF leadership circles, there had been growing concern about the weakness of its external propaganda and, after the split from Sabbe, sources of finance. After the Sabbe split, fighters noted the deterioration of food as the EPLF bought the poorest quality of sorghum from Sudan.

Three significant moves were taken to rectify the former and compensate for the latter. Firstly, the Eritrean Relief Association (ERA) was established in 1975. It was to play a major role in the droughts and famines of the 1980s. Despite the neutral sounding name, it was a para-

---

[10] Over the years I have asked scores of Eritreans why they joined the ELF rather than the EPLF. The answers provide no evidence for the view that the ELF was Muslim lowland and the EPLF Christian highland. Some gave personal reasons: a friend had contacts with the ELF and they went along with them. Others stated that they saw no significant difference; others that the ELF was the founder liberation movement; others that they had been in ELF secret cells.

[11] Two members of the ELF revolutionary council, Abd al-Qadir Ramadan and Ali Muhammad Ibrahim, were killed in Dankalia. Markakis states that they were ambushed by a *fallul* group, *National and Class Conflict*, p. 142. ELF sources have suggested that it was an EPLF ambush aimed at increasing internal conflict within the ELF. Several thousand members of the 'democratic movement' fled to Sudan.

EPLF organization and functioned to assist the internal and external refugees and collect and distribute funds and assistance from outside.

Secondly, the EPLF began organizing communities abroad, particularly in Western Europe and the US. This was done in a fashion somewhat similar to that of the mass organizations of the EPLF inside Eritrea. Most of the leaders of Eritreans abroad were educated highlanders and Christians, facilitating their communication with both political and religious organizations in Western Europe, Scandinavia and the US, where charitable donations and public collections were more established than, say, the Middle East. EPLF organizers of the Eritrean associations abroad worked closely with ERA officials and in many cases were one and the same.

Thirdly, the EPLF began encouraging foreign journalists to visit the liberated areas. With the liberation of the towns in 1977, there was a lot more to show, and journalists from leading North American and European newspapers and radio and television stations were conducted around EPLF-controlled areas. Most were impressed and wrote favourable pieces about the activities of the front, all of which bolstered the international prestige of the organization. These visitors in the late 1970s provided a sympathetic coverage that was in marked contrast to the reports of the mass brutality of the Ethiopian regime, particularly during the period of the 'Red Terror' when opposition members were butchered on the streets of Addis Ababa.[12]

The combination of the external organization of Eritreans, ERA and foreign NGOs became the most important and critical source of finance for the EPLF. Most of it went for arms and food purchases. Additional sources of finance came from small but wealthy states like Kuwait and the United Arab Emirates, with the bulk of that assigned to medicine and humanitarian aid.

Resurgent Ethiopia and the Strategic Retreat

The culmination of the revolutionary process in Ethiopia was the victory of the Derg over its civilian opponents, the concentration of power in the hands of Mengistu Haile Mariam, the adoption of socialism and centralism and an alliance with the Soviet Union. With considerable human cost and the loss of many fighters, the resurgence

---

[12] The author witnessed two murders in a two-week visit to Addis Ababa in autumn 1976. Of the group of Eritreans I met in that period all except one were killed by the Ethiopian authorities.

of Ethiopian central power, the recapture of the towns and large parts of the countryside undermined the power of the EPLF. Direct Soviet and Eastern Bloc support for Ethiopia, including that of the EPLF's former Cuban and South Yemen sympathizers, together with the defeat of the Somali insurgency in the Ogaden war in southern Ethiopia, resulted in the EPLF decision to organize what was called the 'strategic retreat'. Like other EPLF analyses, the conception came from Mao:

> A strategic retreat is a planned strategic step taken by an inferior force for the purpose of conserving its strength and biding its time to defeat the enemy.[13]

In the face of a reorganized Ethiopian army, Soviet advisers, Yemeni pilots and greater Ethiopian force levels, the EPLF retreated from the cities and their rural environs.[14] In so doing, the EPLF took considerable amounts of materials to the base areas. More importantly, it took with it large numbers of civilians and mass organization members. The period of 1977–8 saw as great an influx into the front as the 1974–5 period. By 1978, however, the EPLF had established an extensive infrastructure in the base areas to absorb the refugees and new fighter recruits. Many of the youth of Keren and Decamhare left with the front, as did considerable numbers of peasant youth. One of the elders of Addi Hawasha, a village between Asmara and Decamhare, informed me after liberation that most of the young left the village when the EPLF withdrew and very few returned after liberation.

The scale of recruitment in these years provided the EPLF with a critical mass of young highlanders of peasant origin, in addition to skilled workers and students from the towns and considerable numbers of women. Many from the ELF-controlled highland towns and surrounding areas also went through EPLF transport networks to the base areas. Many families left for the base areas and established a further source of recruitment over the following decade as their younger members passed through the EPLF educational system and trained as fighters.

After the retreat, the strategy of the EPLF closely followed Mao's rubric:[15]

[13] 'Problems of Strategy in China's Revolutionary War', in *Selected Works of Mao Tse-Tung*, Vol. I, p. 211.
[14] See Connell's description, *Against All Odds*, Chapter 10.
[15] According to one interviewer, Issayas Afeworki's preferred reading was the classics of guerrilla warfare. We have already mentioned his training in China. *Eritrea Now*, January 1980.

During the stage of retreat we should in general secure at least two of the following conditions before we can consider the situation as being favourable to us and before we can go over to the counter-offensive...

1) the population actively supports the Red Army
2) the terrain is favourable for operations
3) all the main forces of the Red army are concentrated
4) the enemy's weak spots have been discovered
5) the enemy has been ... demoralized
6) the enemy has [made] mistakes[16]

For the EPLF, all rather than two of these conditions for a counter-offensive were required. Between 1975 and 1978, the EPLF had pursued policies to ensure the active support of core elements of the the population.[17] The retreat to Sahel, with Naqfa as the pivot of defence and symbol of survival and resistance, provided the favourable terrain and, with the reduction of the previous base area by one third, a capacity to concentrate forces and defend the bases. After the re-equipping of the Ethiopian army and airforce by the Soviet Union and the movement of the Ethiopian army northwards, Soviet officers were placed in field advisory positions. By utilizing heavy artillery, air attacks and naval landings on the Sahel Red Sea coast, the Ethiopian army pinned down the EPLF. The EPLF response, however, was to engage the follow-up advances of mechanized units and infantry in close combat and thereby undermine the advantage of air and artillery superiority.[18] In addition, the EPLF returned to guerrilla warfare in areas reoccupied by the Ethiopian army.[19]

In 1978–9, five Ethiopian offensives followed the strategic retreat and, although there were heavy Eritrean casualties,[20] the inability to defeat the EPLF began the process of military demoralization of the enemy.[21] According to EPLF political bureau member Sebhat Ephraim, the failure of the fourth offensive began the decline. In his account, the original plan was to use a mix of regular army and conscripted militia forces. The defeat of this mix in the fourth offensive brought a change of plan, and Task Force 503, specially trained for counter-guerrilla

---

[16] Connell, *op. cit.,* p. 217.

[17] See Chapter 4 above.

[18] See interview with Christian Sabatier in *Eritrea Now*, Vol. 1, No. 4, March 1979. Sabatier had spent many years with the EPLF and is particularly reliable.

[19] See Connell, *Against All Odds*, Chapter 11.

[20] Connell's estimate is around 3,000, a considerable number in one year for a guerrilla army of around 20,000 at that period.

[21] For a lengthier account of military development see Pateman, *Even the Stones*, Chapter 7.

warfare for use after the smashing of EPLA regular forces, was brought in to spearhead the final offensive.[22] The EPLF view is that the mix of regular forces and militias resulted in problems of coordination, a pattern already evident in 1977 as detailed in interviews with Ethiopian officer prisoners of war, and was the beginning of serious military mistakes.[23] It has been estimated that in all five offensives the Ethiopians incurred between 50,000 and 60,000 dead and wounded, although there has been no independent verification of these figures. It was to be another three years before the Ethiopian government was able to undertake further serious offensives against Eritrean positions.

One final advantage for the EPLF arising from Ethiopian resurgence and deriving from a combination of its eastern strategy and the character of the Ethiopian offensive was the negative impact of the latter on the ELF. The ELF strongholds were southwestern Eritrea and a zone stretching eastwards into southern Serai province and the western parts of Hamasin. The initial thrusts of the 1978 Ethiopian offensive hit the ELF first, retaking Umm Hajar, Tessenei in the west and Addi Quala and Mendefera in the highlands, and badly damaging the ELF's military capabilities. Despite the unity agreement between the ELF and the EPLF of 1977, there were constant reports of armed clashes between units of the two fronts.[24] Even though the ELF had units with EPLF ones at the Sahel front after the strategic retreat, there were recriminations from both about the character of their military cooperation. The EPLF, which had conserved its forces better than the ELF during the offensive, was the dominant front, and insisted that there could not be separate military structures. The ELF leadership was equally insistent on maintaining an independent military command structure.

Whatever the causes, in August 1980 the EPLF attacked the ELF forces and drove them to the Sudan border in western Eritrea. By mid-1981 the ELF was a spent force, although it still had about 10,000 fighters. Although the outcome of the second civil war should not be

[22] *Eritrea Now,* Vol. 1, No. 7, September 1979.

[23] Pay differentials were also a problem. Regular soldiers received $E100 and militia members $E20. Many of the militia prisoners interviewed in the base areas and in Keren in 1977 were less than enthusiastic for the war. Most were illiterate, spoke minority languages different from those of their officers and were only fighting because they had been rounded up to fill the village quota.

[24] It is very difficult to establish the accuracy of the different accounts of the origins of these clashes. Each front place responsibility for their occurrence on the other. ELF members assert that the EPLF was hell-bent on destroying the ELF, while the EPLF blames ELF military leaders, particularly Abdallah Idris, head of the ELF military department.

confused with the causes, the EPLF benefited in two ways from the defeat of the ELF. Firstly, western Eritrea was finally opened to the EPLF. It provided the front with a freedom to operate guerrilla units against Ethiopian forces and greater access to the Sudan border. For periods of time, the EPLF was able to operate the large plantations there, providing some food supplies for fighters and the displaced population of the base areas.

The impact of the 1980 military defeat of the ELF brought to an end a long process of political disintegration, the final result of which was a significant number of ELF fighters joining the EPLF. The ELF split into several factions when no Christians were elected to the new executive committee and after the holding of an acrimonious seminar in March 1982 to examine the causes of ELF's problems. The executive committee of the ELF was divided, and Abdallah Idris, in what was described as a coup, subsequently imprisoned other members of the leadership, including Ahmad Nasir and Ibrahim Totil. Abdallah Idris subsequently formed his own group and the ELF further divided into the ELF–RC, headed by Ahmad Nasir, and a group called Sagem.[25] The latter campaigned for a return to Eritrea and then split, with one faction eventually uniting with the EPLF at its second congress in 1987. Almost all of this group were highlanders. With them went Ibrahim Totil, a longstanding ELF leader from the Nara, taking many of the latter community with him.[26]

The disintegration of the ELF placed the EPLF as the dominant military and political force within Eritrea and afforded it an opportrnity to represent Eritrean nationalism. It was able to skilfully use this position until independence to enhance its international prestige in diplomatic circles and through its sole management of famine relief through ERA in the mid-1980s.

Alliance-building

The defeat of the ELF in the 1981–2 civil war was also a product of military cooperation between the EPLF and the Tigray People's

---

[25] Deriving from the Tigrinya '*Sibakh Sagem*', referring to the movement from cultivating fields to the village, and meaning 'return home'.

[26] Pieced together from interviews with Zemheret Yohannes, then of Sagem (Asmara 1993) and Drs Habte and Beyene of the ELF–RC (Bonn, 1995). According to the latter, the departure of the Sagem group was a final military blow, as until then the ELF, though considerably weakened, still had a viable military force.

Liberation Front (TPLF), an important component of the EPLF's strategy of seeking allies among political groups opposed to the Derg. Such alliance-building was made difficult by the Eritrean demand for the recognition of self-determination and independence. Of the myriad opposition groups which emerged to oppose the Derg only the TPLF completely and consistently accepted the Eritrean nationalist position, although the political implications of its conceptions of nationalities raised critical questions about the relationship between self-determination for nationalities and self-determination in multi-national states.[27]

The EPRP, whose first batch of fighters were trained by the EPLF and in 1974 operated inside Eritrea alongside EPLF fighters, subsequently shifted away from supporting Eritrean independence, resulting in a break between the two. The EPLF's relationship with both the TPLF and the EPRP was a development of the links between student activists in the period leading to the Ethiopian revolution. There was a more natural affinity between the TPLF and the EPLF in that Tigrinya was the language of the TPLF and EPLF and of most of the people of the Eritrean highlands and Tigray province. Initially, the TPLF had a closer relationship with the ELF, a result, in part, of the links between the EPLF and the EPRP and, in part, because the ELF operated more widely in Tigray province. The alliance disintegrated as the TPLF came to resent ELF operations in its territory.[28] As the TPLF and EPRP drifted into armed conflict, the EPLF and TPLF moved into a close alliance.

The EPLF's association with anti-Derg Ethiopian political forces initially had had a negative impact on the expansion of the EPLF. In the short term, the recruitment and training of non-Eritreans and their participation alongside EPLF fighters tarnished the nationalist reputation of the EPLF. The highland peasantry, in particular, was confused

[27] There was considerable debate among Ethiopian Marxist groups on this issue during the 1970s, centring on whether Eritrea was a colonial question. See John Young, *Peasant Revolution in Ethiopia: The Tigray People's Liberation Front 1975–1991*, CUP, Cambridge, 1997, pp. 96–105. Young analyses the polemic between the EPLF and the TPLF in the mid-1980s. Of greatest significance were the practical political implications of an ideology of nationalities and their right to secession. For the EPLF, the Eritrean question was a colonial one and Eritrean nationalities had cultural rather than political rights. A right to secession raised considerable problems of Eritrean statehood given the overlapping of Eritrean and Ethiopian nationalities, particularly the Afar, but also the Sahho and Kunama.

[28] One area of disagreement between the two was the precise location of the Tigray–Eritrean border. In May 1998 the dispute over this same area erupted into armed clashes between Eritrea and Ethiopia. Until its military demise ELF cadres taxed in the disputed area.

by the presence of Ethiopians in EPLF detachments and unconvinced by sophisticated ideological justifications about the solidarity of revolutionary forces. The ELF used this cooperation in the highlands as part of its anti-EPLF propaganda. Eventually, the EPLF gave these fighters a choice of joining the TPLF or the EPRP or leaving for abroad. A number of those who were separated from the EPLF were Tigrayans or of Tigrayan origin and joined the TPLF. The paring off of the Tigrinya-speaking Tigrayans made a politically symbolic distinction between them and Eritrean Tigrinyans. In the longer term, the beginning of a cooperative relationship with the TPLF, which became the dominant insurgent organization fighting the Ethiopian central government and a formidable liberation movement in its own right, proved of critical importance.

Despite a break in relations between them in the mid-1980s, the strength of the TPLF in Tigray, a major staging post for Ethiopian offensives against Eritrea, and military cooperation between it and the EPLF in the late 1980s and in the final onslaught against the Mengistu regime the alliance was of the utmost strategic importance. The EPLF's broad strategy of training and supporting the armed Ethiopian opposition, thus, brought considerable military benefits. The decision to remove the EPRP and the smaller group of fighters who joined the TPLF was partly a consequence of Eritrean peasant complaints about the presence of Ethiopians in EPLF units[29] and partly a response to ELF propaganda to the same effect, rather than a purely military calculation that might later bear fruit.

Whatever the causes, having military allies operating within Ethiopia proper and particularly in Tigray province facilitated EPLF operations deep into Ethiopia. The EPLF supported the TPLF's attacks on Ethiopian supply and communication lines through the provision of technical aid and military transfers.[30] It has been estimated that some 3,000 TPLF fighters fought with the EPLF in Sahel during the Red Star campaign.[31] It was to pay great political dividends in 1991 when the Ethiopian People's Revolutionary Democratic Movement, with the TPLF at its core, came to power in Ethiopia. The TPLF had made clear early its programme for a future Eritrea. In one of its 1978 pamphlets, *Tigrai and its National Democratic Struggles*,[32] it sought a solution to the national question through 'referendums under the control of the

---

[29] Interview with EPLF mass administration official in Addi Hawasha village, November 1977.
[30] Young, *Peasant Revolution in Ethiopia*, p. 123.
[31] *Ibid.*, p. 125.
[32] Foreign Relations Bureau, Tigray Peoples Liberation Front, January 1978.

people's government and the vanguard role of legitimate and demo-cratic national organizations'. It was, however, to be another 15 years before the Eritrean independence referendum took place, but it did so with the blessing of the TPLF-controlled Ethiopian government.

The Eritrean People's Liberation Army[33]

After political and military education, EPLF members would be assigned to departments or to military units. To separate the EPLF and EPLA, however, would be to make an artificial distinction between the military and the political, for there was a constant movement of individuals between the two functions. In the EPLF everything served the military function. All were 'fighters', and there was no sense of a separate administrative or military occupation. Members of the mass organizations and the zonal armies were EPLF and members of the EPLF, who had undergone military and political education, regardless of where they were assigned, were EPLA. In general the movement was more one from administrative functions to fighting units in response to periods of intensification of war with the Ethiopian army or civil war with the ELF. Between 1980 and 1981 the EPLF had to confront both simultaneously, and many in EPLF departments were mobilized into dual roles. For those behind enemy lines or in 'contested zones', daily activities fused the political, administrative and military. For the sake of simplicity we shall make reference to the EPLA, as some EPLF literature does, but reiterate that the distinction is only of some analytic use in that increasing military specialization began to emerge and those who possessed it tended to remain in frontline units.

The portrait of the EPLF presented in previous chapters is one of a highly centralized and disciplined military and political organization with spheres for initiative left to cadres. Similarly, battalion, brigade and divisional commanders had significant scope for local initiatives. The EPLF's capacity to withstand Ethiopian offensives and greater power was facilitated by the combination of a highly centralized com-mand structure and scope for individual initiative. Both were reinforced by a learning process of military affairs garnered through practice rather than from a military academy. Other than those with some training in Syria, Iraq, Cuba and China, and soldiers and officers

---

[33] The rewriting of this section has benefited from the critical comments of an anonymous reader, but has resulted in my emphasizing the integrated character of the EPLF.

deserting from the Ethiopian army, most key commanders learned their skills in the field.

Until 1987, the military committee of the political bureau, chaired by Ibrahim Afa, was at the apex of military decision-making and the coordination of the various fronts. Following the 1987 congress, the EPLF established a military staff and a military academy, named after Ibrahim Afa, who was killed in 1985.[34] The military staff had a smaller group of PB members under the chairmanship of Issayas, and included Sebhat Ephraim, Ali Sayyid, Petros Solomon and Mesfin Hagos. Central control and coordination along the Sahel–Keren front during the 1978–84 period was facilitated by the close physical proximity of those responsible for military affairs in one Sahel valley. As the Ethiopian army became increasingly pinned down general staff members were increasingly mobile and coordinated strategy at the frontline and through telecommunications from the Sahel and shifting command points. The centralized command structure left considerable scope for individual initiative at all levels of the structure of the EPLA.[35]

The organization of the EPLA was based on squad units, which formed a *fasila* (platoon), three of which formed a *haile* (force) while three of the latter formed a battalion consisting of around 400 fighters. After the 1977 influx, the EPLA expanded: brigades were formed consisting three battalions, and in the 1980s divisions were formed of three brigades. As greater quantities of more sophisticated weapons were captured from the Ethiopians in addition to infantry brigades, there were tank battalions and heavy artillery units. The pattern of smaller military units within larger military forces permitted flexible shifts between a concentration of large-scale forces for offence and defence and the peeling off of smaller units for guerrilla warfare.

Brigades of a particular division were frequently linked to other divisions. On two occasions in 1977 and 1987, there was a *takhlit*, deriving from the Arabic for 'mixing' but also having a sense of 'confusion', when fighters from the different larger units were reallocated. In part, this was

[34] The prospective abolition of the military committee has been given by ELF sources as a factor in the power struggle between Issayas and Ibrahim Afa and the latter's death. Fighters who observed them together noted no sign of tension or hostility.

[35] The author has no pretence to an expertise in military strategy, and presents this interpretation as an amateur. It is based on accounts of fighters. *Eritrea Profile* has had a long series of personal accounts of battles, and although these are not by high-level commanders they do illuminate the scope of individual military initiative. For a more detailed account of the military ebb and flow and Ethiopian offensives from an EPLF perspective, see Pateman, *Even the Stones*. In his account, however, there is more flow than ebb, and the perilous positions of the EPLF's frontline at various times are not mentioned.

necessitated by the reorganization into the larger units of brigades and divisions. It was also a function of some brigades, such as 51, gaining a considerable military reputation with the consequence that Ethiopian attacks would target less reputed brigades in their offensives.

We have mentioned how in the base area there was skill training within different departments and movement of personnel between them. This was also the case for the frontline units. Individuals and platoons were shifted between infantry, tank and artillery units to expand skills. Both of the latter had specialist training units. In addition, a commando unit was created for special warfare. It received separate military training and political education. Within each ascending level of the EPLA, there was a military commander and a deputy commander, with the latter theoretically responsible for political education. In practice, differences in literacy levels determined who would conduct political education and the criticism and self-criticism sessions. As in the rear base area, political education and discussion groups were continuous. Unlike in the Ethiopian army there was no clear distinction between political commissars and commanders. Although notionally there were functional responsibilities, these were fused in the same individual. If the military commander died, the deputy would take over his command. Not a single fighter I have spoken to had even heard gossip of tensions between those responsible for the political and military spheres. Where it did take place it was a function of personality differences rather than of ascribed roles for the military and political.

Reinforcing the regular units of the EPLA were zonal armies. Their major function was to defend the zone and back up the EPLA. Recruits had only a few months' training. They were usually part-time fighters but on occasions when military activities were heightened and their reinforcements were needed they would operate on a full-time basis.

The EPLF was essentially a voluntary organization, but two caveats must be attached to this statement. Firstly, after joining EPLF fighters could not voluntarily leave: members were in for the duration. Secondly, forms of what can only be described as conscription were introduced. It was partly a response to Ethiopian conscription of young Eritrean men and, in part, a consequence of EPLF losses after 1979 and during the 1982 'sixth Ethiopian offensive' when 90,000 Ethiopian troops were amassed in Eritrea. Indicative of the demand for frontline fighters in this period, in one area of Eritrea three quarters of the EPLF departmental cadres were transferred to the frontline for purely military duties. Most of those conscripted were placed in the zonal armies and for some the zonal army became a conduit into the EPLA.

In areas which had been historically linked to the ELF and where the ELF had had a prolonged presence, as in Barka or Dankalia, conscription was more into the zonal army than the EPLA.[36] Conscription into the zonal armies of these western and eastern zones also had the intent of expanding the representation of Bani Amir and Afar in the EPLF.

Internal Displacement and Refugee Flight

The famines of the 1970s and 1980s reinforced the impact of war and increased refugee flight. While the scale of the refugee problem was a dreadful human tragedy, the nature of it provided a degree of political benefit for the EPLF through a combination of its infrastructure of absorption, its expanding social base in the highland peasantry and the latter's marked preference to stay close to their villages or at least within Eritrea.

The refugee problem began in the 1960s with Ethiopian reprisals against the peoples inhabiting the core areas of ELF military activities.[37] We have already indicated that there were considerable religious, cultural and economic links between the Sudan and Muslim Eritrea, in general, and western Eritrea, in particular. Reprisals against villagers in the Tokombia area brought the first group of 25,000 to Kassala, the majority of whom were local Bani Amir and Marya pastoralists and agro-pastoralists, together with Sahho pastoralists who had earlier moved with their animals from eastern to western Eritrea. In the late 1960s a further group of Sahho from the eastern escarpment of Akalai Guzai came to Sudan. Although there were attacks on villages in the Keren area and north of Asmara in the early and mid-1970s, the settled peasantry generally did not seek refuge in the Sudan on anything like the scale of the Muslim pastoralists and agro-pastoralists.

There was a replication of this pattern of flight in 1978 when the people of villages and small towns in western Eritrea fled to the Sudan and those of the highlands remained in Eritrea. Although multiple factors produced the refugees in Sudan, rarely did the highland peasants flee and, according to the leading authority on Eritrean refugees, nor did those from northern Muslim Eritrea whose mode of life was similar to those of western Eritrea. Among the multiple factors, the

---

[36] The author has no figures for the numbers forcibly recruited.

[37] Much of the following is based on Chapter 2 of G. Kibreab, *Refugees and Development in Africa: The Case of Eritrea*, Red Sea Press, Trenton, NJ, 1987, and personal observations in Sudan betwen 1974 and 1977.

establishment of the EPLF base areas in the north provided sanctuary, sustenance and a degree of safety for internal refugees. In addition, the base areas supplied educational and health facilities. The EPLF, in general, had an express preference for Eritreans to stay put or, in the extreme, come to the base areas. The internally displaced in the base areas were a source of recruitment and a civilian population to defend. One overall consequence of patterns of flight was the increasingly disproportionate numbers of highland Tigrinyans in the EPLF.

Drought and Famine

Along with the constant assaults of the Ethiopian army and combating the ELF, the 1980s brought a different challenge to the EPLF in the form of famine. Yet again, however, the EPLF succeeded in turning this challenge into opportunities for its development, particularly in the arena of international legitimation. Although direct aid to Eritrea and the EPLF was blocked by Ethiopia's assertion that such aid was an assault on Ethiopia's sovereignty, the 1980s saw a rapid development in EPLF's statist role through the expanded capacity of ERA. It was helped in this by the way in which the Ethiopian government managed the famine of the mid-1980s. As Alex de Waal noted:

> control of relief was a major component of the military strategy of both the government and the rebel front[s]. The systematic use and denial of food relief for military ends was the most notable aspect of governmental strategy that also included extraordinarily sustained and widespread brutality against civilians.[38]

Although De Waal attributes an equality of responsibility, the capacity of the Ethiopian government for brutality was far more entrenched.

At the same time that the vivid television pictures of massive starvation were broadcast from Korem in October 1984, the Ethiopian army began organizing a new offensive in Eritrea on a scale akin to the Red Star campaign of 1982. One component of the new military campaign was an offensive in western Eritrea, the aim of which was to cut relief supply lines from Sudan. Barentu, after seven weeks of EPLF occupation, was recaptured in August 1985, then Tessenei, then the Ali Gidir plantation. The EPLF was once again hemmed in to its Sahel base area, and in the Ethiopian advance in the west the EPLF lost one of its grain stores. Since ERA and EPLF were not recognized by foreign

[38] A. de Waal, *Evil Days: 30 Years of War and Famine in Ethiopia*, Africa Watch, 1991, p. 177.

154

governments US relief aid was channelled through NGOs under the auspices of the Ethiopian government.[39] The latter, however, linked the provision of aid to politico-military strategies which included a programme of establishing protected villages and mixing relief and military convoys. In response, the EPLF attacked a relief convoy, claiming that it was military in nature. As a result, relief organizations like BandAid and the Emergency Relief Desk in Sudan were forced to consult with the EPLF and grant it the kind of recognition which the Ethiopian government had been determined to deny.

What is important for our analysis, however, is the growth of ERA's capacity to deal with the famine despite the Ethiopian government's attempts to marginalize it. ERA had an excellent research team that provided credible and, if not verifiably accurate, statistical information sufficient to convince independent observers. For example, ERA claimed that it could deliver food to 85 per cent of the population in October 1984. Even though this figure was difficult to confirm, it reflected the broad control of the EPLF in many parts of Eritrea. As a result, external assistance to ERA, indistinguishable from the EPLF, enhanced the claim of the EPLF to be able to solve the problem of hunger in Eritrea. From 10 trucks in 1984, a year later ERA had more than 250, most of which came from Scandinavian NGOs. It became a major distributor of seeds and tools to the hundreds of thousands of Eritreans in EPLF-organized camps.[40]

In real terms, providing for those Eritreans who were suffering and who could not or did not want to leave placed EPLF/ERA in a legitimate position to claim international recognition of quasi-state control over the relief apparatus and in a position to garner the loyalty of those in EPLF camps.

Ethiopian Disintegration and Military Victory

The Ethiopian government's use of relief did not, however, significantly benefit its war effort. In March 1988, the EPLF won a great victory over the Ethiopian forces at the Afabat front, defeating a force of about 150,000 soldiers and killing about 10,000. With hindsight, this breakthrough in the north was a watershed in the long war. After Afabat,

---

[39] Much of the following is based on De Waal, *Evil Days*.

[40] See J. Sorenson, 'Refugees, Relief and Rehabilitation in the Horn of Africa: The Eritrean Relief Association' in H. Adelman and J. Sorenson (eds), *African Refugees*, Westview Press, Boulder, 1994.

the Ethiopian army gave up western Eritrea, withdrawing forces from Tessenei, Ali Gidir, Agordat and Barentu to concentrate them at Keren. Ethiopian loss of equipment was enormous, particularly heavy artillery and ammunition, the use of which by the EPLF was significant in the fighting in the three years to independence.[41]

With the resumption of EPLF–TPLF coordination and Ethiopian failures, the TPLF further undermined the central government's position by taking Adigrat and the Tigray capital of Mekelle in February 1988. With the EPLF able to seize the initiative in conventional war, the defeat at Afabat and the loss of Tigray province were further devastating blows to Ethiopian army and government morale after a decade of losses and failed offensives. The EPLF had secured the final components of Mao's prerequisites for a successful seizing of the military initiative. Indeed, the failures in the north had already begun undermining the Ethiopian officer corps as Mengistu purged the army in the months prior to the victory at Afabat.[42] For many years, military setbacks had resulted in executions of military commanders, of multiple command transfers and of forced conscription.

Compounding military failure was the evident bankruptcy of economic and finance policies and increasing divisions within the government. Symbolic of these were the dramatic policy reversals signalled by the dissolution of the Workers Party of Ethiopia formed by the Derg in 1984 and the announcement of economic liberalization measures.[43] Both the party and the command economy were closely identified with Mengistu and the group surrounding him. Political problems were replicated within the army, with an attempted coup led by senior officers in May 1989.[44] One of the demands of the conspirators was the opening of a peace dialogue with 'the rebels'.

These policy shifts were a belated and desperate attempt to realign Ethiopia with the decline of the Soviet Union and the shifting balance of international forces. In contrast, the EPLF had earlier moved in this direction at its second congress in 1987, when a new programme replete with the language of the international liberalism of the 1980s was adopted: political pluralism, multi-partyism and the opening to the private sector. It was another example of the EPLF seizing the political initiative. As the disintegration of Ethiopia seemed possible in the late 1980s and international mediation grew, this early EPLF policy shift

[41] Interview with EPLF commander.
[42] See *Africa Confidential*, Vol. 29, No. 9, 29 April 1988.
[43] See Tiruneh, *The Ethiopian Revolution*, p. 356
[44] *Africa Confidential*, Vol. 30, No. 11, 26 May 1989.

paved the way for more comfortable relations with the US. The latter, long committed to the unity of Ethiopia, made pronouncements favouring a return to a federal solution. The military and political tide within Eritrea, Tigray province and Ethiopia forestalled such a solution. Following the Afabat breakthrough, the EPLF captured Massawa and surrounded the Ethiopian forces on all sides. From 1989, the Ethiopian army evacuated Tigray province and the TPLF advanced southwards into the provinces of Wollo, Gondar and Shoa. In 1991, the EPLF launched an offensive from the Decamhare front, taking very heavy losses, advanced through Asmara and pursued the retreating Ethiopian forces to the Sudan border in the west. EPRDF forces entered Addis Ababa, defeating the last stand of the Derg forces with the assistance of EPLF heavy artillery and commando units that for some years had ranged deep into Ethiopia.

After 30 years of armed struggle and 20 years of intense military conflict, Eritrea had attained *de facto* independence and had facilitated the establishment of a government in Addis Ababa that was not opposed to an independent state. Independence had great costs: around 65,000 fighters had died, 10,000 were disabled, an estimated 40,000 civilian deaths were directly associated with the fighting and around 90,000 children were left without parents.

Over the years the EPLF had shaped itself into a state-like organization with a governmental, administrative and military apparatus, and commanded the support of the mass of the population. The EPLF was not, however, a microcosm of the Eritrean population. The bulk of the fighters were highlanders, as reflected in the official statistics: 64 per cent Tigrinya, 24 per cent Tigre, 12 per cent minorities; 63 per cent Christian and 36 per cent Muslim.[45] These figures reflect a contingent set of factors analysed in these last three chapters – including the social origins of the early leadership, the incorporation of the concentrated peasantry through land reform, the EPLF's military strategy and the tendency for the highland peasantry to stay in Eritrea – rather than any drive for Tigrinyan domination of nationalism. In victory, the EPLF secured a territorial base for statehood. It was an immense achievement, but immense tasks lay ahead in the transition from liberation front to legitimate national government.

---

[45] Stefanie Christmann, *Die Freiheit Haben Wir Nicht Von Den Mannern: Frauen in Eritrea*, Horle-mann, 1996, p. 20. Not all of those who survived had fought for a long period: 26,000 of the 95,000 survivors had joined during the last year of the war.

III

Independence

The transition to independence in Eritrea involved the EPLF in a new domestic context that posed challenges to both the will and the capacity of the movement to retain the autonomy developed during the liberation struggle.[1] As it made the transition to government it was absorbed into a politics which embraced all of Eritrea and its communities. Managing a state involved a set of imperatives deriving from membership in the international state system and economy. The broad membership of the front was confronted with a move from a non-monetized economy into direct involvement in a monetized one and into a social context where values and traditions were relatively uninformed by the EPLF. For women fighters, the change was dramatic.

Although less than a decade had passed since statehood at the time of writing, it would seem that the broad framework of politics and policies promoted by the new government had been shaped more by conceptions of authority and power formed during the liberation struggle, with a stress on centralization and control, and that the new domestic and international context had produced only limited accommodations and adaptations. There was, however, a new formality of politics as a constitution and state laws had been promulgated. Instead of Eritrea remaking the EPLF, the EPLF had been vigorous in remaking Eritrea in its image. State-building continued in the trajectory of the front-building we have analysed.

A major challenge facing the government was the need to generate resources for reconstruction and development from a society devastated by war and from a country with a relatively poorly endowed natural environment. Gross Domestic Product per capita is half of the average

---

[1] Much of the following chapter is based on interviews, discussions and observations during visits to Eritrea in 1992, 1993 and 1996.

for Africa, life expectancy is 46 years and infant mortality is 135 per 1,000 births. The political and economic programme had been partly set at the 1987 congress. In political terms, the future had been declared one of pluralism, participation and a multi-party system, with the reservation that parties could not be based on religion, region or ethnicity. The economic future was patterned on a modified neo-liberalism, with the state's role reserved to providing a framework for an economy based on the private sector. The links between party and state and the party's control of considerable economic assets provided a further modification of neo-liberalism. For the new government the opportunity was there to avoid the problems and mistakes made by many African states that reached independence earlier and had, by the time of Eritrean independence, spiralled into unaccountable authoritarianism bedevilled by dependency, debt and corruption. At the same time, statehood provided opportunities to seek external sources of funding to overcome the severe consequences of the destructive war and the devastation of famine and drought. The dual pressures arising from accommodating to broader social forces and the process of absorption into the international economy would severely test the principles of autonomy and self-reliance. The gathering of attributes of stateness by the EPLF during the liberation struggle provided some preparation for independence.

The government had to reconstruct the economy and construct a political system; demobilize fighters without losing their loyalty; and reintegrate refugees, a community which had become geographically and socially differentiated during the years of liberation: highly educated in the market economies of the US and Europe, enjoying commercial success in the Gulf and experiencing marginality but partial economic and cultural integration in Sudan. Diaspora lives have had an unpredictable impact on Eritreans.

The concluding section of this book, then, examines in a tentative way the politics of the conjuncture of the EPLF and broader Eritrean society and the process of state- and nation-building. We shall examine state structures and policy, as well as key issues of language, land and gender. The emphasis will be on the travails of the process of front autonomy transposed to a state and the problems of the transition.

Six

Organizing Eritrea

In 1991, the EPLF entered Asmara and formed a provisional government. After the referendum in 1993 Eritrea joined the United Nations
as a sovereign independent state. The programme decided at the 1987
second congress became the basis of policy until it was superceded by
the national charter formulated at the third congress of 1994, when the
EPLF was renamed the People's Front for Democracy and Justice.

The tasks confronting the new government were myriad. For the
first two years, between *de facto* independence and the conclusion of the
referendum process, Eritrea functioned as a state without many of the
formal attributes of statehood, symbolic of which was the continued use
of the birr, the Ethiopian currency. The economy had been devastated
by the prolonged war, there were hundreds of thousands of refugees
and displaced persons, tens of thousands of orphans and disabled.
There was an extremely limited statistical base on which to formulate
an economic programme of reconstruction. A political system and new
institutions had to be embedded.

At the heart of the new political dynamics was the transition from
liberation front to government and the development of a new relationship between front and society, on the one hand, and front-based
government and the international system, on the other. Such forces were
a test of the autonomy established during the long period of guerrilla
war. As we have demonstrated, save for the brief period in 1977–8, the
EPLF had operated in liberated and semi-liberated rural areas and, in
the 1980s, concentrated somewhat more on military rather than civil
activities. On liberation, the EPLF confronted an urban society.
Asmara, Mendefera, Decamhare and Keren had long been under
Ethiopian military control. International economic and political
pressures on state and government to accommodate and conform to the
norms of the post-Cold War world were immense.

The Transition to Government

The transition to government took place in two stages. The first comprised the transition to internationally recognized sovereignty and involved the organization of the referendum and the establishment of a provisional government to administer Eritrea between independence and the conclusion of the referendum process. The second comprised the formation of a new constitutional order. The referendum was managed in an efficient and relatively smooth fashion, given the antecedent years of military struggle. The referendum proclamation incorporated a straight yes or no answer to the question of whether Eritrea should be an independent and sovereign country, modifying the 1978 proposal of the EPLF, which had included a third option of a return to a federal arrangement. Unsurprisingly, there was a 98.5 per cent turn-out of registered voters and a 99.8 per cent yes vote. From the author's observations in villages in rural Hamasin before the referendum and in Serai provinces during it, these statistics were matched by the engagement in and spontaneous enthusiasm of the highland peasantry. Many of the villages visited during this period had lost a considerable number of the younger generation in the previous decade or more of fighting.[1]

Preceding the referendum proclamation was the Eritrean nationality, proclamation of April 1992. The latter was liberal in its definition of citizenship and had provisions for those born to a mother or father of Eritrean origin, for those of Eritrean birth but with foreign nationality, and for those married to Eritreans. Further provisions were made for naturalization. The extension of citizenship to those born outside Eritrea recognized the citizenship of the large refugee population and the naturalization provisions granted the right to citizenship of the many Ethiopians of Tigray province with long residence in Eritrea.

Unlike the referendum proclamation, that dealing with nationality brought considerable debate and opposition to some of its provisions. It was an indication of the unchanged attitudes of sectors of the population untouched by the organizational outreach of the EPLF. In public meetings in Asmara views were expressed objecting to the equality of rights for children born to mothers of Eritrean origin and to foreigners, by implication Ethiopians, married to Eritrean women. These meetings

---

[1] Compare the rather perverse interpretation of peasant attitudes in K. Tronvoll, 'The Eritrean Referendum: Peasant Voices', *Eritrean Studies Review*, Vol. 1, No. 1, 1996.

on nationality provided an index of an anti-Ethiopian chauvinism, perhaps encouraged by the mass expulsions of Ethiopians remaining in Eritrea, but an initial openness to engage in debate on the part of the EPLF, albeit on chosen issues.

The transition to government essentially involved the movement of the EPLF into positions in government, administration and into a major role in economic reconstruction. Members of the EPLF took almost all the key positions in the ministries of Asmara, the bureaucracy and provincial administration. The transition from guerrilla force to government was most visible in government offices, with khaki-clad figures sitting at desks alongside the more formally dressed civil servants of the Ethiopian era. Issayas Afeworki became head of state. The central committee of the EPLF became the legislative branch of government ratifying proclamations. After the demobilization of 50,000 fighters, a slimmed-down EPLA became the army. Former fighters were everywhere: rebuilding the Asmara factories, restoring electricity and water supplies and reconstructing roads and tracks in the provinces. The only differences from their past lives were that they were involved in peaceful tasks and received a very small amount of pocket money. It was expected that a normalization of the employment of EPLF fighters would take place after the referendum. The EPLF provided food and accommodation. Many of those who worked in the ministries and administration and had no houses in Asmara resided in the former Ethiopian military base and continued to endure a diet similar to that of the liberation war.

Statehood and the New Legal and Political Order

After the referendum, the EPLF began a restructuring of the EPLF and constructing a new constitutional order. The former was undertaken through the third EPLF national congress and the latter by a constitutional commission. Much had already been laid out at the second congress of the EPLF and by Issayas Afeworki in interviews. In these a commitment was given to establish a party system and stress was placed on democracy and pluralism. The same kind of approach was affirmed in the national charter approved by the third congress of the EPLF, which transformed itself into the People's Front for Democracy and Justice (PFDJ). The national charter[2] set the framework

---

[2] *A National Charter for Eritrea: For A Democratic, Just and Prosperous Future*, approved by the third congress of the EPLF, Naqfa, February 1994.

for the political and economic future, and the PFDJ began notionally separating itself from government political structures, a process which will be discussed below.

The programme of the front was based on 'six principles and goals',[3] the congress having debated but rejected anything called an 'ideology', a term smacking of the old Marxist-Leninist days. These principles were to be reiterated in the constitution. The six basic goals were: national harmony; political democracy; economic and social development; social justice; cultural revival; and regional and international cooperation. The six basic principles were predicated on a reformulation of what the EPLF leadership considered the ingredients of its success in combining the political, social and economic factors. Embedded within the principles were obvious tensions. Priority was given to *national unity* on the grounds that

> nationhood is a long, complicated historical process ... this process is not yet concluded [so] we should consider the development and strengthening of Eritrean nationalism and the unity of its people ... It is necessary to build a national government which ... rejects all divisive attitudes and activities, places national interest above everything else and enables participation of all sectors of Eritrean society. All sectarian ... tendencies must be ... rejected [as well as] all forms of discrimination and domination, including ethnic and regional.

There was a stress placed on *a strong relationship between people and leadership* in a modified Maoist language:

> by leadership, we are referring not only to the higher executive body, but to the organized broad political force. We must preserve and strengthen our relationship with the people through our daily presence among them. Our leadership and cadres at all levels must spread to all corners of the country ... Leaders must be free from corruption, refrain from misuse of power, become positive role models ... and be accountable at all times. By clarifying the duties and obligations of leaders, by defined accountability procedures, by constitutionally defining the duration of stay, we must guarantee qualified, accountable and democratic leadership.

In a similar fashion, the language of *active political participation* emphasized the role of organization and mass political education, with a blurring of the means and methods of the organizational process:

> active and organized participation, based on political consciousness, is a basic condition of success ... Participation cannot be successful unless

[3] *Ibid.*, pp. 12–19.

people are organized. People should have the right to establish organizations, they should also be encouraged and assisted to do so.

In a section on *linkage between national and social struggles*, the prerequisite of fair socio-economic development for participation was flagged:

> social justice means narrowing the gap between the haves and the have-nots, ensuring that all people have their fair share of the national wealth and can participate, to creating balanced development ... In the absence of justice, neither prosperity nor stability are attainable ... We should not limit ourselves to talking and teaching about social justice. The movement must provide the most oppressed sections of our society with the means to participate ... as a matter of priority.

Self-reliance was transposed to the national-state sphere:

> politically, it means to follow an independent line and give priority to internal conditions; economically, to rely on internal capabilities and develop internal capacities; and culturally, to have self-confidence and develop one's own cultural heritage.

Human development, a World Bank friendly concept, was given a national character twist in the *the human element*:

> It is primarily the human aspects by which we build Eritrea: strong will, diligence, efficiency, the work ethic, discipline, ability and skills, and inventiveness ... Development strategies must be people-oriented ... and we should put as many resources as possible into human development.

Many of these PFDJ principles were incorporated into the constitution, as EPLF practices were brought into the process of constitution-making. Pre-independence EPLF leaders had made commitments to establishing the rule of law on the basis of constitutionalism. A constitutional commission for Eritrea (CCE) was established in 1994 consisting of a 10-member executive committee and a 50-member council.[4] The executive committee was drawn largely from Eritreans with a legal background and included former ELF members. The chairman was Dr Bereket Habte Selassie, former attorney-general of Ethiopia, an academic and writer on Eritrea and the Horn of Africa; the vice-chairman was Azein Yasin, formerly leading ideologue of the ELF, who died during the process; and secretary Zemheret Yohannes, leading cadre in the Sagem group, which split from the ELF to join the EPLF,

---

[4] The following is drawn from *Constitutional Commission of Eritrea: Strategies, Plans* and an interview with Dr Bereket Habte Selassie, chairman of the CCE, and other members of the CCE in March 1996.

and responsible for research and documentation in the PFDJ. The council members were mainly EPLF figures, with a fair representation of women and members of minorities and some ex-ELF who had joined the EPLF before independence or returned shortly after. Some cynics pointed to an over-representation of wives and sisters of high EPLF cadres, many of whom had been involved in the liberation struggle.

There were four *ad hoc* committees: governmental institutions; economics; social and cultural affairs; and governance and related issues. There was one standing committee: civic education and public debate. While the *ad hoc* committees were involved in shaping the constitutional proposals, the latter had a major role in publicizing, propagandizing and 'making the public conscious' of what a constitution involved. The campaign resembled the EPLF Maoist-style mass political education campaign, although it took place on a much larger scale.

There was a 15-member advisory board of foreign experts, whose comments were unlikely to have been taken seriously unless they fitted with the kinds of assumptions about the constitution made by the executive committee and council. There was also an advisory board on customary laws 'representing the community elders from the various ethnic groups and the administrative regions in the Eritrean society'.[5] This advisory board was of some importance, given the possible tensions between constitutional law, *sharia* and the customary laws of both the Christian and Muslim communities. In the long term, there will inevitably be contradictions between and inconsistencies with the emerging national secular civil and constitutional system and long-established religious courts and customary legal processes.

In many ways the constitution-making process was unique: political education and information at the rural grass roots level, serious debates and seminars in the urban centres. In the provinces and the capital, as well as in the capitals of Europe and the US where there were Eritrean communities, there was vigorous participation. According to one CCE member, who led discussions in small towns like Barentu, Agordat and Naqfa, members of the public asked searching questions as to why there could not be direct presidential elections and two chambers. Others called for two national languages, Arabic and Tigrinya, as had been the case during the BMA and the Federation periods. Neither of these were proposed by the CCE and neither incorporated.

An informal PFDJ and government consensus on many issues either

[5] *Ibid.*

pre-empted or caused the CCE to anticipate an EPLF view of the constitution. The EPLF and PFDJ leader Issayas Afeworki, for example, had been elected from the central committee and central council, respectively. Such a practice was continued in the post-independence period: the head of state was elected by the national assembly, the bulk of whose members were from the front. According to Dr Bereket, there was no government intervention and the CCE had a free hand, although government did lay down a timetable. Both before the constitutional proposals for public debate document[6] and the draft constitution, however, there were various government proclamations that dealt with constitutional issues such as the freedom of the press and rights to land. Indeed, an outline of the press law was published during the work of the CCE, to the surprise of Dr Bereket. Some leading PFDJ members expressed personal views opposing the specific mention of women's rights in the constitution and in favour of a strong presidency. PFDJ leaders, as well as the chairman of the CCE, shared a consensus on a minimal constitution. Insofar as the first draft of the constitution was to be discussed and amended by the PFDJ-dominated national assembly, it would have been foolhardy for the CCE to present a draft constitution divergent from views expressd by leading PFDJ and government members. Dr Bereket asserted that in the discussions about the constitution in the broader executive council there was no apparent common PFDJ line. Given that the PFDJ line had already been laid down at its congress and members followed the decisions taken, the absence of an 'apparent' line makes sense only for points of detail.

The making of the constitution was given a great deal of publicity in Eritrea. With an illiteracy rate of 85 per cent it was no easy task to mobilize opinion about the seriousness of the process. Seminars and meetings were organized across the country, and a record of the questions posed by the public was taken. Reports in the Eritrean press of public meetings to discuss the draft constitution, however, indicated that questions about language, presidential elections and nationality rights continued to surface. Although they have yet to be analysed, their publication would certainly satisfy segments of the intelligentsia who were sceptical of the consultative process, believing that it was essentially a civic education campaign.

Subsequent to the campaigns and seminars, the CCE drafted *Constitutional Proposals for Public Debate*, following which further debates and seminars took place. The legal committee of the CCE presented a

---

[6] CCE, *Constitutional Proposals for Public Debate*, August 1995.

rough draft to the executive council, and a first draft was presented to the national assembly in July 1996. Modifications were taken into account and a final version drawn up, and again presented for public discussion. A final draft was completed and ratified. *The Constitutional Proposals for Public Debate* give a relatively clear idea of both the assumptions underlying the constitution and the kind of constitution envisaged, and we present a summary of them below. The final constitution varied very little from them. The CCE emphasized that

> our constitution has to be based on the history, political circumstances and experience, social structure and culture, level of development and in general on the special conditions of the Eritrean society; and its contents have to serve the basic aims of nation building, equitable development and stability, the building of democracy, the protection of human rights and the assurance of popular participation.[7]

The political system was to be based on the principles of nationalism and national unity and secularism, with the separation of religion from politics. The CCE also stressed the need to balance the rights of citizens with their duties to national unity, and that basic freedoms had to be guaranteed by a 'democratic political culture' and economic and cultural development. Further stress was placed on the need for firm and strong government and governmental institutions in order to create the social, economic and cultural foundation for the growth of democracy, which 'has to develop gradually, taking root through a process of struggle and change'. A multi-party system and competitive elections were viewed in a rather negative light and were described as 'procedural as opposed to an essential'[8] aspect of democracy. As to the specific institutional recommendations the CCE proposed separation of powers with the legislature able to hold the executive body accountable, an executive with a 'strong leadership with clear vision for development'[9] and an independent judiciary. All of these views were in line with views expressed by EPLF leaders prior to the appointment of the CCE.

The constitution closely followed the proposals of the CCE. The preamble stressed the centrality of the liberation struggle for building the future Eritrea: 'it is necessary that unity, equality, love for truth and justice, self-reliance … which helped us to triumph must become the core of our national values.'

Article 2 asserted that the constitution was the source of government

[7] *Ibid.*, p. 6.
[8] *Ibid.*, p. 11.
[9] *Ibid.*, p. 20.

legitimacy, the guarantor for the protection of rights, the supreme law of the country and the source of all laws of the state. All laws, orders and acts contrary to both its letter and spirit should be null and void. Article 3 assigned citizenship rights to anyone born of an Eritrean mother or father. This provision followed the nationality law, which had been opposed by conservative circles favouring citizenship restricted to those born of an Eritrean father. Chapter 2 dealt with national objectives and principles. First mentioned was the guiding principle of 'unity in diversity'. Article 7, 'Democratic Principles', stressed equality of participation but also stated that the 'organization and operation of all political and public associations and movements shall be guided by the principle of national unity and democracy'. Although the party law had not been promulgated, such a provision presaged government control of party registration. Article 7 contained a strongly worded clause concerning women: 'Any act that violates the human rights of women or limits or otherwise thwarts their role and participation is prohibited.'

Chapter 3, 'Fundamental Rights, Freedoms and Duties', provided for equality before the law, with comprehensive prohibitions against discrimination, torture and degrading treatment. Article 7 detailed due process of law in relationship to arrest, detention and trial, including *habeas corpus*. The right to a public trial was limited for reasons of 'morals, the public order or national security'. Article 9 of Chapter 3 listed comprehensive freedoms of thought, conscience, belief and religious practice, as well as rights to assemble, demonstrate peaceably and form organizations. Property, other than land, water and natural resources, could be owned, disposed of and bequeathed. Article 26, dealing with limitations on rights and freedoms, stated that

> The fundamental rights and freedoms guaranteed … may be limited only in so far as is necessary in a just and democratic society in the interests of national security, public safety, or the economic well-being of the country, health or morals, for the prevention of public disorder or crime or for the protection of the rights and freedoms of others.

There were, however, no limitations to equality before the law, discrimination and the freedom to practise religion. The general phrasing of the circumstances of limitations on fundamental rights and freedoms left considerable interpretive scope for the supreme court, which had the sole jurisdiction of interpreting the constitution and the constitutionality of all laws.

Following the CCE's proposals, provision was made for a separation of powers. The key institution was the presidency nominated and elected by the national assembly. He or she had extensive powers of appointment, and was head of state, leader of government and commander-in-chief.

The constitution and the PFDJ national charter incorporated seemingly contradictory principles and raised complex questions. To what extent was a commitment to pluralism and freedom of expression and assembly compatible with the stress on national unity? To what extent was social justice, balanced regional development and a stress on empowering the most oppressed compatible with a macro-economic policy 'framework designed to stimulate private investment' that gave the 'private sector the lead role in the economic activities of Eritrea'?[10] To what extent were the political practices of the EPLF, in the past so successful in mobilizing and organizing Eritreans for the liberation of Eritrea, a hindrance to the stated goals of developing a democratic and pluralist polity for all Eritreans? Indeed, could the culture of equality and strong leadership which the EPLF combined in the liberation movement and in the liberated zones be a model for state-building? Could cultural diversity, reflected in the continuing commitment to the policy of nationalities, be harnessed to national unity and be depoliticized without an authoritarian state? To what extent could any devolution of power from the EPLF to non-EPLF institutions take place given the centrality of the EPLF to the liberation of Eritrea and its running of Eritrea since independence? Could the solidarities and loyalties developed between leadership and cadres of the EPLF in the form of democratic centralism be transformed into a set of checks and balances between executive, legislature and judiciary and an institutionalized system of accountability when all three separate areas were staffed by former EPLF personnel?

The texts of the constitution and the national charter can be read in two different ways. Firstly, they could be interpreted as the basis for establishing an elitist, exclusionary and tutelary authoritarian system that eschews liberal democracy on the grounds that the party-based institutions and the electoral processes of the latter are procedural and corruptible. Thus the stress on building national unity. Secondly, they could be interpreted as creating the basis of a participatory democratic order in the longer term through establishing the social and economic basis for equal citizenship and participation. Thus the stress on social justice. In both these cases, national unity and development imperatives

---

[10] *Macro-Policy*, Government of the State of Eritrea, Asmara, November 1994.

operate as justifications and joint constraints and are actually embedded in the legal and constitutional framework and impinge on citizenship rights.

The intention of the following sections is to assess, in a tentative but critical way, the operation and practices of the government and to question whether the EPLF can create a government and society that is successful in a context different from the liberation struggle.

There have already been political strains arising partly from the weak financial position of the government and also from a rapidly emerging gap between leadership and EPLF members. Immediately after the referendum fighters took over parts of Asmara and the airport in protest against the continuation of the policy of no salaries. Subsequently, a further demonstration of disabled fighters protesting against their lot took place and ended in the shooting of several of them. These incidents will be discussed in more detail below.

Although measures were rapidly introduced to accommodate the demands of the fighters, these incidents highlighted the urgent need for economic development and the interconnectedness of economic growth and political stability. Given the distressed state of the Horn of Africa and the prevalence of internal wars which have raged there, the new Eritrean state, nevertheless, had an opportunity to make a fresh start and develop a formula for peace, stability and development that incorporated a concern for social justice and human rights. As we have illustrated above, the PFDJ had set the agenda for the new state. After a prolonged history of internal conflict, at times between communities, at times between organized political forces and at times manipulated by external forces, was the stage being set for a period of peaceful development and, to quote the title of the PFDJ's national charter, 'a democratic, just and prosperous future'?

The Emerging Political Dynamics

Certain trends have already become evident. As Issayas Afeworki emerged as the key figure in the EPLF and his power was formalized at the 1987 congress, so that power has been constitutionalized. He is both the guardian and at the apex of the system in control of an interlocking set of state and party institutions. He ensures the respect of the constitution, the integrity of the state and the efficiency and effectiveness of the public service, the interests and safety of all citizens, including the enjoyment of their fundamental rights and freedoms.

Cabinet ministers are accountable individually to the president and collectively to the National Assembly *but* through the office of the president. The president, then, acts as a buffer between ministers and the national assembly.

It would be a brave member of the National Assembly who attempted to confront the student nationalist activist, dominant figure in the Ala group, key founder of the EPLF and of the secret party within it and architect of the ideology and organizational structure of the front. His publicly expressed views on democracy are somewhat similar to those expressed almost two decades earlier in his response to the *manqa* criticisms and are mirrored in the institutional arrangements of the new Eritrea. Issayas is president, commander-in-chief of the armed forces, chairman of the national assembly, secretary-general of the PFDJ and chairs ministerial meetings. He has wide-ranging powers of appointment: ministers, heads of commissions like the constitutional and land commissions, provincial governors, high court judges and ambassadors. It is unclear how wide are the consultations on appointments and policy decision-making but ultimate decision-making lies with the president, assisted by an increasingly powerful presidential office which has functions paralleling ministerial ones in the spheres of economy, security and foreign affairs. The presidential office is at the core of the executive and indicative of his power.

Most key ministries have been held by former EPLF political bureau members, with secondary ones held by central committee members. There has, however, been considerable movement between portfolios, an index of presidential power and the use of powers of appointment. Six years after independence, many of the top tier of leadership had been shifted to the second tier, to technical ministries or to administrative positions. Ramadan Muhammad Nur, secretary-general of the front from 1977 to 1987, became minister of justice, then governor of Dankalia and subsequently left politics. Mesfin Hagos, a very close second in the vote at the 1994 PFDJ congress, was removed from defence minister to a provincial governorship. Petros Solomon, EPLF security chief and subsequently at foreign affairs, was demoted to minister for fisheries. Ali Sayyid Abdallah, EPLF military commander and interior minister, was demoted to ministry of trade and industry. Others from the EPLF central committee with powerful positions after independence were also sidelined. The deputy minister for interior, Naizghi Kiflemeariam, responsible for internal security, was sent as ambassador to Moscow. Adhanom Gebremariam, a key military commander, was sent to Scandinavia as ambassador.

Only a few EPLF PB members had retained powerful positions. Sebhat Ephraim was moved from defence to health and back to defence. Both Mahmud Ahmad Mahmud 'Sharifo' and Haile Woldetensai were shifted between different ministries but remained in key positions. Al-Amin Muhamad Said, who was minister of information, was appointed to the PFDJ.

Although the volatility of ministerial appointments has been explained by the need to fit appropriate people to portfolios, the frequent transfers emphasized the dominant position of the president over the former top EPLF leadership. It has also been reliably reported that the president occasionally made biting attacks on the personal capacities of ministers. Parallelling the increased presidentialism has been the growing power of the presidential office over ministries through directives that undercut ministerial authority, particularly in the sphere of expenditure. Internal security and economic policy become centralized in the presidential office under the rapidly promoted Abraha Kassa and Berhane Abraha, respectively.

The internal workings of post-independence Eritrean politics continue to reflect the secretive nature of the front. Notionally, decision-making within the EPLF had been based on debate aimed at generating consensus on a particular issue at front congresses. The decision-making process of both central committee and political bureau, however, was secret, unsurprisingly given the liberation war. Although foreign observers attended debates at pre-independence front congresses and attested to their frankness,[11] it was without the knowledge of the existence of the secret party. After independence, national assembly debates have not been reported in the official media. The press generally presents government news and decisions but provides little in the way of political analysis. Controversial policy decisions do surface tangentially through media interviews with ministers and officials. A bizarre example of the secrecy occurred after the government reshuffle of early 1997 when no public announcement was made and no ministers' names appeared in the Eritrean press for some considerable time. A greater degree of openness would give some confidence in the projected development of pluralism.

The increasing shift to presidentialism and the specific changes in governmental portfolios is not only a mark of the political and intellectual dominance of Issayas Afeworki within the EPLF but also a

---

[11] See R. Leonard in Cliffe and Davidson, *op. cit.*, p. 122. It should be noted that there was no mention of party activity.

consequence of a crisis of authority after independence. In some ways, it was a historic parallel to the *manqa* crisis of the early years of the front. Like the latter it was shrouded in an atmosphere of secrecy. All the accounts in the Eritrean and international press, as well as those by experienced writers on Eritrea, including the author, depicted the 'fighters' rebellion' as a struggle for the normalization of their lives. In brief, the accepted account is that EPLF members expected that they would receive salaries after the two-year period between independence and the referendum. When it became clear that this was not to be forthcoming a spontaneous revolt occurred, with armed units taking over the airport and other parts of Asmara. Along with criticisms of the treatment of disabled veterans and the families of martyrs, they complained about their lot in comparison with the incomes and lifestyles of the leadership. The crisis was resolved by the president meeting with disaffected units and promising a change from their dependence on 'pocket money'.

The protest, however, was as much against the emergent political order as against the fighters' impecunious position. From within the heart of the liberation front came opposition to the direct transfer of the formal leadership of the EPLF into state leadership. A socio-economic protest by rank and file fighters became entwined with the political transition directed against the proposed ratification of the EPLF central committee as the legislative body of the new state. Although the party had supposedly been abolished, within some ministries party members campaigned, on the same basis as in 1977 and 1987, for an EPLF list for membership of the national assembly. Meetings within ministries and units were acerbic, with some junior cadres expressing strong opposition to the automatic list system. After independence the *nomenklatura* had clearly broken down. Since independence there was already a visible rift between fighters on pocket money and members of the PB, central committee and military who had better housing and expenses. Some of the latter, in any case, came from prosperous Asmaran families and had succeeded to elegant villas or had relatives abroad who subsidized them. Others took over villas which had been inhabited by Ethiopian officers.

Like the *manqa* crisis of the early 1970s, the rebellion was resolved through a combination of accommodation and repression. Leaders of and participants in the rebellion were imprisoned and the personnel of some military units dispersed. A gradual shift to salary was initiated for EPLF fighters in administrative positions together with a regularization of a new Eritrean army. As with the early crisis, there was both a demonstrative and a reactive response to the challenge to the authority of an embedded leadership. It was the impact of this crisis, occurring while many international observers of the independence celebrations were still in Asmara, that resulted in the transfer of key commanders and security officials and the centralization of decision-making in the presidential office.[12] Of greater political importance, however, was the inability of the leadership to grasp the increasing gap between their lives and those of others in the liberation struggle, during which differences in social status had been hidden in the equality of the field.[13] With the formalization of executive centralization in the person of the president, there also developed an increasing centralization of state structures, raising questions about the extent to which grass roots participation and building a 'democratic culture', stressed by the leadership as a pre-requisite for democracy, were in train.

Building Grass Roots Participation

An intrinsic part of the new political structure is local government, a cornerstone of its new democratic system based on creating the circum-stances for participation through grassroots involvement in decision-making rather than on representation through parties.[13] In addition, the restructuring of provincial administration was intended to serve development strategy and nation-building.

Patterned on the system of peoples' assemblies formed during the liberation struggle, after independence the EPLF established a system of elected provincial assemblies. At the base of the local government system was the village committee or *baito*, a traditional forum for decision-making on community issues. Although provincial affairs were under the guidance of centrally appointed governors, provincial assemblies were directly elected and had the power to formulate some few development priorities, albeit within a framework of national ones. They had the power to tax specified economic activities and promote particular projects. In practice, a limited amount of funds was provided by the centre, with shortfalls made up through local taxes or through

---

[12] The president reportedly blamed officials who had their own power networks within the front. Asmara rumour mongers had it that powerful figures in the ministry of defence supported or turned a blind eye to the movement. Given the historic internal controls of the EPLF it was surprising that the scale of discontent and anger was not monitored.

[13] Most of the following is based on interviews with Habtab Tesfazion, deputy minister for local government, in April 1993 and March 1996.

contributions to province development funds from the refugee population and Eritreans abroad. Elections to provincial assemblies appear to have been competitive, with government guidance limited to specifying representation for women and minorities and EPLA provincial units. In Akalai Guzai province in 1993, for example, there were 575 candidates seeking the votes of 56,228 voters for 67 seats, with six seats reserved for fighters.

In 1995 the local government system was radically transformed. The old provinces were abolished, as were the village *baitos*. The latter were replaced by another traditional village structure, the *megaba'aya*, a meeting of the whole village community. According to Habteab Tesfazion, then deputy minister for local government, the previously elected village leaderships promoted prestige projects that did not benefit the community, an indication of the tension between grass roots participation in development and state guidance. In 1996 a proclamation to redraw the old provincial boundaries centralized authority in the ministry of local government. Unlike the public discussions on nationality, there were no meetings to debate what were sensitive changes, particularly for the highland provinces. The overall result was that the local administrative officer guided the regional assemblies to ensure that their resolutions were in keeping with government policies.[14]

Following the EPLF 1994 congress, which resolved to abolish the old provinces on the grounds that they were a legacy of colonial structures, the ministry of local government set about delineating new provinces on the basis of development criteria and resources. According to the minister, breaking down traditional regionalist sentiments and mixing different ethnic groups in the new provinces was a derivative, albeit beneficial consequence. The new provinces were: Dubub (South), bringing together parts of Akalai Guzai and Serai provinces, with Mendefera as capital; Centre (Asmara and 20 km surroundings); Southern Red Sea, from Ras Andadai to the Djibouti border, with Asab as capital; Northern Red Sea, incorporating parts of Samhar and Sahel, with the capital at Massawa; Gash Barka, formerly Gash-Setit and southern Barka, with Barentu as capital; and Anseba, incorporating northern Hamasin, Senheit and northern Barka, with Keren as the capital. The administrative changes were very radical and a degree of disquiet was expressed by some Eritreans. Unlike the

---

[14] See K. Tronvoll, 'The Process of Nation-Building in Eritrea', *Journal of Modern African Studies*, Vol. 36, No. 3, 1998, pp. 466–9.

process of constitution-making, there was no popular consultation on this radical change.

Accompanying the redrawing of the old provincial boundaries was a policy of devolution. The intention was to develop and strengthen the new provincial capitals through devolving administrators and technicians away from the central ministries based in Asmara, thereby cutting down bureaucracy and bringing government and technical advice closer to the people. If this process were operationalized, a boost would be given to underdeveloped towns like Barentu, the new capital of Gash Barka and centre of the Kunama minority. Alongside the formalization of presidentialism, participation at the local level is constrained by a form of institutionalization that associates the rural people with state institutions without any real devolution of power.

In many ways, the nature of participation in post-independence rural Eritrea is rather similar at the local level to the relationship between the cadres of the mass administration and the peoples' assemblies during the liberation war. Most of the local government administrators were former EPLF fighters accustomed to a tutelary role under the guidelines set by the political bureau. In post-independence Eritrea, however, the guidelines derive from the national development strategy rather than the strategy of liberation war. The PFDJ as successor to the EPLF has been central to the definition of the former and has been assigned a direct role in it.

The Popular Front For Democracy and Justice[15]

After the referendum, preparations began for the EPLF 1994 congress, the major goal of which was to revitalize the front and reinforce the ties between it and the broader population by transforming it into a mass party. EPLF members were automatically signed up. By mid-1996, there were about 1,000 branches with a membership of around 600,000, a figure embracing most of the adult population. In both Africa and the Middle East, mass parties have usually been instruments of control by a small elite rather than vehicles for participation, with the mass membership unable to do more than follow the policies set by the leadership. As one PFDJ leader told the author: it is up to the members to make it a vital organization.

---

[15] The following is based on interviews with Yemane Ghebreab and Zemheret Yohannes, responsible for PFDJ political affairs and research and documentation, respectively.

As successor to the EPLF, the PFDJ is a formidable force. Although formally it became a separate institution from government, there was an overlapping membership of its central council of 75 and the national assembly and ministers. Not only did it inherit the EPLF's legacy of popularity for liberating Eritrea, it succeeded to its non-military assets built up during the struggle. Considerable resources in Eritrean terms, these assets provided it with economic and political power and the potential to establish an extensive patronage network to reinforce its dominance. In the course of sustaining myriad social, economic, political and military activities, the EPLF had administered a transport network, commerce, construction, finance and small-scale workshops in the base areas. On liberation it took control of a variety of concerns nationalized by the Ethiopian government.

By 1995, the PFDJ owned a large number of enterprises. Smaller businesses included a bookshop, garages, a pharmacy and a shop specializing in imported audio-visual goods. Small industrial concerns included metal works and tyre retreading. In the finance sector there was a foreign exchange bank, which gave the best exchange rate in Asmara, and a housing bank. It owned internal transport concerns and a shipping line, as well as a construction firm that built both low-cost housing and modern apartment complexes. Complementing PFDJ economic concerns was the government-controlled Red Sea Corporation, involved in international trade. The latter was staffed by former EPLF members. When the government began privatizing the nationalized sector the PFDJ took shares in both the denationalized manufacturing and service sectors.

The intention was that the assets would be held by a holding company, functioning rather like a trust fund. It would operate as a commercial concern but also invest profits in non-profit-making sectors and underdeveloped regions. Through its trading arm, the Red Sea Corporation,[16] it has played a role in controlling prices of basic commodities and essential development materials in line with the principles of the national charter. After liberation the PFDJ imported grains and sugar and sold them at a profit, but below the market price, and did the same for construction materials and consumer items like televisions.

In conjunction with its profit-making market operations, some of its activities were orientated to social justice and correcting uneven regional development. Profits were invested where the private sector would be unlikely to invest: enterprises in Afar areas of Dankalia and

[16] Worth US$25 million by 1995. *The Economist*, 6.5.1995.

public transport in southwest Eritrea, for example. The PFDJ has already set up a technical school outside Keren and is planning to rebuild hospitals for women and children. It was an innovative experiment in using the former EPLF's assets for development in regions relatively lacking in infrastructure and in educational and health provision. Although it operates as a private corporation, the size and range of its enterprises effectively provide it with control of the market in many areas. Its role has resulted in complaints by the merchant community that its activities undermine the operation of the private sector, much of which is involved in small-scale manufacture and petty trade. At the same time, its financial institutions provide loans to private sector business in return for a stake in ownership.

The combination of political and financial power has the potential both to block the emergence of a flourishing private sector and decrease the space for the development of a credible opposition. In the absence of a critical opposition, how internal mechanisms of accountability and transparency develop will become crucial. How the assets are managed and the nature of accountability within the PFDJ are crucial determinants of the development and shaping of Eritrean politics given the strategic position of the PFDJ in the economy. It is as possible that the mass support garnered through the liberation struggle can be maintained in the longer term through the performance of government and front, as it is possible that it can be eroded when policies fail to fulfil popular expectations. It is not unusual for political structures like the PFDJ to become moribund, authoritarian and corrupt, especially when there are close and long-established connections between government and party members. Incidents of corruption did occur in 1996, involving officials of the Red Sea Corporation and highly placed EPLF members. They were dealt with in a closed trial by a special anti-corruption court.

There is an imbalance emerging in what will be a combined presidential-dominant party state, on the one hand, and the stated intention of establishing a pluralist political system where opposition parties would have a realistic opportunity to function, on the other. Organized opposition has so far been prohibited, and there has been a growing list of individuals who have been arrested and imprisoned for lengthy periods without judicial process.[17] They have included former EPLF members involved in the 1993 fighter protests and those accused of corruption, ELF returnees and some few Tigrinya-speaking

---

[17] There have been various petitions to the government naming those imprisoned as well as reports from Amnesty International in 1997 and 1997 expressing concern about human rights violations.

Jiberti who demanded nationality status on the grounds that as a Muslim community they were distinct from Christian Tigrinya speakers. While some former individual members of ELF factions have returned, ELF groups as organized forces were not permitted to participate in state formation and constitution-making, the political consequences of which will be mentioned below.

There are obvious tensions between the avowed goal of encouraging the private sector and the economic power of the PFDJ. It partly reflects an historic EPLF antipathy toward the leading role of petty traders in the rural economy. Although the majority of urban and rural Eritreans benefit from price controls through market mechanisms, the urban merchant and business strata involved in internal trade face considerable dents in traditional areas of profit-making. The formal and informal nature of government–party and army links, the extensive inclusionary character of membership and the breadth of its goals and functions impose severe constraints on the development of social and economic structures independent of the state. Indeed, they set the stage for the emergence of an interlocking cohesive ruling group whose ideological justifications are the promotion of development and national unity, tempered by the benevolent provision of social justice. A similar kind of trend can be observed in the operation of the EPLF's former mass associations.

The leaders of the women's, youth and workers' organizations were all longstanding EPLF members and on the executive council of the PFDJ. They represented the face of government and PFDJ policies to their members rather than vice versa. In many respects, they continued the mobilizational and educational activities pursued during the liberation struggle and provided fora for debate about the new state laws in covering their functional interests. Together with language, education and land policies, the issue of gender and the role of the National Union of Eritrean Women illuminate emerging state–society relations in independent Eritrea.

Women

As we have demonstrated, there were contrasting legal provisions for women EPLF members and those in broader Eritrean society. The kinds of principles that underpinned the 1977 EPLF law on marriage were carried over into post-liberation Eritrea. Article 22 of the constitution, for example, provided for the right to marry based on consent. By liberation, women EPLF members had undergone a qualitatively distinct experience both in their roles and in their relationship to men. They had become orientated to a set of norms, expectations and behaviour different from those of the wider society and, indeed, different from the families they had left. The sharpness of the contrast was more marked for those from rural backgrounds. Since liberation, however, there have been some expressions of disquiet as some women fighters accounted for a soaring divorce rate after liberation by reference to male fighters seeking new and more submissive partners and the erosion of the equality of the field as couples returned to civilian roles. There is no statistical evidence available on the scale of marriage breakdowns, nor is there any analysis of causes, but I mention it because it was strongly asserted by many Eritrean women. For these women, such divorces were considered symbolic of the problems of sustaining gender equality in the post-liberation period, even with male fighter counterparts.

Strains also emerged among Eritrean women over the role of the National Union of Eritrean Women (NUEW) after independence and the place of women's rights in the constitution. Although the NUEW was, in effect, a mass organization of the EPLF, since independence it has functioned, in part, as an arm of the government in raising finance for projects particularly targeted at women (literacy, skill training, credit for establishing businesses, training for demobilized fighters) and, in part, as a lobby for women's interests. Eritrean women seemed divided on the duality of these two functions, with some believing that a greater distance from government and front would enhance and make more effective a role as an independent pressure group. In practice its role has been developmental and supportive of government policies.

Indicative of the radicalization of some women fighters, at a NUEW workshop in 1994, a more radical interventionist position than that of the government on the treatment of women was taken.[18] It called for the legal prohibition of premarital virginity testing, circumcision and infibulation. It proposed that domestic violence be grounds for divorce and that decisions about divorce by committees of elders could be vetoed by civil courts on the grounds of abuses of the rights of women and children. This position stands in marked contrast to that of government, which favoured change through education and persuasion. More controversially, the workshop proposed that the civil code on family, marriage and divorce should embrace members of the Islamic faith.

[18] Cited in M. Iyob and Z. Jaber, 'Social and Cultural Rights', *CCE Issue Paper No. 6*.

Although this view was based on the principle that religious and customary law should be subordinated to secular law, religious elders of the Islamic communities would certainly oppose such compulsory change in the relationship between *sharia* and state law, and in practice government has been unwilling to dramatically change the role of Islamic courts in personal status issues.

These debates do not necessarily herald a contest between Muslim and Christian communities, although there are significant implications for them, but between the forces of secularism and modernization developed within the EPLF and the younger generation, on the one hand, and traditional social forces, which are equally strong among Christian communities, on the other. The position of women, with its highly sensitive political ramifications, is likely to be fought over in the arena of religious, customary, civil and constitutional law and, in defining the relationship between them, the women's issue is likely to become a barometer of the broader contest between forces of change and conservatism.

Already, some communities in the Muslim west and the Afar area have resisted the participation of their women in the compulsory national service programme, a duty required in the constitution and a means of socializing the younger generation into the values of the EPLF. Insofar as there is more resistance to change in Muslim areas and some opposition factions like Eritrean Jihad mobilize support on uncompromising Islamist positions, it is possible that womens' rights could be sacrificed to counter such opposition.

There was a debate within the NUEW and the constitutional commission about the place of women's rights in the constitution. The prevailing view within the commission appeared to be that mentioning gender equality in the preamble was sufficient, and that if women's rights were specifically mentioned recognition should also be accorded to children's rights and the rights of disabled fighters and the elderly. Many women members of the NUEW asserted the necessity of mentioning women's rights explicity in order to assure the gains that women had made during the liberation struggle and ensure that there would be no retreat from them. The individual views of some PFDJ leaders was to oppose the specific inclusion of women's rights. Some Muslim members of the advisory board on customary laws were concerned that mentioning women's rights in the constitution would be detrimental to the position of the *sharia*. As we have pointed out, the statement about women in the constitution was stronger than the author had expected from his discussions in Asmara prior to the issuing of the draft constitution.

In the area of formal party and state institutions, women are well represented, even though this form of representation is a symbolic rather than a real indication of power. Although the quota does not match their proportional membership of the EPLF, 10 of the 75 members of the PFDJ central council are women, and are thus automatically members of the national assembly. In local and provincial assemblies women have been allocated a quota of 30 per cent and the opportunity to stand in general constituencies. There has been some debate on the issue of women's representation. Saba Issayas argued that quotas marginalized women and that women could best assert their position in Eritrean society by competing with men. In *Women in the Constitution* she pointed out that women can achieve a stronger position than allowed by the quota system through which women do not achieve representation proportional to their numbers. In support of her claim, she cited the example of the Carneshim district elections of 1994 when women participated in general elections and successfully elected the chair, vice-chair and secretary in three village assemblies.

Although this kind of debate was restricted to an elite of educated urban woman and the educated and self-educated fighters, for the 200,000 members of the NUEW, education, literacy, credit and health are probably more important. The struggle of the former, however, is likely to shape the fate of the many and will continue to raise difficult questions about the relationship between secularism, the role of the state, religion and law. Accommodating opposition to the expansion of gender equality from the EPLF to all of Eritrean society is likely to provide a test of pluralist politics.

The role and position of former women fighters in independent Eritrea and the likelihood of organizations autonomous of government and party structures emerging can be illustrated by an account of BANA, the Eritrean Women War Veterans Association. It was established in 1995 by three women fighters as a share company the initial capital of which came from the 10,000 birr demobilization money of 1,000 women ex-fighters. It registered as an NGO with the ministry of internal affairs and had an advisory board drawn from government officials, including the minister of justice, and attracted considerable funding from foreign NGOs. Its goal was to provide financial and technical support for demobilized women. Among the projects were a fish-marketing cooperative and a bakery.

In 1996, a ruling from the president's office closed it down on the grounds that it duplicated the work of other organizations. It would seem, however, that the explanation for its closure was considerably

183

more complex and was a function of a set of interrelated factors that can be directly or indirectly linked to a broad disfavouring of organizations independent of government and quasi-government institutions. Both MITYAS, a department of the Eritrean Relief and Rehabilitation Authority, and NUEW, semi-integrated with the PFDJ, had programmes for the rehabilitation of fighters.

Even if the outcome was a result of the resolution of bureaucratic rivalries or a duplication of activities, the closure of BANA illustrated that subsidiary governmental organizations were favoured by the authorities rather than independent and autonomous ones. The case of BANA is particularly interesting in that it originated with former EPLF fighters. The argument that it challenged the principle of national self-reliance because it combined self-funding with external funding[19] is hardly convincing insofar as both MITYAS and NUEW were dependent on external support for their programmes. Whatever the case, the auguries for the growth of civil organizations outside of governmental control are poor, as the experience of BANA has been replicated in the closure of other organizations.[20] It also seriously undermines the argument that extensive power of the post-independence government of Etitrea is a function of the lack of any civil society, an argument made by Alemseged Tesfai, a prominent EPLF intellectual.[21] Controversial policy areas along with gender are language and education.

Language and Education

These issues are entwined with development and nation-building as well as religious and ethnic cleavages. The language issue is also politically contentious in that the ELF groups have consistently proposed Arabic and Tigrinya as official languages. Providing greater access to education at all levels but particularly at the primary level has been one of the major goals of the Eritrean government, as education for fighters and those in the liberated zones during the war had high priority. Language and education policies of the post-independence government have been based on an extension of EPLF policies deriving from the principle of nationalities formulated during the liberation

[19] As claimed by Dan Connell, *Against All Odds* pp. 330–2.
[20] *Ibid.*
[21] Alemseged Tesfai, *Diversity, Identity and Unity in Eritrea: A View from Inside*, African Studies Unit, University of Leeds, 1997.

struggle. The national development objectives, as laid out in *Macro-Policy*,[22] stress the need to provide a broad-based education, widespread dissemination of skills and languages and the development of human capital. Past educational provision had been marked by significant disparities between the urban and rural sectors, regions and the sexes. The lowland areas were particularly deprived and female education there has been minimal.

The EPLF came to power with extensive experience of providing education and managing an educational system for fighters and the civilian population of the liberated and semi-liberated areas. Whereas all communities share aspirations for the education of the next generation, the language question is a more controversial one.

Underpinning language policy was the development of Eritrean languages based on the EPLF's principle of the recognition of Eritrea's nine nationalities, although as we have pointed out Tigrinya became the operative language of the front. Considerable success in educational provision has been achieved in a relatively short period given the run-down state of the school system, a prolonged history of interruption of the school year and limited resources. Primary school enrolment in 1990–1 was 109,087 and in 1994–5 224,287. The school system is one of mixed government and non-government schools, with the latter following the national curriculum. The commitment of the government to expanding education provision and enhancing quality is not in doubt. Nor is its commitment to bolstering the languages of the diverse nationalities.

Government policy is that pupils should study in their mother tongue at the primary level as far as is possible. Government textbooks, building on those used in the base areas, have been produced in most of the languages: Kunama, Tigre, Sahho and Tigrinya, as well as Arabic. In addition, all children study English, Arabic and Tigrinya as subjects, moving at middle school level to the use of English for all subjects. It is a demanding package of language study and is aimed at sustaining minority languages, making study at the primary school level easier for pupils, socializing pupils into the languages of other communities and, at the post-primary school level, providing skills in an international language.

During the first years of independence there was a degree of flexibility based on community choice of language of primary instruction. Flexibility was as much a matter of the availability of facilities and the

[22] *Macro-Policy, op.cit.*

limited number of trained teachers of minority languages. Several Muslim minority community leaders expressed preferences for study in Arabic rather than a minority language on the basis that it was the language of the Quran and a higher international culture, that knowledge of minority languages was transmitted through the household and that there was nothing written in languages like Sahho and Bileyn. In some areas, where there has been a number of returnees from the Sudan, Arabic became the language of instruction. And in some provinces, where there were largely Muslim populations, there was considerable teaching in Arabic: in Dankalia, of the 26 primary schools 20 were taught in Arabic and four in Tigrinya; in Sahel, 11 in Tigre and four in Arabic; in Barka, 33 in Arabic and 3 in Tigrinya.[23] Although some Sahho community leaders favoured Arabic, in 1994–5 the bulk of that community's children were in Sahho primary schools: 12 in Akalai Guzai and one each in Hamasin and Samhar.

In areas which were highly heterogeneous, it was difficult to provide choice. At one school I visited on the outskirts of Keren in early 1996 I questioned students in a middle school class about languages spoken at home. Thirty spoke Tigre, nine Bileyn, 24 Arabic and one Sahho. Although the language of study in middle schools is English and all study Arabic and Tigrinya, all the children were from Muslim backgrounds and the vast majority had some passing knowledge of Arabic from studying the Quran in the *khalwa* or residence in Sudan. There is, then, something of a tension between competing principles: right of language choice, preservation of cultural heritage and educational development criteria. According to one high official in the department of education, there have been examples where parental or community choice proved to be to the detriment of children's education. In Gash-Setit, the Nara community opted for Arabic but that resulted in relatively high failure rates. To allow total freedom of choice, however, would result in a chaotic educational system.

Decisions on language provision can also create intra-community divisions.[24] Many Bileyn Muslims favoured the Arabic language and script. Bileyn Orthodox Christians preferred the *Ge'ez* script, while Catholics wanted the Latin. Some opted for either Tigrinya or Arabic on the grounds that there was nothing in Bileyn for children to read. As a consequence, by the late 1990s there was no text in Bileyn.

---

[23] *Basic Educational Statistics.*

[24] The following comments are based on random conversations in Keren between 1992 and 1996.

The language of instruction is a sensitive issue and would involve difficult choices and complex problems for any government in Eritrea. Given the relatively small numbers that proceed to middle and secondary school at present, it makes educational sense that students are taught in their native language and develop some literacy skills. The desire of some Muslim communities to study in Arabic, however, suggests that in the longer term there needs to develop a greater range of publications in languages that have no written literature. As it is, children who are taught in Arabic and Tigrinya will be advantaged for the two language subjects taught in middle and secondary school.

Although the range of language teaching seems excessive, it reflects a determination on the part of government to use language and education for the dual purposes of creating national unity and promoting a recognition of the diversity of cultures in Eritrea. Community demands, however, are indicative of the difficulties of establishing a consistent set of practices for the language of education in contrast to those established during the liberation struggle, when the EPLF leadership was able to remain impervious to such pressures through its tight infrastructure of absorption of recruits. Introducing a centralized policy of language use and education at the primary level for all of Eritrea has been more challenged.

One area in which EPLF poicy has changed since independence is that of religious education. Religion was not part of the curriculum of EPLF-established schools. After independence, however, it was incorporated and as long as the national curriculum was followed religious schools were permitted to be established.

In choosing English as the language of instruction of middle, secondary and tertiary education the government has attempted to moderate the identification of language with religious community and, in particular Arabic with Islam. The same principle was behind the decision that there be no official language. Although some official documents are written in both Arabic and Tigrinya, the government opposed that they both become official languages. In effect, however, Tigrinya has become the working language of the administration, a function of the proportion of Tigrinya speakers in the EPLF, the Tigrinyanization of non-Tigrinya EPLF fighters and the proportion of former EPLF members in government and administrative positions. For non-Tigrinya speakers government and its institutions can present an alien face in courts, at airports and offices. Like the gender issue, language has the potential to be manipulated with divisive social and political consequences.

The Land Proclamation,
Land Rights and Development[25]

Prior to dealing with the rural land question, the new government first sought to resolve the urban land problem. The latter derived from the Ethiopian government's nationalization of houses owned in addition to an individual's place of residence. Denationalization was an essential prerequisite for encouraging private and foreign sector involvement in housing construction to alleviate the housing shortage, particularly in Asmara. It removed the anomaly of the existence of nationalized private housing and the government's desire to encourage private sector housing construction,[26] some of which was undertaken by PFDJ-owned construction companies. Peri-urban land, particularly land claimed by village communities close to Asmara, was also freed for construction. Resolving urban land questions created problems mainly of a legal and administrative nature.

Land tenure in the rural areas, however, was an issue which was central to the lives of 80 per cent of Eritreans, linked to refugee return and the demobilization of fighters, and a pivot of government development policy. The Eritrean government emphasized food security, improving agricultural productivity, the development of commercial agriculture and its own role in the removal of critical bottlenecks. To achieve these goals property rights had to be defined and a land commission was established in 1993. At the third congress of the EPLF the principles of a national land policy were stated and, in 1994, the land proclamation was issued. It fundamentally changed rights to land and traditional land tenure systems by proclaiming that all land was government-owned and that all Eritreans should have equal access to land, regardless of gender. These provisions were included in the constitution.

The implementation of the land proclamation in the rural areas had an impact on peasants, agro-pastoralists and pastoralists and commercial farmers. The basic principles of the proclamation were:

(1) ultimate ownership of all types of land lies with the state;
(2) security of tenure should be for a lifetime;
(3) the right of every member of an Eritrean community, regardless of gender to have access to land;

---

[25] This section has benefited greatly from discussions with Lionel Cliffe.
[26] See Pool, 'Eritrean Independence', pp. 396–8.

(4) land redistribution on the basis of equal holdings; and
(5) the state to pay compensation for land taken for development purposes.

Although these were relatively clear principles, their specific implementation engendered complex problems. Prior to the land proclamation divergent views were expressed as to the best way to increase production. Some favoured a shift to private property, others a retention of a modified version of the communal system. Inserted into this debate was the development priority. The preamble to the proclamation described the existing system of land tenure and the laws and customs associated with it as the major obstacle to agricultural and industrial development, to both private and public investment and to the improvement of agricultural techniques. In addition, it viewed the systems of land tenure as a source of rural conflicts and expensive and time-consuming litigation.

The situation prior to the proclamation was exceedingly complex, and reflected both the evolution of and reforms to 'traditional' systems, a simplified version of which we have treated. These systems were modified by land reforms carried out by the ELF, the EPLF and the Derg in different areas they controlled at different periods, and produced an even more complex picture. In simplifying and universalizing the legal framework extensive powers accrued to the state and its agencies, providing it with theoretical powers at least to dispose of land after usufruct for a 'lifetime'. In addition to the considerable expansion of state powers over land, the implementation of the terms of the land proclamation could impact on national unity.

The principle of equalizing access to land is a sound one and complementary to the principle of social justice, but it entails possible problems in some Muslim areas where the *sharia* enshrines both the principle of the right of inheritance and unequal inheritance between men and women. In practical terms, it depends on whether the state authorities make much of the power of ownership or whether they leave undisturbed current local practices of access to land. In development terms, freeing unproductive land for investment purposes makes sense, as long as mechanisms for adequate compensation are in place. On the other hand, it could create a vast new area for litigation with peasants pitted against the state.

So far there is no publicly available land survey, but the assumption that there are significant amounts of land available for the state, as owner, to distribute is possibly wide of the mark, unless new irrigation schemes are developed. Notionally, most parts of Eritrea have some form of community claim over them. If anything were to inflame rural communities in Eritrea it would be the encroachment of others, under the aegis of the state, on land traditionally considered theirs. There has historically been a tension, at times turning to violence, between highlanders moving to the eastern and western lowlands for cattle grazing and between settled peasants and agro-pastoralists in the western lowlands. Disputes over the boundaries between villages frequently took a violent turn, particularly in Serai, the richest of the highland provinces.

By 1996, there was reportedly no available land in the highlands, and without long-term conservation more land is likely to go out of production. Indeed, some have argued that environmental rehabilitation will require that some land in the highlands be taken into reserves for rehabilitation. The main source of available land for demobilized fighters, returning refugees and the development of commercial investment is the Gash-Setit area. Since the majority of fighters to be demobilized were highlanders, the disposition of land to them in a largely Muslim area that was the birthplace of the defeated ELF could be a source of conflict and, not least, a fertile source of political mobilization of sectarian sentiment by former ELF leaders.

Some writers, in part drawing on this author's earlier work, have suggested that a further politically divisive consequence of the land proclamation is the lack of attention paid to pastoralists and agro-pastoralists and the stress on permanently settling the latter.[27] While this has been a long-standing feature of EPLF policy, based on the best means of delivering health, education and veterinary services, the new government does pay attention to grazing rights in its *Macro-Policy* document. To assert that settlement is simply a reflection of the social base of the EPLF among the highland peasantry in contrast to the pastoralist base of the ELF is an oversimplification.

While it is true that the ELF originated the struggle in the pastoralist heartland of the west, by 1975–6 there was a majority of highland fighters in that organization. While there remains a considerable retention of support for the factions that emerged from the ELF and strong antipathy to the EPLF, it has ceased to be based on an axis of pastoralist–peasant division. The bulk of the western pastoralists lost the economic rationale for their way of life through war and famine

---

[27] See S. F. Joireman, 'The Minefield of Land Reform: Comments on the Eritrean Land Proclamation', *African Affairs*, No. 95, 1996, p. 275.

and have become poor refugee farmers or farm labourers in Sudan. At the core of this population are the Bani Amir, who have remained alienated from the EPLF and have found a political home in supporting Eritrean Islamic Jihad or the ELF faction of Abdallah Idris, a Bani Amir.

A further source of conflict could arise from the promotion of commercial market gardening along the Gash-Setit through state allocation of land to commercial farmers and demobilized EPLF fighters, particularly if the bulk of them are highlanders. This area has been a traditional source of water, grazing and subsistence cash crops for local people. In addition, all key staff of the ministry of agriculture in the area are from highland Tigrinya-speaking backgrounds and thus present to the local inhabitants an ethnic dimension of state authority.[28] This reflects the historically differential access to education between Eritrean regions and peoples, and the imbalance of representation within the EPLF rather than government policy, save that the government has favoured the employment of former EPLF fighters and administrators. This combination of state power, the highland origin of local administrators, and government agricultural policy could become politicized on an ethno-religious basis.

Unless handled in a sensitive way, developing the underdeveloped west has some of the ingredients for political conflict witnessed between Eritreans in the 1940s and within the ELF in the late 1960s, if highlanders increasingly gain access to land. As it is, the spread of highland Tigrinyans into the whole of Eritrea has gone on apace over many decades, although largely in urban areas, as evidenced by Tigrinya primary schools dotted all over the urban centres of the lowlands. Like the language issue it provides excluded oppositions with an opportunity to politicize ethnic and religious cleavages. Developments in the new state's external relations have provided space for these oppositions.

Foreign Policy

When the new government came to power, it sought to retain the principle of self-reliance as the cornerstone of its foreign economic relations and to build peaceful relations with neighbouring states on the basis of mutual non-interference. As I have pointed out, the influence of external powers had been a major factor in denying Eritrea independence after World War II. The involvement of Israel and Arab

---

[28] A. Hansen, *Final Report to the GTZ Integrated Food Security Project, Gash-Setit*, Asmara, 1994, p. 6.

states, and the Soviet Union's support for post-revolutionary Ethiopia, had a multi-faceted impact on the course of the armed struggle.

The aspiration to peaceful relations with neighbouring states rapidly turned sour and by the end of the 1990s Eritrea had been in conflict with every state with which it had a land border, as well as Yemen with which it had a maritime border. Clashes have taken place with Djibouti and Sudan, serious fighting with Yemen over the Red Sea islands of Hanish, and a full-scale war along most of its border with Ethiopia. The latter conflict was perhaps the most surprising insofar as the Ethiopian government was formed from the TPLF, the alliance with which brought down the Mengistu regime and paved the way for independence. It was a savage welcome to a world undergoing globalization but still based on territorial-state boundaries.

It might be expected that independence for Eritrea would bring to the fore unresolved border problems with its neighbours that had been masked by the Italian succession to Ottoman control, provincial boundary changes during the Italian expansion into Ethiopia between 1936 and 1941, and Ethiopian incorporation of the Italian colony and subsequent provincial boundary changes. Whereas the dispute with Yemen and Djibouti was about the definition of the territorial state, the conflicts with Sudan and Ethiopia were multi-dimensional. The former involved ideological differences, reciprocal interventions in domestic politics, the politics of refugee return and their impingement on secularism and Christian–Muslim relations in Eritrea. During the prolonged stay in Sudan, many refugees, the great majority of whom were Muslim, became increasingly integrated through residence and education into northern Sudanese Arabo-Islamic culture. Saudi Arabia had initially been a major supporter of refugee education and of a strong Islamic emphasis in the curriculum. After the Sudanese National Islamic Front government took power it supported Eritrean Islamic Jihad (EIJ) and provided sanctuary for factions of the defeated ELF. After independence, both EIJ and Abdallah Idris's group began guerrilla activities in western Eritrea. Both portrayed the new government of Eritrea as Tigrinyan and Christian. The close relationship between the Eritrean government and Ethiopia was portrayed as an ethnic alliance between the Tigrinya speakers of the Eritrean highlands and those of Ethiopia's Tigray province. The secular nationalist ELF–RC, which had not taken to arms at the time of writing, portrayed the government as an EPLF dictatorship that had established an EPLF rather than a national constitution and state, and called for a referendum on official languages, implicitly favouring Arabic as one of them.

In combination, these opposition forces challenged the secular ideo-logy of the government and its political legitimacy. When allied to the military activities in the west, the Eritrean government responded in the same fashion as the Sudanese, and provided political and military support for the Sudanese opposition, the National Democratic Alliance. The vision of open trade across the borders of eastern Sudan and western Eritrea, to the benefit of the peoples of both areas, had given way to mutual political and military interventions. Whatever the responsibility, the existence of a particular community of refugees and a disaffected opposition was a function of their exclusion from Eritrea physically and politically.

While the fighting in the west was through surrogates, the eruption of conflict between Eritrea and Ethiopia in 1998 was a direct one. The Ethiopian–Eritrean conflict, which began as a boundary problem, involved economic issues and the domestic legitimacy of the post-Mengistu government in Ethiopia. It was the more surprising given the initial, relatively harmonious process of the disentanglement of the new Eritrean state and Ethiopia after *de facto* independence. Ethiopia effectively ceded its access to the sea and ports when it accepted without protest the independence referendum, despite opposition from Ethio-pian opposition quarters. In return, rather than declare immediate independence, the EPLF waited two years to hold a referendum, providing the TPLF with the time to settle into government and manage the tensions arising from Tigrinya speakers ruling the previously dominant Amharans and insurgent Oromos. Although there was no taste for any resumption of hostilities in Ethiopia, there was a widely shared opinion in Amhara political circles that Eritrea was an integral part of historic Ethiopia, that a loss of access to the Red Sea ports was a national disaster, that a return to federation should have been part of the referendum proposals and that behind it all was a sinister Tigrinyan conspiracy.

The Ethiopian and Eritrean governments took very different approaches to the ethnic/nationalities question. In contrast to Eritrea, Ethiopian regional administration was based on a recognition of ethnic-based provincial administrations, some of which, like that of the Afar, overlapped with the Eritrean Afar minority.

Immediately preceding the armed conflict was a period of political tension emerging from Eritrea's assertion of monetary independence. This disentangling of currencies had been projected for some time, but took place after several years of resurgent Eritrean business and com-mercial activitites in Ethiopia as the statist economy of the Mengistu period was dismantled. In 1997, the Eritrean government established its own currency, the *naqfa*, in response to which the Ethiopian government demanded that all trade should be paid for in hard currency. Given Eritrea's dependence on trade with Ethiopia and its lack of hard currency, these responses were savage economic blows but also a function of increasing domestic criticism of the TPLF-based government for its accommodation of Eritrea. For some considerable amount of time, Eritreans had formed a significant part of the the small business class in Ethiopia and there was a perception that this kind of economic role had burgeoned since 1991, with Eritreans moving into control of transport from the ports as well as expanding into internal trade. Given the large numbers of Eritreans resident in Ethiopia and that Eritrea was more dependent on Ethiopia than vice versa, the Eritrean military occupation of the poor triangular piece of land in dispute was surprising.

It is possible that the Eritrean government had considered that the control of the ports provided it with a sizable bargaining chip in negotiations subsequent to the military action. Whatever the calculations made by the Eritrean government, the Ethiopian government's riposte could not have been rationally calculated. Under criticism for representing the Tigray people, the TPLF-controlled ruling organization, the Ethiopian People's Revolutionary Democratic Front, was presented with an opportunity to defend Ethiopia and Ethiopian nationalism. Tens of thousands of Eritreans were deported and houses and businesses confiscated. During 1998 and 1999 both states mobilized tens of thousands, and bombed and shelled each others' civilians. While international mediation attempted to resolve the problem, the most devastating impact was human and economic.

Although the war with Ethiopia generated an upsurge of nationalist sentiment, it diverted resources from economic development, ate the proceeds of the privatization programme and curtailed economic growth. Without any significant tax base the capacity to redistribute without economic growth is minimal. The conflicts with the neighbouring states have been in stark contrast to the astute seizing of opportunities by the EPLF on its path to independence.

Conclusion

The liberation and independence of Eritrea was a function of a multiplicity of factors, including Ethiopian government collapse, the success of the TPLF, the end of the Cold War and the bankruptcy of the former Soviet Union. Central to the outcome was the EPLF's capacity to sustain itself and the armed struggle. It has been argued in this study that there were a set of factors accounting for the latter. In the first place, the EPLF remained autonomous from Eritrean society, insulating it from, and at least containing, historic multi-dimensional social and political cleavages. As we have shown, the organizational discipline and the imprinting of an EPLF *Weltanschaaung* on its members were key factors. Even though dissent emerged, it was based more on a mix of personality and semi-organized ideological groups. Political control by the leadership was underpinned by an equality of hardship and of applied organizational rules, although this feature became less marked in the 1980s. Finally, the EPLF took on state-like characteristics, which enhanced its control over the Eritrean population in liberated and semi-liberated areas and its international standing.

The EPLF changed the social base of Eritrean nationalism through the incorporation of the highland peasantry and the educated urban youth and women. Instrumental to the incorporation of these key groups were a combination of EPLF ideological positions, Ethiopian repression and the disintegration of an alternative national banner around which Eritrean nationalists could rally. The demise of the ELF was brought about not only by internal tensions but by EPLF subversion. In the same way Ethiopian regime collapse was a consequence of the alignment, fraught and tense though it was, between the EPLF and the TPLF. A critical factor in sustaining the armed struggle was the financial support of Eritrean refugees organized

195

almost as tightly as those under EPLF authority in the liberated and semi-liberated areas.

In the post-independence period, the new government faced internal dissent, paralleling that faced by the early EPLF, resulting in heightened political controls. Internal EPLF dissent has been matched by opposition from former ELF factions, including secular nationalist and newer Islamicist. In part, this was a dual legacy of the past: of the conflict between ELF and EPLF and the EPLF approach to unification of nationalist forces. Justified or not, the exclusionary character of politics after independence, the refusal to permit organizations to participate in deciding the shape of the new Eritrean state while appointing some individuals from them to lesser positions, has resulted in significant numbers of disaffected Eritreans, largely but not wholly outside Eritrea, excluded from the EPLF-designed political system.

For the new Eritrean government, developing a more inclusionary system has been premised on social and economic development and creating national unity devoid of past ethnic and religious tensions. The framework for this has been a relatively authoritarian government modelled on the policies and practices of the EPLF, and a recognition that whereas the EPLF instilled nationalist sentiments and values in its members, unreconstructed sub-national loyalties lurked in the hearts of broader Eritrean society. EPLF professions of the necessity of first establishing the socio-economic basis for a democratic polity and pluralist society can only be verified in the longer term. In the short term, a highly centralized state is emerging as the embryo of the new polity with the EPLF as its heartbeat. Those who make ethnic and sectarian calculations have pointed to the disproportionate numbers of Tigrinyans in positions of authority without indicating (as this book has tried to do) the complex development of the EPLF and the contingent historical, social, economic and cultural factors that have shaped it. If former cadres and supporters of the EPLF use their positions to enrich themselves and an embourgeoisement of fighters occurs, opposition critics will not draw attention to the poverty of the mass of Tigrinyan poor peasants but to a class-sect. The transition from a centralized and tightly organized liberation front is fraught with difficulties, not the least of which is putting aside the components of victory. Perceiving threats to national unity has frequently provided the justification for the maintenance of secretive and unaccountable political systems, which in their turn generate division. None of the above comments should detract from the impressive successes of the EPLF and positive aspects of developments since independence, particularly in education and the efficient delivery of services, more remarkable given the legacy of war and poverty.

Eritrea will not be an easy state to govern. We have already mentioned the controversial nature of decisions about education and language, provincial reorganization, the tensions between secular state law and religious traditions and practices among conservative Muslim communities. All provide opportunities for marginalized and excluded opposition political factions to mobilize on issues that do not have unified popular backing. The exclusionary character of post-independence politics provides a basis for the opposition to portray the system as essentially undemocratic, EPLF justifications for its dominance notwithstanding.

The conflictual relationship with its neighbours has presented further problems for the new state, the most disastrous of which has been the war with Ethiopia, ostensibly over a small piece of contested territory. Post-independence foreign policy stands in stark contrast to the astute management of external relations during the armed struggle analysed in Chapter 5. While the EPLF was a beneficiary of support from states hostile to Ethiopia in the 1960s and 1970s, it has become a participant in and victim of the replication of patterns of reciprocal subversion after independence. The Sudan government's support for Eritrean opposition has been matched by Eritrea. With the war against Ethiopia, a broad coalition of Eritrean opposition groups has found a new haven, and in the process of 'sleeping with the enemy' in time of war hardly generated sympathy among Eritreans. Nevertheless, this debilitating cycle of state subversion in the Horn has a particularly harsh impact on a state like Eritrea, with its limited resources, and is a mark of problems arising from excluded oppositions in an area of fragile multi-ethnic states. It can be expected that the future will bring dramatic realignments between states in the Horn of Africa as changing constellations of domestic power impinge on inter-state relations, national unity and development prospects. While the EPLF was able to insulate its organization from historic sources of internal division during the liberation struggle, formal statehood has brought a new challenge.

Bibliography

Official Sources

British

Foreign Office, 371 Files, Public Record Office
Nadel, S.F., *Races and Tribes of Eritrea*, British Military Administration, Asmara 1944
Trevaskis Papers, Rhodes House Library, Oxford: *Hamasein; The End of the Italian Empire; The Tribes and Peoples of the Cheren District; The Tribes and Peoples of Northern Eritrea; A Report on the Tribal Reorganisation of the Western Province Eritrea and its Future*

Eritrean

Constitutional Commission for Eritrea, *Constitutional Proposals for Public Debate*
—— *Draft Constitution*, English version, Asmara, 1996
—— *Issue Papers*
—— *Strategies, Plans*
Government of Eritrea, *al-Iritiriya al-Haditha* (Arabic: Modern Eritrea) – biweekly newspaper published by the Ministry of Information, 1991–8
—— *Macro-Policy*, Asmara, 1944
ELF, *The National Democratic Revolution versus Ethiopian Expansionism*, Beirut, 1979
EPLF, *al-Talia* (Arabic: Vanguard) – official EPLF publication, 1975–8
—— *A National Charter for Eritrea: For a Democratic, Just and Prosperous Future*, 1994
—— *Creating a Popular, Economic, Political and Military Base*, Research and Information Centre on Eritrea, 1982
—— *Eritrea: Eyewitness Reports*, Belgium, 1979
—— *The Destructive Movement* (translation from Tigrinya), April 1978
—— *The EPLF and its Relations with Democratic Movements in Ethiopia*, February 1985
—— *The Historical Background to the Eritrean Civil War*, December 1972
Liberation, 'Our Struggle and its Goals', March 1973

Bibliography

United Nations

Report of the Four Power Commission, 1948
Report of the UN Mission to Eritrea, 1950
Report of the UN Delegate in Eritrea, 1951
Final Report of the UN Delegate in Eritrea, 1952
UNIDO, Eritrea: A New Beginning, 1996

Secondary Sources

Aberra, Y.M., 'Muslim Institutions in Eritrea: The Asmara Awqaf' *Journal of the Institute of Muslim Minority Affairs*, 1983–4

Adelman, H. and Sorenson, J., *African Refugees*, Westview Press, Boulder, 1994

al-Amin, Muhammad Said, *al-Thawra al-Iritiriyya* (Arabic: The Eritrean Revolution), Asmara, 1992

Ammar, Wolde-Yesus, *Eritrea: Root Causes of War and Refugees*, Baghdad, 1992

Balsvik, R., *Haile Selassie's Students: The Intellectual and Social Background to Revolution 1952–1977*, African Studies Center, Michigan State University, 1985

Bender, M.L., *Language in Ethiopia*, OUP, Oxford, 1976

Chistmann, S., *Die Freiheit Haben wir Nicht von den Mannern: Frauen in Eritrea*, Horlemann, Berlin, 1996

Clapham, C., *Transformation and Continuity in Revolutionary Ethiopia*, CUP, Cambridge, 1988

Cliffe, L. and B. Davidson, *The Long Struggle of Eritrea for Independence and Constructive Peace*, Red Sea Press, Trenton, NJ, 1988

Connell, D., *Against All Odds*, Red Sea Press, Trenton, NJ, 1993

de Waal, A., *Evil Days: Thirty Years of War and Famine in Ethiopia*, Africa Watch, New York, 1991

Doornbos, M. and Cliffe, L., eds, *Beyond Conflict in the Horn*, Institute of Social Studies/James Currey, The Hague/London, 1991

ELNA, *In Defence of the Eritrean Revolution*, n.p., n.d.

Erlich, H., *The Struggle over Eritrea 1962–78*, Hoover Institution Press, Stanford, 1983

Faddab, T.H., *Harakat al-Tahrir al-Iritiriyya wa Masiratiha al-Tarihkiyya* (Arabic: The Eritrean Liberation Movement and its Historic Fate), Sharuf Press, Cairo, 1994

Gebre-Medhin, J., *Peasants and Nationalism in Eritrea*, Red Sea Press, Trenton, NJ, 1989

Ghaber, M., *The Blin of Bogos*, Baghdad, n.p., 1993

Hansen, A., *Final Report to the GTZ Integrated Food Security Project, Gash-Setit*, Asmara, 1994

Iyob, R., 'The Eritrean Experiment: A Cautious Pragmatism', *Journal of Modern African Studies*, 35, 4, 1997

────── *The Eritrean Struggle for Independence: Domination, Resistance, Nationalism 1941–1993*, CUP, Cambridge, 1995

Joireman, S.F., 'The Minefield of Land Reform: Comments on the Eritrean Land Proclamation', *African Affairs* 95, 1996

Bibliography

Keller, E.J., 'Drought, War and the Politics of Famine in Ethiopia and Eritrea', *Journal of Modern African Studies* 30, 4, 1992

Kibreab, G., *Ready and Willing: Eritrean Refugees in Sudan and the Dilemmas of Return*, Life and Peace Institute, Uppsala, 1996

—— *Refugees and Development in Africa: The Case of Eritrea*, Red Sea Press, Trenton, NJ, 1987

Killion, T., 'The Eritrean Economy in Historical Perspective', *Eritrean Studies Review* 1, 1, 1996

Leonard, R., 'Popular Participation in Liberation and Revolution', in Cliffe, L. and Davidson, B. (eds), *The Long Struggle of Eritrea for Independence and Constructive Peace*, Red Sea Press, Trenton, NJ.

Markakis, J., *National and Class Conflict in the Horn of Africa*, CUP, Cambridge, 1987

Negash, T., *Eritrea and Ethiopia: The Federal Experience*, Nordiska Afrikainstitut, Uppsala, 1997

Pateman, R., *Even the Stones are Burning*, Red Sea Press, Trenton, NJ, 1990

Peninou, Jean-Louis, 'La Réforme Agraire à Azim' [For Azim read Azen] in *Revolution in Eritrea: Eyewitness Reports*, Research and Information Centre on Eritrea, Belgium, 1979

Pool, D., *Eritrea: Towards Unity in Diversity*, Minority Rights Group International, London, 1997

—— 'Eritrean Independence: The Legacy of the Derg and the Politics of Reconstruction', *African Affairs* 92, 368, 1993

—— *Establishing Movement Hegemony*, Manchester Papers in Politics, 1992

—— 'Revolutionary Crisis and Revolutionary Vanguard: The Eritrean People's Liberation Front', *Review of African Political Economy*, 19, 1980

Sabbe, O.S., *Judhur al-Khilafat al-Iritiriyya wa Turuq Ma'lajatiha* (Arabic: The Roots of Eritrean Differences and the Means of Treating Them), Beirut, n.p. 1978

—— 'The History of Eritrea', Beirut, 1974

Silkin, T., 'Changes in the Negotiation of Marriage in those Areas Controlled by the EPLF', unpublished M.Phil thesis, Goldsmith's College, University of London, 1989

Tesfagiorgis, A., *A Painful Season and a Stubborn Hope*, Red Sea Press, Trenton, NJ, 1992

Tiruneh, A., *The Ethiopian Revolution 1974–1987*, CUP, Cambridge, 1993

Trevaskis, G.K.N., *Eritrea: A Colony in Transition 1941–52,* OUP, Oxford, 1960

Trimingham, J.S., *Islam in Ethiopia*, OUP, Oxford, 1953

Tronvoll, K., 'The Process of Nation-building in Eritrea', *Journal of Modern African Studies*, 36, 3, 1998

Wilson, A., *The Challenge Road: Women and the Eritrean Revolution*, Red Sea Press, Trenton, N.J., 1991

Yohannes, O., *Eritrea: A Pawn in World Politics*, University of Florida Press, Gainesville, 1991

Young, J., *Peasant Revolution in Ethiopia: The Tigray Peoples Liberation Front 1975–1991*, CUP, Cambridge, 1997

Index

Index

Index

Haykouta 51
Hazu tribe 10, 30, 116
healing 15
health services 81, 100-2, 115, 124-5, 154, 179
Himbirte 139
history and historical factors 1-3, 31, 34-5, 37-8, 47, 51, 57-8, 88-9, 100, 104, 105, 197; *see also* descent
Horn of Africa 197; *see also name of country*
hospitals *see* health services
households 117
housing 14, 122-3, 141, 188

Ibrahim Afa 84-5, 151
Ibrahim Sultan 25, 46-8
Ibrahim Totil 87, 147
identity cards 122
Idris Muhammad Adam 48-50
Idris Muhammad Awate 50
Idris Osman Galewdewos 49, 91
imperialism *see* empires and imperialism
income 16, 52, 124
Independence Bloc 41, 47, 53
industry 16, 23, 102-3, 107, 178-9; *see also* Asmara - factories
infibulation 128
inheritance 19, 44, 96, 189
Intile Shaykh Are clan 22
Iraq 56, 69, 150
irrigation 114, 189-90
Islam 26, 30-1, 33, 37, 53-4, 57, 68-9, 114-15, 118, 157, 180-1, 190, 192, 196-7; and Ethiopia 52; and nationalism 24, 36, 40, 44-6, 48, 57, 86; and Sudan 39, 153; Arabic language 29, 73, 186-7; Bileyn 9, 25, 186; Jiberti 7, 32, 89; Keren 42, 123; law 22, 166, 182, 189; lowlands 2, 11, 17-22, 34; Nara speakers 10; refugees 129; Tigre speakers 6, 8, 11-12, 71; women 96, 116, 128; *see also* Muslim League; Sufism
Israel 54, 56-7, 69, 191
Issayas, Saba 183
Italy 2-3, 7, 13, 16, 18, 23-8, 34, 38, 41-3, 45, 47, 52, 88, 116, 129, 192

Jiberti people 7, 11-12, 32, 47, 89, 179-80
journalists 143
judiciary 122, 168

Kagnew Military Base 39, 138
Kahsai, Wolde 51
Kassa, Abraha 173
Kassala 22, 48-9, 54, 153
Keren 6, 22, 24-5, 27, 32, 51, 61-2, 120, 123-4, 126, 133, 139, 156, 161, 176; and serf agitation 41; *awqaf* committee 20; Bileyn 9, 121; Ethiopian garrison 107, 135; hospital 125; migration 31; *Qadi* 47; school 186; Tigre speakers 8; youth 101, 144
Khartoum 141
Khatmiyya family 20-2, 25, 48
Kidane, Habte-Selassie 79
Kiflemeariam, Naizghi 172
Kiflu, Afeworki 76-7, 79
Kiflu, Kidane 54-5

kinship 26, 42; see also clans; descent; families
Korem 154
Kunama language 9, 185
Kunama people 6, 9-10, 50, 52, 177
Kuwait 143

Labka river 114
labour 16, 23, 103
land 12-17, 32-4, 42, 46, 61, 100, 102, 104, 106, 108-18, 128-9, 157, 160, 167, 188-91
Land Commission 188
Land Proclamation (1994) 188-9
languages 28-30, 57, 68-70, 75, 160, 184-7, 197; *see also name of language*
Latin script 186
law 15, 21, 30, 42, 44-5, 96-7, 113, 122, 127-9, 159, 165, 169, 180; Islamic 22, 166, 182, 189
Lebanon 52
Liberal Progressive Party 39, 41, 47, 53, 64
Libya 56, 98
life expectancy 160
literacy 28-9, 98, 100-1, 115, 124, 127-8, 137, 187
livestock 6, 81; *see also name of animal*
local government 175-7, 183

Macro-Policy 185, 190
Mahmud Ahmad Mahmud 'Sharifo' 84, 173
Mahmud Dinai 51
Mai Habar 140
manpower *see* labour
manufacturing *see* industry
Maoism 54, 57, 61, 63, 78-9, 81, 93, 104, 106, 133, 136, 144-5, 156, 164, 166
Markakis, J. 78
market gardening 191
marriage 44, 68, 96-8, 128-9, 180-1
Marxism-Leninism 54, 57, 81, 93
Marya people 8, 18, 30, 51, 65-6, 153
Mass Administration 119-22, 125-6, 177
massacres 51, 55
Massawa 7-8, 20, 22, 27-8, 34-5, 51, 73, 90, 98, 101, 104, 107, 125, 133, 136, 139, 157, 176
me Embera people 22
medicine *see* health services
Mekelle 156
men 127-8, 181, 189
Mendefera 16, 134, 139, 146, 161, 176
Mengistu Haile Mariam, Major 136, 143, 156
Mensa people 8, 18, 30, 65
merchants 11-12, 23-4, 47, 121-4, 179-80
Middle East 177; *see also name of country*
migration 13, 19, 29-33, 111; *see also* urbanization
militias 122, 126, 135, 145-6
Miniferi people 10, 116
ministries (government) 172-4
Mirghani family 20-1, 45, 48
missionaries 7
MITYAS 184
monasteries 33-4
money *see* currency
mortality rates 160
Mufti of Eritrea 20
Muhammad (Prophet) 22, 30
Muhammad Ahmad Idris 67

204

Index

Muhammad Ali Umaru 51, 65, 72-3
Muhammad Osman al-Mirghani 21-2
Muhammad Sa'id Barih 71
Muhammad Umar Abdallah *see* Abu Tayarra
Musa Rabi'a 85, 94
Muslim League 39, 41, 43-8
Muslims *see* Islam

Nadel, S. F. 9, 12, 14, 19, 45
Naqfa 6, 139, 145, 166
Nara language 10, 68
Nara people 6, 9-10, 42, 50-1, 87, 147, 186
National Assembly 167-8, 172-4, 183
National Charter 163-5, 170, 178
National Democratic Programmes 88, 93, 108-9
National Service Programme 182
National Union of Eritrean Women 180-4
nationalism xiv-xv, 1-2, 5, 34-5, 37-8, 42-3, 51, 55-6, 59, 68, 70, 133, 138, 147-8, 157, 168, 195-6; Afar 8; and Christianity 47, 69; and Islam 24, 36, 40, 44-6, 48, 57, 86; Egypt 49; Ethiopia 39, 136-7, 194; Keren 25; Obel Group 73; Sudan 54
nationalities and nationality 7-11, 87-90, 148, 162-3, 180, 184; *see also name and* citizenship
nationalization 122-3, 178, 188; *see also* privatization
naturalization 162
Nefasit 135, 140
Negash, Tekeste 40-3, 45
Nilotic peoples 9-10
non-governmental organizations 143, 155, 183; *see also name*
North America 129-30; *see also name of country*
Norwegian Church Relief 130

Oromo people 193
Orthodox Church 6-7, 9, 11, 16, 25, 30-1, 33, 39-41, 186
Osman Ajib 67
Osman Azaz 70
Osman Salih Sabbe 49, 56-7, 64-6, 69, 71-3, 83-4, 98, 134, 140-2
Ottoman Empire 27, 33, 192
Our Struggle and its Goals 68-9, 88
oxen 53, 113

pastoralism 5, 9-11, 17, 19-21, 23, 26, 28-9, 32, 34-5, 45, 49-50, 52, 81, 100, 153, 190-1; *see also* agro-pastoralism
peasantry 2, 11-13, 28, 53, 60, 98, 118-19, 121, 126, 136, 149, 157, 189-90, 196; Akalai Guzai 52; and politics 80-1, 100; Christian 39-40, 55; highland 106-14, 144, 148, 153, 162, 195; Italian colonial period 16; rich 116; *see also* agriculture; Eritrea – highlands and highlanders
Peasants' Association 120
Peninou, Jean-Louis 113
people's assemblies 119-22, 126-8, 175, 177
pluralism 170, 173, 179, 183, 196
politics 20, 28, 34, 52, 55, 70, 109-13, 131, 142, 152-3, 159-60, 161, 168, 171-5, 190-1, 195-7; and Muslim League 43; and nationalism 48; and regionalism 3; Bani Amir 18; BMA 2, 56; Ethiopia 148-9, 156; Keren region 25; land 33;

peasantry 80-1, 100; pluralist 179; village 14-15, 41-2; *see also* education - political
polygamy 117
Popular Liberation Forces *see* Eritrean Peoples Liberation Front
Popular Front for Democracy and Justice 65, 78, 91, 161, 163-7, 170-3, 177-80, 182-4, 188; *see also* Eritrean Peoples Liberation Front
populations 10-11, 16, 23, 111
Port Sudan 29
presidency 167, 170, 172-3, 177, 179
press 167, 173
prices 122, 124, 178, 180
priests 14-16, 113, 117-18
privatization 141, 178, 188, 194
propaganda 80-1, 109, 111, 126, 137, 142, 149
property rights 169, 188
prostitution 125
Protestantism 7, 41
proverbs 127
provincial assemblies 175-6, 183

Qarora 120, 134, 139
Quran 22, 29, 115, 118, 186
Quraysh tribe 30

rainfall 5-7
Ramadan Muhammad Nur 66, 72, 82-4, 87, 92, 172
Ramadan Osman Awlay 54, 72, 84-5
Rashaida people 10
Red Sea Corporation 178-9
Red Star campaign 149, 154
referendums 149-50, 161-2, 192-3
refugees and emigres 81, 129-31, 137, 143, 153-4, 160, 192-3, 195-6
regional assemblies *see* provincial assemblies
regionalism 3, 5, 38, 76n, 86, 89
religion 2-3, 5, 28-31, 33-4, 40, 57, 88-9, 115, 168, 187, 191; *see also name and* sectarianism
Research and Information Centre for Eritrea 61
robbery 52
Roman Catholicism 7, 9, 25, 41, 186

Sabbe *see* Osman Salih Sabbe
Sahho language 10, 12, 30, 185-6
Sahho people 10, 22, 31, 51, 80, 116, 134, 153, 186
Sa'id Barre 84
Salih Hayouti 67
Salih Titu 66
Saudi Arabia 29, 129, 192
Sayyid al-Hashim 22
Sayyid Ali Mirghani 48
Sayyid Ja'far 22
Sayyid Mustafa wad Hasan 21, 48
Sayyidna Hamid Hamad 48
Scandinavia 143, 155; *see also name of country*
schools *see* education
Sebhatu, Yohannes 77, 79
secrecy 95
sectarianism 52, 69, 89, 164, 190, 196
sedentarization 5-6, 9
Segeneiti 133, 139

205

206